THE STORY OF INFANT
DEVELOPMENT

THE STORY OF INFANT DEVELOPMENT

Observational Work with Martha Harris

Romana Negri

edited by

Meg Harris Williams

Published for
The Harris Meltzer Trust
by

KARNAC

Published in 2007 by
Karnac Books Ltd
118 Finchley Road
London NW3 5HT

British Library Cataloguing in Publication Data

A C.I.P. for this book is available from the British Library

ISBN 978 1 85575 414 0

Edited, designed, and produced by The Studio Publishing Services Ltd
www.publishingservicesuk.co.uk
e-mail: studio@publishingservicesuk.co.uk

Printed in Great Britain

www.harris-meltzer-trust.org.uk

www.karnacbooks.com

CONTENTS

A stunning experience; a state of normal non-integration
and evacuation of sensations; the pull of the nipple;
maternal depression and the difficulty of introjecting the
object; digesting emotions; problems of identification in
the mother; the breast that comes and goes away; the
bottle, and a distance from the mother.

The end of breastfeeding; feelings of aggression and
seduction; representations of the breast; the lost breast

and the nipple lifeline; mother returns to work—the new sweetheart; the only baby; the relationship with the father; how the new baby is made; the little chair—the new place in the family.

Feminine and masculine qualities; the value of fairy tales; the epistemophilic instinct; one day it will be his turn; a point of "catastrophic change"; birth of the next sibling; the "imbecile" infantile self that damages its objects; the second day at nursery school (*with Donald Meltzer*); the third birthday.

Summary of the first two observation sessions; the gang and circularity of time; the parents' unfulfilled childhood (*with Donald Meltzer*).

Eleanora: redefining a diagnosis of child psychosis as neurotic anxiety; Daniela: redefining a diagnosis of epilepsy as psychosomatic illness; Vittoria: redefining a diagnosis of brain pathology in terms of mental deficiency.

Two infant observations: Matteo (early internalization of the object) and Giuseppino (the child's look and the mother's emotional state).

This book is dedicated to Mattie's grandchildren: Gawain, Duncan, Giuliana, Euan, Elena, Andrea, Francis, and to all their generation.

ACKNOWLEDGEMENT

I wish to express deep thanks to Meg Harris Williams and Adrian Williams, without whose contributions I could not have brought this book to realization. Meg transcribed most of Mrs Harris's supervisions and examined all the material with me. In particular we discussed the titles of the chapters and of the concept of "windows" and the subtitles. Meg's valued interventions helped to perfect the language used in the book. I am also very grateful to Adrian for translating all my observations with great skill and patience.

Romana Negri

ABOUT THE AUTHORS

Martha Harris (1919–1987) was born in Beith, Scotland, eldest child of a farming family who moved to Sussex when she was eight. She read English at University College London, and then Psychology at Oxford. She taught in secondary schools for some years before training as a psychologist at Guy's Hospital, then as a child psychotherapist at the Tavistock Clinic, where she was responsible for the child psychotherapy training at the Department of Children and Families, from the 1960s until the time of her retirement. She also trained as a psychoanalyst at the British Institute of Psychoanalysis and practised privately until her death. Her main mentors were Melanie Klein, Esther Bick, and Wilfred Bion. Together with her second husband, Donald Meltzer, she taught widely in Europe, North and South America, and India. Her books have been published in many languages and include *Thinking about Infants and Young Children* (1975) and *Your Teenager* (new edition, 2007), and many of her papers in English have been reprinted in *Collected Papers of Martha Harris and Esther Bick* (1987).

For a biography of Martha Harris see www.harris-meltzer-trust.org.uk.

Romana Negri was born in Bergamo in 1942, youngest of three sisters. Her father was a veterinary surgeon and her mother a primary school teacher. She graduated in medicine and trained as a child neuropsychiatrist at the University of Milan. She began work at the Child Neuropsychiatry Institute of that university in 1968. From 1970 onwards she attended the seminars of Martha Harris and Donald Meltzer and commenced work projects inspired and influenced by their teaching, meanwhile training as a psychotherapist. From 1976 to 2004 she was a consultant in the Special Care Baby Unit at the Caravaggio Hospital, Treviglio, publishing some of her research findings in *The Newborn in the Intensive Care Unit* (Karnac, 1994; also published in Italy, 1994 and 1998, and Greece, 2002). Since 1982 she has been a professor at Milan University, teaching in the paediatric department of the School of Medicine and the School of Psychiatry and Psychology. She is also responsible for early pathology consultation at the Sacco Hospital in Milan. In addition to *The Newborn* she has published over one hundred papers in the field of early psychopathology and child psychiatry in Italy, Germany, France, Spain, and England.

Gianna Williams, a psychoanalytic psychotherapist, taught at the Tavistock Clinic from 1970 and became head of the Child Psychotherapy discipline in the Adolescent Department. She worked closely with Martha Harris in the development of the course in Psychoanalytic Observational Studies and was organizing tutor of the course between 1979 and 2000. She has initiated similar courses in Italy, France, and Latin America, and founded the *Centri Studi Martha Harris* as their containers. She has published articles and books in England and abroad. She has been Visiting Professor at Pisa and Bologna Universities and in 2003 was awarded an Honorary Doctorate in Education by the Tavistock and the University of East London.

EDITORIAL NOTE

The idea of this book was welcomed by Donald Meltzer a few months before his death in 2004. He had begun to accompany his wife, Martha Harris, on her teaching trips to Italy in the 1970s, and his contributions appear at certain points in Chapters Three and Four. After his death it was decided that this book of clinical work, together with a reprint of Mrs Harris' earlier book on teenagers for parents and teachers, would constitute an appropriate inauguration of the Harris-Meltzer Trust.

The seminar scripts have been edited from the tapes in such a way as to try to convey some of the spirit of the way in which Mrs Harris thinks about the material. This is in line with the modern appreciation that it is not the ideas alone but also the thinking processes of the teacher that are important for the student.

Emphases in Mrs Harris's speaking voice are given in italics. In order to help the reader navigate the evolution of her thought, "windows" have been inserted in the text.

Meg Harris Williams

PREFACE

Gianna Polacco Williams

This precious book, based on verbatim transcriptions of supervision recordings, provides an opportunity for a valuable emotional and learning experience, particularly for those who did not meet Martha Harris when she was alive. Romana Negri says in her introduction, quoting Martha Harris, "The emotion is the thing which gives the meaning, and the thought is a way of organizing that meaning and giving form to it". It is a great gift to recapture the *feeling* of the seminars held by Mattie (as all of us who worked with her used to call her). She had an inimitable style and she was one of the most facilitating persons I have ever met. One of her favourite quotations was a sentence she paraphrased from Bion, saying that we should worry not so much about our inhibitions as about our tendency to inhibit others.

A very large part of this book is based on the observation of one normal child, Simone, from birth to three years; another chapter, which includes an enriching contribution from Donald Meltzer, concerns a young child not suffering from psychological disturbance, and there is also a chapter that includes a differentiation between psychosomatic and physical illness. Martha Harris was an exquisite clinician and supervisor of clinical work but she felt passionately that the study of *normal* development "against which psychopathological development can be measured" was an essential foundation for the training of all in the helping professions as well as for future clinicians.

She wrote, "Change and expansion need to be facilitated so that psychoanalytical ideas can travel and take root amongst workers who are ready to receive them so that their usefulness may find homes in which to flourish". She gave impulse to a project, found by many to be very daring at the time, which transformed a small pre-clinical training into what was to become a course in Psychoanalytic Observational Studies, open to all professionals interested in learning about normal development. The intention was that only a small proportion of them would opt to become clinicians; many others (nurses, teachers) used the opportunity to deepen and widen their approach to the work they were involved in. The first year Mattie accepted fourteen students for this course (there are now over 300) was called "the year of the bulge". Mattie brushed aside criticism by saying, "If you plant many flowers the weeds cannot grow." It was not meant to make gardening sense and Mattie knew it, as she was a keen and excellent gardener.

This book, where we can hear Mattie speak with her own voice, is a marvellous opportunity for people who did not have the chance to meet her to get to know her; and it is an incredible privilege to re-establish contact with her twenty years after her death for those of us who found her—and still find her—a unique source of inspiration. I will conclude by paraphrasing something I have heard her say more than once: "the only way to develop resides in an intimate internal relationship with people, dead or alive, who have inspired us".

Introduction

Romana Negri

In this book I would like to present some of the observation work
that I had the privilege of presenting to Martha Harris for supervision between 1970 and 1984. These cases include infant observation,
young child observation, and play observation of three children
who, for various psychopathological problems, were in hospital at
the Institute of Child Neuropsychiatry at the University of Milan.
Martha Harris's supervisions were recorded and in almost all
instances preserved, and the tapes have been transcribed here. The
case of Simone, which constitutes a major part of the book, particularly delighted her, since it afforded in great detail a record of an
infant's normal development, highlighting the passions, struggles,
and vicissitudes inherent in ordinary life, so providing a role model
against which psychopathological impediments may be measured
and more clearly seen.

The material in this book demonstrates the high importance
accorded by this Scottish psychoanalyst to close observational
work. In the process, it provides illuminating illustrations of
the theories of Esther Bick and of the Kleinian model of child
development, including such themes as states of normal non-
integration, establishing a rapport with the breast, problems of

weaning, and the operation of the epistomephilic instinct. The influence of Bion's theories of the structure of the personality is very evident.[1] Mrs Harris, along with Bion, sees the child's emotions as crucial in the development of a capacity for thinking. She says, "The emotion is the thing that gives the meaning; and the thought is a way of organizing that meaning and giving form to it" (see below, p. 101).

In addition to being a teaching analyst of the British Psychoanalytical Society, Martha Harris always manifested a lively interest in the people, both children and adults, whom she encountered in daily life. As Rita Parlani writes, "This attentive sensitivity to others derived from her 'mystical' and at the same time realistic vision of how her analytical work supported her commitment, which was always inspired by her search for the truth" (Parlani, 1989, pp. 6–7). Mrs Harris never ceased reformulating concepts and hypotheses, judging that dogmatic and uncritical assumptions encouraged omnipotent attitudes. Her rigorous adherence to the Kleinian school co-existed, none the less, with a free and lucid intellectual approach. For example, she believed the Kleinian idea of "correct" interpretation had a certain omnipotent component, as if the patient was to be "stamped" with the right interpretation. Instead, she searched not for the right interpretation but for the "enabling interpretation". By "enabling" she meant that which aids the patient to express more clearly their emotional state in a way that leaves space open for further experience. The "right" interpretation closes off the experience. Referring to Bion's terminology, she described how "alpha function forms in the child's mind with the introjection of a thinking object (that is, an enabling reasoning power), not with the introjection of an object that formulates omniscient judgements ('right' interpretations)" (Brutti & Parlani, 1979, p. 181).

Her interest in promoting the use of psychoanalytic ideas extended to all fields where there was a chance of furthering the development and education of the individual and, in particular, the child—whether at home, school, hospital, in consultation, etc. In her paper on "The Tavistock training and philosophy", she expressed the goal of the members of all socially concerned institutions as one of "promoting the healthy growth of the individual, the family and society, concentrating attention not just on pathological conditions but on those which foster change and harmonic development of both the personality and of social structures" (Harris, 1987, p. 261). The work–study seminars devised for workers who came from a variety of different disciplines entailed the use of "no particular technique", since their aim was the general but essential one of "sharpening perceptions and enlarging imagination". "Disparate elements" in the material could be evaluated from different perspectives in a way that was mutually enriching.

In all the study seminars of the Tavistock course, the emphasis on detailed observation and reporting was paramount. Focusing on the material, rather than on the reactions of individual participants, meant that when childish emotions were inevitably aroused these could be recognized and discussed as inherent in the situation. For "distortions of perception happen at all times with us all" and the key to understanding projections is to focus on "renewed scrutiny of the situation in question" (ibid., pp. 262–263). Attention to detail is not a function of academic obsessionality but is a psychological facilitator of "free and honest reporting" (ibid., p. 268).

Observation work, says Harris, helps the student learn "to endure 'living in the question' (as Keats put it)",[2] a capacity that she insists is "indispensable" for the psychoanalytic student, whether they wish to practise with children or with adults. Living in the question is enabled by the struggle to observe phenomena minutely and correctly without seeking refuge in "premature, anxiety-ridden interpretation and intervention. It helps relax undue therapeutic zeal, allows us to learn to feel and to respect the drive towards development that exists in every patient, as in every baby. It cannot be hurried" (ibid., p. 267).

The observational methods for the mother–child relationship and for "young child" and play observation (of children over two years) were established by Esther Bick in the 1950s (Bick, 1987). These are the methods followed in this book and they are described below. In each category, the observation lasts approximately fifty minutes and is transcribed by the observer in the most detailed way possible. It is subsequently presented to a work group of others involved in a similar activity, led by a psychotherapist who has extensive experience in the observation of infants and in analytical therapy with children and adolescents.

Infant observation

In the same paper on the "Tavistock training" Martha Harris describes the procedure for conducting the mother–infant observation seminar, which she regarded as "more valuable than any other" in honing observational skills:

> The mothers are asked if they are willing to have an observer who, although he may be a professional worker with children and may even be a parent himself, would like the opportunity to learn by observing for one hour each week how an infant grows and develops within a family. The mother is also told that it will be helpful and interesting for the student to be informed of any changes and developments which she has noticed in the baby during the intervening week. Her thoughts and feelings about the baby are welcomed, and one often finds that the interest of the observer seems to encourage the mother to take more notice of the baby as a developing individual. [Harris, 1987, pp. 265–266).

The observations are carried on at these regular weekly intervals (excluding holiday periods, etc.) for the first two years of the child's life. In the case of Simone, reported in this book, they continued until age three, at Mrs Harris's request, to include the story of the birth of the next sibling and also the child's entrance to nursery school. When other family members are present (as frequently in Simone's case) the mother–infant observation also becomes a family observation, and the observer needs to pay the same unobtrusive attention to everyone present, learning to "retain and record complicated details of interactions and conversations". The observer's task is not to "over-identify" with either mother or baby but to concentrate on feeling his own countertransference. In this way he will come to appreciate "the impact on the mother of the responsibility of the baby" and the difficulty of her own task of being "open to reverberations of [the baby's] gropings and disturbances" rather than following what she has learned "by precept, hearsay or academic psychology" (*ibid.*, p. 266).

This is an education in "living in the question", in which the observer is in a potentially privileged position of learning from the "wise mother", who knows that "it is illusory to believe that, if she is good enough, she can help [her baby] grow up without any frustration". Mrs Harris points out that "not every mother is able to respond in this way" to the emotional turmoil aroused by the baby's needs: "There is every possible variation in degree and in areas of responsiveness and blindness between mothers, and at different times within each mother, as within all of us" (*ibid.*, p. 266)

For the observer likewise needs to metabolize his own frustration at the inevitable stirring of "intense feelings deriving from his own infancy", and to beware of the common tendency to find fault with the mother (or therapist or other caring person), which Harris denominates the "voyeuristic eye". (There is an example of this in the material about Simone, see Chapter One, p. 52.) The counterpart to this is idealization of the mother–baby and a failure to appreciate their difficulties. Both these projective attitudes constitute "impediments to accurate observation" (Harris, 1987 p. 268), while the struggle to observe accurately, and to report and discuss the details in honest totality, allows for the containment of infantile feelings within the group, away from blame or idealization. Attention is focused scientifically on "the material itself, rather than upon that comparison and measurement of individual performance which so inhibits honesty and spontaneity" (*ibid.*, p. 268).

Ultimately, the fruit of accurately observing in minute detail the growth and strengthening of an infant's capacity for trust in his internal objects is to provide the observer with "a model and source for their own development as a therapist with patients", an education that is available also to the other members of the seminar. This "thrust for development", in Mrs Harris's view, may vary in strength from one individual to another, but "is present in all who live" (*ibid.*, p. 267).

Young child observation

This is the weekly observation of a child aged between two and a half and five years of age carried out in the institution he or she attends. Usually, the observations are made in a nursery or kindergarten and the work lasts one year. In the case of Angi, the child presented in the book, the observations were initially carried out in hospital, and then later in the family environment.

Play observation

For play observation sessions of a child over two years of age a simply furnished room is used with a small table, a desk, two chairs, and a standard selection of toys: a doll, a furry animal, two little cars, an ambulance, a fire engine; wild and farm animals with fencing; toy pans, plates, cutlery, cooking utensils; if possible, also a little house containing dolls; animals and cars, and a basket with plastic cubes. On the table there are drawing paper, crayons, plasticine, and a "family" of little dolls. Melanie Klein (1952) described how this simple selection of toys was designed not only to interest the child but also to allow him to transfer to them imaginatively his feelings and anxieties. Mrs Klein thought of play as the means of expression of unconscious phantasy, which was in turn the mental representation of the instinctual life, so the toys she provided served as the vocabulary for the children's expression in the same way that words, free associations, and dreams would do for adults (Klein, 1948). She thought that projective processes present in play and personification allowed the child to communicate his inner world. As Shirley Hoxter writes, "Play is of particular value to the child, as it provides possibilities for anxiety situations to be faced in a symbolic way. The anxiety itself is reduced to tolerable and manageable levels" (in Camhi, 2005, p. 213). Mrs Harris also emphasized the usefulness of the indirectness of play as a means of expression for the latency child, by contrast with the difficulty of verbalizing emotions.

The observer does not intervene in the child's play; he must not interfere with whatever the child wants to communicate, because only when his presence is emotionally receptive, and not directive, can he really make contact with the child. He is then able to register in his mind everything the child did, right down to gestures that may seem casual or apparently insignificant, remembering the exact sequence of the different stages of play. All this, once the session has finished, will be written down with the greatest possible accuracy.

Mrs Harris was invited to conduct our observation seminars at the Institute of Child Neuropsychiatry at Milan University from 1970–1973. Our first experiences enabled us to understand that changes are necessary in the attitude of the observer, particularly when dealing with psychotic children. We saw how we must give more to the psychotic child than to the neurotic child. It becomes up to the observer to employ his particular sensitivity and experience to understand if he should intervene occasionally during the session so that the child, under the influence of his phantasies of destruction, does not feel too persecuted by the doctor, against whom his defences are generally directed at that moment in time. With non-psychotic children of over eight years of age, it is best if the person who is trying to understand the child's anxieties and worries helps him to recognize them during the course of the session itself.

Mrs Harris, along with Klein and Bick and other analysts, emphasizes that notes should not be taken during the session itself. Writing interferes with the observer's free-floating attention and, in the case of newborn babies, "prevents the student from responding easily to the emotional demands of the mother" (Bick, p. 241). An experience of my own confirms this point. My first observation of a psychotic child of seven, named Stefano, was conducted in our clinic at a time when it had not yet been established whether note-taking during the course of the session was a good idea or not. Some time after the session had started, when I wrote some words on a sheet of paper, Stefano approached me to ask what I was doing. He then said I was writing "to a man" and later "to a man on the phone", i.e., to a person he could neither see nor hear. Thus, he showed that he saw me in the same way as he saw his mother, who was interested only in his father, excluding the child totally from their relationship. Stefano then showed me a scar on the back of his hand and said loudly, "One of granny's cats." This was how he wanted to show me his anger, the part of him that scratches. He feels scratched himself and reacts angrily: he scratches and expects to be scratched. So I asked, "Does it really hurt a lot?" He answered very quietly, "No", and again, softly, "Doctor . . . medicine", making me understand that his anger could be alleviated if the doctor would really concern herself with him. This experience demonstrated to our group the meaning and purpose of not taking notes during observation sessions.

Only seven or eight doctors took part in the seminars at the Institute and each of them reported a case from time to time. We realized that only those directly involved in this type of work were interested in a way that could contribute to the discussion and derive practical benefit from the session. The principle of play observation became a recognized part of the overall assessment of a child admitted to the Institute. It was taken into account together with the history, psychological examination, and complete test evaluation—intelligence quotient, projective tests, neurological evaluation, and instrumental examinations such as the EEG, etc. The play observation method turned out to be a precious instrument for arriving at a correct clinical diagnosis.

Martha Harris described the value of the method in the terms Freud used in his funeral speech for Charcot (also frequently quoted by Bion):

> He used to go on looking at the things he did not understand in order to get a deeper and deeper impression, until the moment came when their meaning suddenly became apparent. Then the symptoms, apparently so chaotic, fell into shape. [Harris, 1980, p. 189][i]

As a result of being able to see what underlies the symptoms of the disorder, it became possible for us to modify wrong diagnostic orientations and to set up appropriate therapeutic measures.

Notes

1. Martha Harris had personal supervision with both Klein and Bion.
2. A reference to the "negative capability" passage in Keats (letter to G. and T. Keats, 27 December 1817).

References

Bick, E. (1964). Notes on infant observation in psychoanalytic training. International Journal of Psychoanalysis, 45: 558–566 [reprinted in M. H. Williams (Ed.), Collected Papers of Martha Harris and Esther Bick. (pp. 240–256). Strath Tay, Perthshire: Clunie Press, 1987].

Brutti, C., & Parlani, R. (1979). La terapia dell'autismo come laboratorio di ricerca: una discussione con D. Meltzer e M. Harris. Quaderni di psicoterapia infantile, 3: 170–204.

Camhi, C. (2005). Siblings of premature babies: thinking about their experience. *Journal of Infant Observation, 8*(3): 209–233.

Harris, M. (1980). L'osservazione dei bambini. In: R. Speziale Bagliacca (Ed.), *Formazione e percezione psicoanalitica* (pp. 175–223). Milan: Feltrinelli.

Harris, M. (1987). The Tavistock training and philosophy. In: D. Dawes & M. Boston (Eds.), *The Child Psychotherapist* (1977), reprinted in: M. H. Williams (Ed.), *Collected Papers of Martha Harris and Esther Bick* (pp. 259–282). Strath Tay, Perthshire: Clunie Press.

Klein, M. (1948). *Contributions to Psycho-Analysis*. London: Hogarth.

Klein, M. (1952). *Developments in Psycho-Analysis*. London: Hogarth.

Parlani, R. (1989). Un omaggio a Martha Harris. *Quaderno di psicoterapia infantile, 18*: 5–9.

CHAPTER ONE

The pattern of normal development: forming a relationship with the breast

T he story of Simone starts with the mother's expressing her absolute need to tell the observer the intensity of the emotional experience of the birth, an experience that Mrs Harris defines as "stunning". Simone in the first observation is in a state of restless sleep that Mrs Harris (following Mrs Bick) describes as "ordinary" or "normal" non-integration. In the following sessions we see how this is modified and overcome, when the nipple through the force of its attraction pulls together the functioning of the baby's eyes and mouth and starts the process of integration. The sessions in this first period demonstrate how for the mother the overwhelming impact of the birth is followed by the emergence of depressive anxiety relating to her uncertainty about her capacity to nurture the baby and to take on a genuinely maternal role. For this reason the mother maintains a certain distance from the baby that interferes initially with the process of the baby's introjection of the object.

A stunning experience

First observation of Simone Paolo, five days old,
born 26 October 1979[1]

RN (*reads*): Simone is the much-wanted first child of Rita and Gigi, the mother aged twenty-nine and the father thirty. The couple moved from the Marche to Romano in Lombardy for their work. The father's elder sister, a teacher, was already living there. The mother is also a teacher at a secondary school. The father, a pharmacist, is employed in the town pharmacy. The pregnancy proceeded uneventfully, the mother following all the specialist advice and regularly attending all her check-ups at the hospital in Treviglio, where I first met her after a consultation. At her final consultation in September, while waiting for the obstetrician, she saw me and communicated to me her visible anxiety; she seemed depressed. Her husband and his sister were with her. At the end of the check-up, she came and told me that everything was fine, and that the baby was due to be born at the beginning of November.

On the 26th of October, at the beginning of the clinic, the sister-in-law came to tell me that Rita was in the labour ward. For two days she had not been well, and at 1 p.m. had gone into hospital when the waters broke. At 7 p.m., a paediatric colleague told me that Simone had been born and that his presence had been required. Everything had gone well, but the baby was very big, at 4.210 kg. The mother had had a tachycardiac crisis and it had been necessary to apply the vacuum extractor twice. I went down to the labour ward and met the father and his sister in the corridor; they were exhausted from waiting and from the crisis at the moment of birth. I went to see the baby who was big and very beautiful, his wide eyes closed. There was an obvious cephalohaemotoma in the left occipital region, with light abrasions to the skin, but the baby did not seem to show the usual evidence of suffering caused by the suction process; he seemed full of life. I showed the nurse who was with me the light cyanosis of the hands and feet. She responded that it was the same with all newborn infants. I went over to the mother who was still in the labour room; she was very tired and had been given valium. Even though she was a little confused, she was very keen to recount her experience to me. I saw the mother twice more in hospital. She was not sure whether she had really seen me after the birth or if it were a dream, and confirmed the fact by asking the nurse. She was worried about the impression she might have had on the paediatrician during the birth—"I grabbed her and held on to her tightly"—and asked me if she was a friend of mine. She was very happy with the hospital and felt they had been very helpful.

By the third day Simone had latched on to the breast and started to suck. At one point, in his mother's arms, he had suddenly opened his eyes and looked attentively at his mother, "You should see how he looked at me!", she commented. She told me that gradually as the time went by (he was now five days old) she felt far more attached to him. The first day he'd been given to her she had felt very distant; now things had changed enormously. We agreed on a date for the first observation at home.

MH: You get some hint from this of what a stunning experience the birth can be for the mother. I was also thinking about how the mother says she absolutely *has* to tell you her experience; she is really looking forward to having the observer as somebody to whom she can communicate her feelings about it. It is as if already she has formed what one could call a maternal transference to you; and she hugs the paediatrician—is the paediatrician a friend of yours? Now let us hear the observation from seven days old.

A state of normal non-integration
and evacuation of sensations

Second observation of Simone, 7 days old

RN (*reads*): Simone had come home from hospital the previous day. The mother and paternal grandmother were in the kitchen. The baby was sleeping in his cot by the double bed. The mother seemed well, if rather pale. She told me yesterday had not been a good day; she didn't know how to dress the baby, because in hospital they had never encouraged her to do this herself; she felt inadequate. In the night Simone had cried long and desperately; she had not known why, nor how to console him. She thought he may have been disturbed by the change in ambience; in hospital it was warmer, so she had put an extra cover over him in the night to comfort him. He hung on to the breast, even when she knew he was not hungry.

We go into the room and sit down by the cot. The mother wonders if it is rather dark and there should be more light; I say it is all right. She sits for a moment on the bed by the cot, then goes out, leaving me alone with the baby in the room. The baby sleeps, his head turned slightly to the left (towards me and behind me the window blinds are almost lowered). He stretches his arms, frowns, sticks out his tongue, shakes his whole body, straightens up, becomes still, with his mouth slightly open, his hands with fingers bent but slightly apart. He stays like this for a few moments, then his face puckers again, and it seemed to me (though I was not sure) there was a slight smell of pooh. He puts his hands to his face and stays like that, not moving. Suddenly, brief sucking movements occur, accompanied by his head moving up and down. His hands move, tongue between his lips. He stretches clenched hands and turns towards me. He lightly shakes his left hand like a boxer, sticks out his tongue, and yawns. His left fist stays in front of his mouth. He remains asleep, and opens and closes his mouth as if swallowing. He waves, making a sound, puckers his eyebrows and grimaces, his hand raised to his head. He sighs, and becomes calm, remaining still.

The mother comes in with coffee for me, and tells me she is preparing a large glass of milk for herself. She likes milk; as a child on the farm, with many cows, she drank a lot of it. She tells me about the problems with Simone the night before. Her husband, she says, loves the baby and often says "How have we managed to make him?" The baby stirs but does not wake up, bringing his hands together, moving his mouth. He puts the back of his hand against his face and seems on the point of crying, but doesn't. He sleeps. He knits his brows, then is peaceful. He becomes restless again, bending his arms in front of his face. He lets out a groan and his arms change from flexion to extension. Now he is still, face turned towards me, fingers slightly flexed. He moves his mouth, waves his arms, puts his tongue between his lips, then puts his hands in his mouth. He turns his head and his eyes open slightly. Now he is still.

His mother comes in and, leaning over him, says "Still asleep?" The baby opens his mouth, makes sucking movements, puckers his face and then is still. Then he shakes his arms, sighs, closes his mouth, makes noises, moves his arms, holds his hands and writhes, still in his sleep. Again he seems fairly still, then he breathes deeply and moves his head, going "eh . . . eh . . . eh" accompanied by sucking movements. It is time for him to wake up, but his mother says: "I am not waking him, he can wake up himself." She calls to him but the baby appears not to notice. He waves his arms, closes his eyes, becomes still. The mother goes out, saying "In that case I will go and have a wash." The baby closes his eyes, his left fist in front of his mouth, lying still.

Meanwhile, I hear the sister-in-law and a friend come into the house and begin a conversation with the grandmother in the kitchen. Simone softly moves his left arm, opens his mouth, opens his eyes, stirs, opens his mouth wide, his left fist in front of his lips, makes smacking noises with his lips, yawns, and opens his eyes—but does not awaken. His eyelids are open and he seems to look up above him. The mother comes in but goes out almost immediately. Simone opens his mouth and a smile seems to form, then seems to change into a moan. He stretches his arms out and waves them. He opens his eyes, his mouth; his eyes are often slightly open, and again the lips form a smile that changes into a grimace. His right arm is alongside his body, his left arm close to his mouth. I hear his mother saying to the visitors, "He is sleeping blissfully now, making up for last night." Then she comes back into the room. The baby lets out a sigh, puts his tongue out, shakes, grimaces, stirs. His eyes are clearly open now. He yawns, arms slightly bent, looks ahead, but his look is like a blind child. His mouth is half open. He turns, waves his arms, makes a drawn-out light hiccupping [noise].

He goes back to sleep, mouth and eyes slightly open. His hiccuping continues. He seems about to cry. The mother comes in and says, "He's got the hiccups." She takes his hand. He hiccups but continues to sleep. She strokes the nape of his neck. The hiccups stop for a few moments, then start again, then stop. Then he sleeps completely still.

> Not dreaming

MH: There are two things here to think about: the mother, and the baby. At seven days old, the mother says the baby is sleeping "quite happily"; but it is not what one would call a happy sleep if one looks closely. It would seem to me to be the sort of sleep where the baby is constantly being disturbed by some sort of sensation, in some part of its body. He makes these constant little movements with his face, his mouth, his arms, the tongue that goes out and comes back in. One might think of them as more or less random movements that have not as yet got much meaning to them; he has not yet reached the stage where you could say there is a definite division between sleeping and waking. This is the sort of sleep that is not deep and tranquil, in which you feel the baby is held and enfolded. He remains, you might say, *barely* asleep: not enough disturbed by the various sensations that he seems to be evacuating with the various movements of his body to really cry and in that way draw his mother's attention to him. This type of uneasy sleep is not a state that one would call *dreaming*. It is a state of constant little evacuations of disturbing sensations, which one sees very often with babies in the early days.

The change in temperature

Now the mother said that the night before he cried for a very long time, suggesting that what was disturbing him was *too much* to be simply evacuated through these little movements. It was not because he was hungry, because she had fed him; she puts it down to his being upset by the change in temperature—in hospital it was warm, but here it is cold. In a sense there is some truth in this; but the *real* "change in temperature" is from being in the warmth of the womb, to being outside. Dr Bion talks about changing from a "liquid" to a "gaseous" environment. What a major change this must be for the baby, whose contact with the mother has been not only through the amniotic fluid but also through the placenta, whereas now he is outside, breathing in with his nose, and having to take in with his mouth. It is a major change.

In these constant little movements we see the disturbance that has to be evacuated in some way or other before the baby has becomes really established in a quite different way of relating to the mother. You also get some indication from the mother of what a change it is for her: instead of holding the baby inside her, feeling his movements inside her as she said, and being able to relate to him this way, she now has to be able to hold him *outside*. Here she is saying that yesterday she could not dress him—she did not do that in the hospital.

At the beginning, when the mother tells you about his crying the night before, and the change in temperature, pressing him to her even though she knew he was not hungry, and then goes out leaving you with the baby . . . I would think that at that moment she is using your observation and attention to be able to put the baby out of her mind for the moment, just to escape. This would be escaping from the responsibility of thinking and worrying about the baby, just for a moment—leaving that with you. One gets some idea of the heavy responsibility that it becomes for a mother to have this baby *outside*, having to try to understand just what the baby's disturbance is about. You also get these reminiscences from her own girlhood, of how she had always loved milk and her father had many cows. In this way she is going back to her own infantile experiences with her own parents.

When she talks about her husband being in love with the baby—I take it she is saying, "How did we manage to produce such a marvellous baby?"—is that what this means? She is so pleased with the baby; yet what a heavy weight of responsibility. Although the mother has had some anxieties about the baby, she is being very careful not to intrude these on the baby. So she says she does not want to wake him; it is better for him to waken by himself.

Comment [on the baby's looking]

MH: That looking that you describe there, is not really *looking* towards something, fastening on an object; it is more an opening of the eyes, like some of those other movements; they are not directed towards anything in particular, they are more in the nature of an evacuation of a disturbing stimulant. Even earlier on when once or twice he puts his tongue out, it is not the movement of reaching towards the breast, or even of sucking in his sleep as if seeking the breast.

I would think that with most babies, if you observe them, you can probably see the point at which there becomes a definite division between sleeping and waking, when the movements in sleep become *the beginnings of dreaming*, if you can see dreaming as a form of thinking in your sleep that takes place in relation to an object. At the moment, you cannot see much sign in his sleep of his recollecting a relationship to an object—really to the breast.

> The quality of crying

You have not heard him crying yet, as the mother said he did the previous night; but you can also study differences in the quality of crying. It can have an evacuatory feeling, but this can change at some point to the kind of crying that is not just evacuation of pain, but a cry that wants something, is seeking something. The cry will *come* to have meaning, as a result of the mother's interaction with the baby, and the baby's needs being met, and having some feeling that there is an object that can respond to his needs. The problem is

then to learn to differentiate the meaningless evacuatory movements from those that do begin to have some meaning.

> An ordinary evacuation of sensations

The baby's present movements, I would say, are random and relatively meaningless. All the various parts of his body—the mouth,
the face, skin surfaces—sense some feeling of disturbance, and he
evacuates the stimuli. Every part of him is in contact with a very
different medium. He has to get used to being *held together* in a very
different way from when he was inside the amniotic fluid. Yes, I
would think that what one is seeing at the moment with this baby
is a very *ordinary* evacuation of sensations; though it is something
that is very much prolonged in atypical, autistic-type development.
It is an area that I think does exist in everybody, at certain times. I
would imagine that one will see a very decided change in this baby
during the next few weeks.

We have not actually observed a feed at this early stage; but I
would think it quite likely that when you see the baby having a
feed, you will see he is more held together, with the nipple in his
mouth and the mother holding him; and these random movements
will probably be much less. When the baby feels he is *held*, he will
not need to evacuate his disturbance.

The pull of the nipple

Third observation of Simone, fourteen days old

> RN: When I entered the room, Simone was sleeping, and remained
> asleep for half an hour. In his sleep he makes little grimaces. The
> mother enters the room, approaches him, tries in vain to wake him up
> and says, "Nothing." She kisses him on the neck and calls him. He
> opens his hands, his mouth, twists his face as if unwilling to wake up.
> He moans, rolls his head, and starts to cry. The mother, standing above
> the baby, says "Where are you—you're away somewhere else!" She
> takes him in her arms and says he has done a big pooh. Simone does
> not cry but fixes his eyes on his mother, who puts his cheek against hers
> and says, "Are you hungry, it is amazing how he feels close to me when
> he is hungry . . . do you want to go back to sleep? I will change him,

though, because he is very dirty." She says he has finally opened his eyes. She calls the sister-in-law to hold the baby while she gets his clean clothes. On the changing table, once he is undressed, Simone moves, wriggles, seems to control himself, putting his hand in his mouth and opening his eyes, and seems to hold himself together better than the previous time.

The father comes in and says, "You should have seen him last night, the little animal!" The mother takes him in her arms. He looks at her, then at the window. The father comes back in and says to the child, "Look at Daddy." Instead, he looks out of the window. The mother puts him to the breast and he latches on hungrily, such that she lets out a yell. He sucks hungrily, then stops to look around, and starts sucking again a little less forcibly.

MH: In the way he is sucking there, as you describe it, you can see how both his eyes and his mouth are going in the same direction, to the same point—towards the nipple, towards the breast. When the father picks him up and says "look at me", you can see that the father's face and voice do not have the same *pull* on his attention. It would seem that, at that point, it is the light that *pulls* his attention. When he is at the breast, the nipple *pulls* his eyes and mouth together. We may find later on that the baby's attention is pulled towards the mother's face, by her talking to him and looking at him. But here, he is concentrated on the breast and nipple.

I take it this observation is about a week later than the first one? ("Yes.") I suppose one also has to consider that at the seven-day session, after a slightly difficult birth, and the mother having had valium, it may be that the valium had slightly affected both her and the baby himself. And being born via the vacuum extractor was a slightly traumatic experience, that had not yet been really dealt with.

Maternal depression and the difficulty of introjecting the object

Fourth observation of Simone, age one month, twelve days

MH: So this is the first observation we have had of the baby when he is awake. We remember that this is the first baby of a couple twenty-nine and thirty years old, who do seem to be very close, and the baby is very much welcomed. The mother seemed pleased to have Romana as an observer, but we also had the grandmother in that first observation, and she seemed rather less pleased and more critical. That early observation was very much to do with the mother's anxieties and wish to do everything she could for the baby—to drink a lot of milk, because her father had many cows. She wants to prepare herself to be a very good mother to this child.

RN (*reads*): I found Simone lying on the big bed in his room, with his mother by him. He was looking intently at her, with his arms outstretched. "Rascal!" she says to him. The baby makes an "Ehh . . ." sound, shakes his head, looking at her and seeming to wish to speak. He follows her with his eyes. "Little rascal!" she repeats, and the baby smiles. "He's certainly smiling, he must feel good to be like this", says the mother. Simone looks long at his mother and she says, "Smile, sweetheart", and Simone smiles at her. She puts him on his tummy. He stays still, looking around him. He goes "Ehh . . .", and holds his hand in front of his mouth. The mother takes his elbow: "Are you all right like this?" she says, "shall I leave you like this? Or shall I cover you?" The baby looks up with his mouth open. He smiles, while his mother touches his chin. Simone moves the fingers of his left hand, wriggles a bit, moves his head and goes "ehh . . .". He seems restless, his movements more jerky, then he stops and stares in front of him. "He seems fine like this, you should see him when he doesn't want something, the little chick!" He moves his fingers, his mouth, making noises. He smiles, then looks round restlessly, saying "Ehh . . .", wriggles, and moves his head.

The mother goes out. The baby opens his mouth, looks in front of him, seems restless. The mother comes into the room, stands near me and looks at him. The baby touches the end of his nose with a finger, raises his head and appears to laugh. "Be careful you don't fall off the cushion", says his mother. He continues to look in front of him, seems restless; his body shakes and he sighs. "Are you falling?" says the mother, and puts him in the middle of the bed. "We went out three times when it was fine weather." The baby raises his head and puts his cheek on the cushion. He puts his thumb in his mouth and sucks. He looks ahead, seeming restless, puts his finger in his nose with his thumb in his mouth, sucks strongly for a few moments. Now he seems calm but keeps looking for his finger. Then he gets restless and extends his body symmetrically, still on his tummy. He moves as if to try to extend his field of vision; his mother above him says, "Go to sleep because you've already had your feed." With his thumb firmly in his mouth, Simone sucks strongly for a few moments. He raises his head, his hand in his mouth.

His mother goes out of the room; I hear her say to the paternal grandmother in the kitchen, "He's been very smiley." She seems more cheerful than during the last observation. Meanwhile Simone looks in front of himself and yawns; raising himself decidedly, he looks at the lamp, but he is still restless. The mother, who has come back in, says, "He's tired . . . do you want me to pick you up, have you wet your nappy again?" She picks him up, holding his cheek against hers. The baby now seems calm as he looks around. "What a yawn!" says the mother. The baby looks towards the window, his eyes wide open, often fixed, directed towards various points in the room—the bookcase, the table, etc. His mother kisses his cheek repeatedly. The baby shakes his head and it hits her shoulder; he appears stunned, almost absent. He stares in front of him. He seems uneasy and cries. His mother asks him, "Do you want to go into your cot?" and the baby goes "Ehh . . .". Mother says, "Have a little sleep; I'll put the little bees on for you." "Ehh", he repeats, and she says, "Shh . . . I'll let you listen to the bees." She sits on the bed, repeating, "You can listen to the bees," winds up the toy— "here you are, look"—and goes out. Simone looks intently at the bee-toy that circles to the music of "Für Elise". He raises his arms and wriggles, looking at the bees as they go round.

In the kitchen I hear the mother and grandmother talking about food. Simone stops looking the bees, but towards me. Then he looks at them again, but not calmly; he moves his arms and head as though searching for something. He looks at the bees and laughs with his mouth open. He seems to be trying to do a pooh. He sticks out his tongue. His mother has come back and stands over him, saying the music has finished. He looks intently at her and smiles. She says, "Shall I wind it up again?" and he seems content, follows the bees as they go round, waving his arms, while the mother again speaks to the grandmother in the kitchen. The musical toy stops. Simone looks at the bees unhappily. The mother returns, comes near and says *"Toh"*. Simone calms as he hears the toy being wound, and waves his arms as he watches the bees.

The mother's uncertainty about her maternal role

MH: So, by the end of the observation, the baby had not gone to sleep—he is still awake? ("Yes.") It does seem as if the mother is, you might say, *hypersensitive* to what the baby might want; she always asks the baby, "Do I leave you like this? . . . or should I cover you up . . .? Are you falling . . .?" as if her mind is filled with questions about what the baby is feeling or wanting or what might be happening to him. She has a lack of confidence in really being able to *hold* the baby herself. So the mother-in-law's presence may be very helpful to her, enabling her to just remove herself from the baby for short periods, not to feel so close and constantly worrying about whether she is finding the *right* answer to the baby's needs. I would think her continued worry about the effect of the induced birth upon the baby is becoming a kind of focus for the anxiety that she feels—it gives it an explanation.

I don't know if I am getting the right impression, but the baby in the large bed gives a feeling of being rather un-held, in a wide open space. You see, when the mother comes and looks at the baby and says, "Be careful, you are falling off the cushion—are you falling?", I was wondering about some feeling in the mother about not being able to provide a completely secure situation—the baby seems somewhat *precarious*.

RN: No, it is a single bed; there is a cradle next to it.

MH: I would think that is some reflection of the uncertainty she still feels about being able to be close enough to hold, keep the baby together, understand him sufficiently. She does talk to him very tenderly and very respectfully, but with just a little uncertainty as to quite how to please him. She seems to feel terribly grateful when he smiles; she says that he does smile and laugh, but "he has to feel very well to do this". Then she asks him to smile. Later, when she goes to the grandmother and says, "Simone was smiling a lot", it is as if she feels very reassured and gratified, almost in a childlike way herself, as if she were receiving some kind of confirmation that she was doing the right thing for him.

Now . . . have you actually seen the baby being fed, in these observations?

RN: In the next session . . .

MH: It seems to me that after this, with the thumb, and poking his finger up into his nose, he is trying to recreate some close relationship with the breast, and of somehow holding himself together through this. The mother feels uncertain about him; when she says after this, "Do you want to go into your cradle?", it is almost as if she is wondering whether the baby is happy after his feed. She hasn't *decided* that, after his feed, he will be wrapped up and put into his cradle to sleep; she seems to be waiting to find out what he wants. She is again rather uncertain when, from what you say, he seems to moan or cry a little and not be completely settled.

RN: Only recently has the baby been quiet after being fed. He is a baby who changes quickly from crying to being quiet, but does not stay like that for long periods.

MH: He is constantly moving. Yes, that is the impression he gives after the feed—of being not quite settled. He and his mother between them are unsettled—she trying various things to see what would make him happier. When she picks him up and puts him on her shoulder, she is not sure whether that is going to help or not; and falls back on that little toy with the bees. So you get the impression that what she communicates to the baby is a kind of *questioning and uncertainty*; as if she has not yet grown into a really maternal role. She is almost more still the little girl who is trying hard to be a good mummy, and looking for the baby to tell her what to do. When the baby is anxious and uncertain, she finds it difficult to remain close, with that feeling, and tries to "shift the position" so that he might feel better, and she might feel better.

Digesting emotions

Fifth observation of Simone, age one month, nineteen days

RN (*reads*): I enter the room, find the baby in his mother's arms, cheek to cheek with her. He is looking at a little bookcase next to the window. His mouth is slightly open. The mother talks about the weather, saying that she would like to be in Bergamo (I have come from Bergamo, and it was sunny there), or she would like to go down to her house in the Marche. She holds the baby cheek to cheek and asks, "Are you comfortable?" He cushions his head against her breast and makes some sounds. She says, "You're sleepy, aren't you?" The baby closes his eyes then opens them. "He has already had a feed, at 10.30, then he kept crying and I didn't know how to comfort him." The mother appears very tired. The baby holds his hand slightly open on the breast, with his other arm hanging down under his mother's arm. Meanwhile the mother talks to me about a mutual acquaintance.

We sit down with Simone on the swing seat; the baby keeps his mouth slightly open on the mother's blouse over her breast. Cuddled close by his mother, he goes to sleep. "If you're tired but then he starts to smile, you feel better," she says. The baby wakes up and looks around. "Do you want to see things?" asks his mother, and holds him on her knee, "You don't want to sleep?" Simone yawns, and the mother says him, "You're sleepy really, aren't you?" He looks at the toy with the bees, that is to his left. The mother says, "Do you see the bees?", and he looks out of the window. She picks him up, covers him, and turns round and round with him. He seems anxious, makes sounds "Ehh . . . ehh . . .", and she again puts him cheek to cheek. Now Simone looks at me, then at the window, then again at me. He looks around, at the ceiling, mouth open, and looks at me. He looks at the mother but not into her eyes and makes a sound. The mother says, "I don't suppose he will go to sleep again." The baby yawns. Mother says, "Lazy thing, I'll put you down. Do you want to look at them?" He is put in his cot, looks at the bees and waves his arms. He moves his mouth and body, making hiccupping sounds, looks as if he is going to cry but does not.

The mother says to him, "Do you want the dummy?", and he accepts it. She sits near him, and he sucks it, looking at her. He looks at the bees, moves his arms. Mother says, "Don't you like the bees?" She holds his hand. Simone looks at her; she strokes his hair and he goes "Ehh . . . ehh . . .", almost crying. She touches his face and comments, "The bees are so nice, don't you like them?", and he puts his hand in his mouth, stretching it. In response to the mother, the baby gurgles. The mother says, "The bees aren't singing any more." He appears surprised, and the mother adds, "Do you want to hear it again, then?" She rewinds the toy. Simone looks at them excitedly, moving his arms, and looks at his mother. "What do you want?" The baby looks at the bees, waves his arms, starts to cry. The mother puts the dummy in his mouth and he becomes quieter. He accepts the dummy but seems on the point of crying, saying "Eh . . . ehh", with arms outstretched. He looks at the bees, shakes his head. The mother holds his hand and asks, "What's the matter?" The baby says "Ehh", and seems angry, and the mother says, "Don't you want the little dummy?" The baby seems unhappy, going "Ehh . . .ehh" emphatically.

Meanwhile, the mother goes out, then comes back in and picks him up. "What crying!" She holds him cheek to cheek, but the baby is not consoled and the mother continues, "It's impossible you're still hungry." The baby goes "Eh eh", and cries louder. He stops and looks around. "Do you want to lie on your tummy—have you got a tummy ache?" Simone starts crying again. The mother says, "Let's go for a little walk." Then, "Do you want to eat something?" Simone starts crying, then stops, then starts again. The mother rolls him round on his tummy and says, "Surprise . . . but you're smiling too." Simone cries again and his mother turns him back to face her, changing his position, and says, "Do you want more to eat?" She offers him the breast. The baby latches on to it voraciously, looking first around him then into his mother's eyes, intensely. She takes his hand, and strokes his neck. His half-closed fist is next to the breast. He sucks strongly and noisily, but is restless and waves his arm. He looks at his mother through half-closed eyes, then around him, then intensely at the mother. Then he seems to be going to sleep on the breast with his mouth open, shakes his arm, jerks his mouth open on the nipple and starts to suck again. He looks at the mother, continues to suck, then stops, still looking at her. He sucks again, stops as if to go to sleep but doesn't; he starts again while looking around him. He sucks strongly, stops, then sucks strongly with eyes closed. He loses the nipple, continues for a little with an empty mouth, and becomes still with his mouth half-open on the breast and his eyes closed.

Feeling and digesting emotions

MH: It is very clear in this observation that the mother is depressed. She speaks of the fact that in Bergamo it is sunny—and the observer comes from Bergamo. The mother seems to feel that there is sunshine somewhere; and that seems to be related to her own home, like her saying earlier that her father had many cows, in the context of producing milk. There is sunshine, there is happiness, there is a good object somewhere; but where she is at the moment, it all seems foggy and depressed. She seems to feel that there *is* a "good way" for the baby, if she could only just find the "right position"; but somehow she has not found it yet, and the baby is not quite contented. It is as if she has difficulty conceiving that the baby may *need* to feel a bit unhappy or a bit uncomfortable sometimes, and she could perform a useful function by *being with him* when he feels unhappy, and letting him have enough time *to feel what he does feel*. So there is this constant changing of position, asking him what he'd like, then feeling delighted when he smiles, as if she wants to shift him into a position where the sun can break through. She very much needs his approval, his sunshine, his smiles, to reassure and warm her, and help lift her depression. Yes, she expresses it quite clearly—when she says that if she is tired, and she sees Simone begin to laugh, she feels happy. It is interesting that she has chosen this particular toy with the bees. There is sunshine and honey, as if she is trying to provide her good object.

So the baby is again offered the breast. It seems very likely from the observation that the baby has really had enough to eat; and the problem is rather one of managing to sort out his *emotions* about the breastfeed that he has just had. He needs to digest his food, both physically and mentally. In a sense he does not get much opportunity to really cry very hard; if he is feeling upset he does not have the opportunity to fully express that. So—the dummy, and then later on it becomes the breast—is put back into the mouth, to keep [this distress] from emerging ("to stop his mouth"), yes, to stop his mouth. This is quite a common situation, with a mother who wants to be a good mother and who is very sensitive to any disapproval, not to be able to really *bear* the baby's feelings—to *feel what he feels* and have a wholehearted experience. So the breast is made the solution; but he feels a bit unhappy, a bit discontented, so he is given more breast. But he is not given the *mental space* in his mother's mind, or the time, to be able to really express his upset. So at the end here he is drifting off to sleep with his mouth on the breast. He hasn't separated from it, and he hasn't yet had the opportunity to introject an experience that he can turn to inside himself when he goes to sleep; he is still clinging to the *external* object. He drifts off, rather than having had an intense experience with an object that allows him to turn inwards.

I think one can see here one of the very usual difficulties in the mother–baby relationship. It is difficult for the mother to feel she has given the baby a good-enough experience, then to give him some time to *digest* that and to express what his angry feelings are, while having the confidence that he has got something good enough inside for him to find his object. It is very much related to her feeling of depression—that her sunshine, her happiness, is not actually with her, so she is not able to give it from herself to her baby. At the moment what she is having to struggle with are her own nostalgic and infantile feelings of loss and longing for her own mother and her breast; and these infantile feelings are interfering with her being close to the baby.

I think you do get, handed down from generation to generation at some level, something of this infantile attachment to mother that continues to be invested in the external object, and it is not entirely transferred to the internal establishment of a good mother, a good breast. It is a perpetuation of the dependence upon an external object—either the mother or one that represents mother.

Problems of idealization in the mother

Sixth observation of Simone, age two months, seven days

RN (*reads*): Simone was in his mother's arms while she opened the door to me. (The paternal grandmother had gone home the day after Christmas.) He had already been fed, but was not sleepy and was looking around. The mother says she wants to put him down so she can make me a coffee. I offer to hold the baby instead. The baby is restless in my arms, frowning a lot and looking in other directions. After a bit he gives me a long stare, resting his gaze above my head, frowning first to the side then in front of him, crying. The mother returns and puts him on the little bed, saying that he's lost his dummy. She leans over him: Aren't the bees nice!" He looks at her and smiles contentedly. She goes out for a moment and Simone looks at the bee-toy above him, seems restless, waves his arms. The father comes in and puts the dummy in his mouth. The baby becomes quieter and smiles a lot, but frequently spits out the dummy. With the dummy in his mouth, he pays more attention to what the father is saying to him. "How serious you are, little one (*pisello*), with your wide open eyes!"

When the father goes out, the baby protests loudly, with his arms stretched out. The mother comes in and he suddenly stops; she says, "Do you want me to start up the bees?" He sucks his dummy firmly. She says, "All the nasty things have gone now", and touches his cheek: "Do you want to hear them, little rascal?" The bees go round to the music of *Für Elise.* He looks at them, but also looks often at his mother, smiling. His arms are open and his hands are moving. He looks at the bees, the mother, as though holding her with his eyes.

The mother gives him the dummy again but he doesn't seem to want it. He says, "Eh eh"; then he accepts it and sucks rapidly. She takes his hand, he seems restless, and cries. "The bees aren't singing any more," says the mother. He shakes his arms and goes "Eh . . . eh", staring at the bees that have stopped moving. The mother says, "You are a rascal" the baby continues to cry. She picks him up: "I'll pick you up for a bit and all those bad feelings will go away." The father comes in and asks about something to do with the cooking. The mother holds the baby cheek to cheek, looking in front of him. "Don't say you're hungry." He looks at me fixedly for a few moments, then cries and she holds him up to her shoulder. She shows him the coloured pattern on the curtains. He is calmer; the mother moves swaying around the room with him. She says, "You're sleepy, why don't you go to sleep?" She brings his mouth to her cheek and removes the dummy, while he seems decidedly unhappy. He then stops crying and looks around.

The father comes in; he often jokingly calls the baby "Arthur". He wants to give him the dummy, saying, "I know he's hungry." "Yesterday", says the mother, "he ate a lot at 11.30, and he also ate first thing." The baby, held tight by the mother, sucks the dummy strongly and looks around at things at her eye-level, jerkingly interrupting his sucking. He stops, eyelids a bit closed; his mother touches his forehead and nose with her own mouth and nose. He seems to be trying to go to sleep, eyelids closed, sucking the dummy noisily and often strongly. His hands are together in front of him. The father, standing up in the room, says, "I can tell you that last night he didn't sleep at all, the little beast."

MH: I am just wondering, where does the baby sleep at night?

RN: In his little cot, in the room where these observations are being made.

MH: In a way, from the observation here, it would be not too surprising that he doesn't sleep at night, because he is not getting that much help in turning to his own resources when he is upset. Again, the father comes with the dummy; the mother comes with the little bees; all the time, his distress is kept at bay and some solution is immediately provided to take it away. I was thinking how, in this first part, when the mother goes out for a moment, he does immediately look at the little bees and shakes his arms. It is as if the thought of the mother outside is unbearable to him, and he immediately looks towards them instead. He is immediately responsive to external objects. When the father comes in and gives the dummy he accepts it, but he also smiles at his father. When the father then goes out, the baby protests again; then the mother comes in, and he *immediately* stops when he sees her. He is almost being *encouraged* into a situation of expecting distraction or attention all the time.

This is a situation where the parents are delighted with the baby, yet seem to be over-anxious, over-sensitive, *trying too hard* really to have an ideally happy, satisfied baby, and concentrating on trying to find the "right sweets" for him. In a way they are trying to put into practice this fantasy that most of us have at an infantile level, that if only the world were nice enough to us—if only we had nice enough parents or nice enough people—it would be sunshine all the time. The reality in fact is that every human being—which does include babies!—has to struggle with the demands and disturbance of *his own nature.* Simply living, being alive, is a situation that at times is a very disturbing one. And obviously the good experiences are very important: the baby should have a satisfactory experience in being loved and given the food that it needs; but that does not mean to say that that is *all* it takes from that experience.

> Toleration of bad feelings

Q: [about the nature of the mother's idealization]

MH: Yes, I would think it is an idealization that is really perpetuated by some problem in really coming closer to that whole area in the person that is not able to appreciate the goodness of the good object, or that might treat it badly. This mother, one feels, is a very sensitive, tender, well-meaning person. There is very little that seems to emerge from her of feelings of anger or resentment or hostility—of anything one could think of as *bad feelings.* It is a problem of being able to tolerate bad feelings in oneself.

RN: The grandmother has left because she had a disagreement with the aunt (her own daughter). Simone's mother said she was pleased also, because she finds her a little authoritarian; however, she said she herself could adapt because she had been to college and was flexible; and she was interested only in the baby.

MH: There you get a picture of the mother *placating* her persecutor; because another mother, for instance, might feel very annoyed and resentful, and even fight with a mother who was too authoritarian, for her right to decide what she wants for herself. This suggests that this mother somehow submits to authority, and has not really got a sufficient hold on her own aggression to be able to use it when it would be useful. That would really imply a kind of idealization of parental authority—she believes they really are right. That idealization might come about because her parents are in fact very authoritarian, or she might feel that if she allowed her aggression to emerge they would be [too] frail to stand it. As a result of this, what comes over to the baby is a feeling of having parents who are constantly preoccupied with trying to please him, and who would be terribly distressed if he got angry or into a rage; they would fall apart.

Q: Would this mother be stronger if she was physically near to the good object, to her mother?

MH: I doubt it; because the problem is really that of getting in touch with the good object inside herself. That is related to not being in touch with her own nastier feelings. Her depression, I would think, is to do with her fear that she may do something that would spoil things for the baby, and would hurt him. But she cannot let herself be aware of that, and of whatever her anti-baby feelings and resentment may be—the aggression in herself that may separate her from her good object. The depression is fundamentally to do with inability to reach the good feelings internally; and that is to do with the inability to manage the bad and aggressive feelings. This is not to say that she doesn't actually need some maternal support in the external world, which in fact could help to mitigate this a little. The observer, for example, is used as a good mothering figure in the external world; and her husband also supports her. But the lack of place for, grasp of, her negative feelings does make it difficult for her to allow the baby to be really angry or upset, and to remain *with him* while he is in that state. She always tries to shift it, so that situation cannot arise. That has a kind of placatory quality, which is different from the desire to meet the baby's needs as far as she can (though this is also present). It is quite difficult for mothers, when the baby is very small, to be fully in touch with the *intensity*, the *force*, that exists in that small body. There is this paradox about babies: that they are helpless and vulnerable, but also, there can be a very fierce spirit, or life-force, in their very small bodies.

Q: Would this aspect of the mother's internal situation repeat her experience with her own mother?

MH: I would think it very likely that there is a tendency to repeat the same pattern. The extent to which these patterns are repeated is very much determined by the degree to which the child has not been able to internalize and think about its experience with its mother. This mother does think about the child a great deal. But everything comes under one heading: how to make him happy, how to be nice to him. It may be she is beginning to think about something else, when she says that during the night he doesn't sleep, "the little beast". Oh, that's the father . . .! ("The dummy . . .") The dummy, yes, is always being put in the mouth to *stop* the bad feelings, almost as if to say "stop it, I don't want to know about your upset".

Q: I would like to know whether the mother was worried about the child during pregnancy?

RN: She was very careful throughout the pregnancy, undertaking all the tests and check-ups. She had a period of depression a month before the baby was born, fearing that he had something wrong with him. She paid attention to all his movements, and when she didn't feel any she gave him a little tap to make him move.

Q: [about whether the mother has aggressive feelings]

MH: Well . . . whether this mother is any more aggressive in herself than anybody else, is a moot question—she wouldn't strike me as being somebody who has got a "bad nature" in the sense of being very aggressive. But I think she does have the problem that so many "good girls" or "good boys" have, of getting some conscious *grasp* of what the bad or aggressive parts of their nature are feeling.

Q: Grasp?

MH: By "grasp" I mean conscious awareness and toleration of her own bad feelings. She may be someone of a naturally tender and loving disposition who was therefore always *expected* to be tender and loving, and was not given the space to feel the other side of her nature and to fight with it, allowing it a real place in her personality.

I don't know what Romana knows of this mother's place in her family—were there many children, was she one of the eldest?

RN: No, she is the only daughter of farming people who, as a result of becoming well educated and getting a university degree has changed her social level. But she has a great affection for the farm and everything in her background; she is a simple, sweet, and unaffected person, and very emotional; she is afraid of sleeping on her own; and when she feeds the baby, although she only wears a light shirt, she is always drenched with sweat from her emotion.

The obligation to be good

MH: The situation could be, then, that she herself has had so much done for her, by her parents, that she feels a sort of *obligation* to be especially good; and any other side of her personality has had great difficulty finding room to express itself. So I would not think that she is *not* a good and well-meaning mother—I think that in fact she *is*. But I also think that the nastier and more aggressive side of her nature is pretty split off, and along with that is likely to go quite a lot of her *strength*; because this timorousness, fear of being on her own, does derive from the more forcible parts of the personality being split off, allowing fears to come in from the outside.

Q: Why does she have this need to split off her aggressive part?

MH: Well, we can perhaps see it happening with this child. It may be that if a child has a naturally affectionate and outgoing disposition, and that is approved of by the parents and pleases them, there is a terrific tendency for *collusion* between them, for the child to be like that *all the time*, in order not to hurt the object of which he feels so appreciative and fond.

If she was a mother with a nastier disposition, this part of her would not be split off so successfully; you would find it coming out in unconscious aggressive acts towards the baby, or she would feel more cut off from him. Instead, her aggressive aspects have been split off into a feeling that she has frail internal objects, who would not be able to stand it if she were nasty. You see this in her attitude to the baby, feeling that he is frail if left to himself, so she must constantly try to keep away from him all feelings of upset. You can see reflected, in the mother's attitude to the baby, the attitude that she has toward her own internal objects. So the fear that she had about the baby not being alive, being dead inside her—does indicate something of her anxiety about not really having strong, live, internal objects inside herself. This makes for what you might call a sense of *over-responsibility*—a sense that everything depends on her; so she has to worry excessively about doing everything possible herself to keep the baby alive. She can't really delegate to him, however little, some responsibility for managing his *own* feelings to some minimal degree.

Comment: The opposite kind of mother would let the baby cry, saying that it is good for him.

MH: That is another rationalization for not being able to empathize with the baby's upset feelings, when the baby is crying. She tells herself she is "doing the right thing". It is, also, to avoid the uncertainty that one inevitably has at times with a baby, of *not really knowing* whether one is doing the right thing; and sometimes feeling helpless that one can't do any more, so the baby will just have to cry a bit—because one simply doesn't know what else to do.

Q: [about whether the mother might possibly change her behaviour into this alternative or opposite type].

MH: I doubt it. It depends a bit on how the baby will be. I would think it possible with this mother, as with many mothers, that as the baby himself survives and grows and becomes stronger, her anxieties may be allayed and she may feel better about being able to be angry with him sometimes or to leave him to his own resources.

Q: [about the other kind of mother].

MH: From what you say, the mother you are speaking of has the attitude that she knows all about babies, but she is actually a bit deaf to their communication of their needs. Whereas Simone's mother gives the impression that she doesn't really know anything. She is asking the baby, all the time—looking to him to tell her what he needs.

There is a general problem here that one doesn't always think about, for people who have very positive characteristics—very loving people, very beautiful people, very intelligent people. They may find they utilize their good qualities or their gifts in a way that enables them to avoid the *other* aspect of their personality. The very intelligent person may use his intelligence to avoid getting into a situation which would make him experience being stupid; the beautiful girl can use her beauty to avoid the experience of ever feeling left out or jealous; a very loving person can use those very qualities of sensitivity and making people happy to avoid being in a situation where lovingness and sensitivity are not enough, and they may be faced with having to cope with the *misery* of somebody else.

I think that this mother is possibly in this last category—somebody who has natural sensitivity and good feelings, which enabled her to be a good child who pleased her parents, but who used these qualities also to avoid facing the aspect of her nature that would have made her rebel and get into fights with them. Now, bringing up a baby of her own, there is a problem in *staying with* the baby's bad feelings, without having to believe that somehow if she does the right thing she will be able to *make it feel happy*. So, I would say, this mother has not split off her aggression because she is a very aggressive person, but because other factors in her situation have always enabled her not to have to confront her own aggression. If, for example, this mother had been a more turbulent, aggressive person, she might not have been able to split it off quite so easily; it might have forced itself on her attention. She might then have had to fight with it more. This is a very general statement; but it is worth thinking about. The people who develop their own capacities best may not always be those who are most gifted in some respect; they may be those who have been forced to have a struggle with different aspects of their nature, forced to *notice* them, from an early age. One would have to see, for instance, how a mother like this may possibly develop in her own personality *through* having children, through being forced up against the conflicting emotions that children can arouse. "Nice girls" can—and many do—grow into being mature women through the process of having children.

The breast that comes and goes away

Seventh observation of Simone, age two months, twenty-four days

> **RN** (*reads*): Simone's mother opens the door, holding the baby in her arms. He cries because he had been feeding. She sits down quickly; seems slightly depressed. Simone sucks, looking at her, with his hand on the breast. He goes "Eh . . . eh." From time to time he suddenly spits out the nipple. At times he sucks with an empty mouth and says "Eh . . . eh." He stretches out his arms, raises his head from the breast, often jerks his left arm. Then his mother offers him a finger, which Simone holds, but not for long. He sneezes, raising his head from the breast with his mouth half-open. He looks at his mother, who says, "Don't you want any more?" He moves his mouth, puts his hand in his mouth, still looking at his mother, who says, "How nice his hands are . . . do you want more? No, enough . . .." She puts him to the breast several times. He looks intently at his mother and seems to wish to play with the breast with his mouth. Mother says, "That's enough", and holds him to her, cheek to cheek.

The baby notices me and looks at me with wide-open eyes, then looks at the window. The mother says to him, "Who is it?" He takes a long look at me. The mother takes his hand, but Simone does not stop looking at me. She turns him towards herself. Simone burps so loudly that the mother and I burst out laughing. He turns again very quickly towards me, and carries on looking at me. The mother kisses him. He looks in her eyes, holding out his arm. He seems a little unsettled, but only for an instant; then turns and looks fixedly at me with his mouth partly open. He looks at the window, then at me and says, "Eh . . . eh." The mother says, "What is it—what are you trying to say?" A little milk escapes from his mouth. Now he is calm.

The mother goes out for a few moments, carrying the baby. She returns with him, cheek to cheek. The baby opens his mouth against his mother's cheek and looks at me, gurgling and smiling, and seems to recognize me. Then the mother puts Simone on her knee and says, "Sit here for a bit." He puts out an arm, smiles, and says, "Eh . . . eh." "Rascal . . . who's a little rascal", she says. He looks at me and smiles. "Where are you going, little one, what a darling you are!" she says. He burps, held upright against his mother's chest. "You have had a good feed, dearest," she says. The baby brings up a little milk, and she says, "What a *merlo* (silly)!" He rubs his open mouth against his mother's face. He looks attentively at my lap, then begins to cry. He looks at me over his mother's shoulder and seems to recognize me: "Mm . . . mm . . ." He looks at the floor beside me. The mother says, "I'll put him down for a bit." She puts him down on the big bed and goes into the kitchen. The baby, on his back, looks at me with his finger in his mouth, looking in front of him. He kicks his legs and is restless. The mother comes in. "Tell me now, what would you like?" she says. Simone kicks his legs, looks at her, smiles. "See now," she says, "you don't know how to talk. Say what you want—do you want to be a little rascal . . . ah, you're smiling."

She is standing above him; he goes "Eh . . . eh." The mother picks him up, and Simone, in her arms, turns and looks intently at me. Then he looks around; then turns and stares at me. He rubs against his mother's face. "Do you want to sleep a bit now?", she says. He looks at me around his mother's face and breaks into short bursts of laughter, then he cries. "Up we come," she says, "say—do you want your dummy? Do you want to sleep? Ah . . . what is it, what have you seen?" At this point Simone is looking at different parts of the room, but he is restless. He looks at me, seems to smile at me, then suddenly hangs his head. Then he observes me prolongedly, putting his hand next to his mouth.

His mouth is now nearly next to his mother's. He is restless and his mother puts the dummy in his mouth, but this does not settle him. She cuddles him and rocks him. She embraces him tightly and sits down. He sucks his dummy, spitting it out against his mother's mouth. She gets up, rocks him, goes "Shh . . . shh", but he is still restless. "No, no— don't throw it away, baby! No, no, no" she chants, rhythmically. He calms down, dummy in his mouth, pressed against his mother's cheek.

Simone now seems sleepy even though his eyes are open. He looks fixedly above himself and sucks rhythmically on the dummy. He pulls his mother's hair and starts to cry. The mother walks with the baby in her arms and hushes him. The baby pulls a tuft of his mother's hair, touches her on the cheek, then on the mouth. She is now rocking him up and down and he is calmer. He is still, and closes his eyes. The mother strokes his neck. The baby sucks rhythmically on the dummy. Mother says, "First it was the sun, or so it seemed to me." The baby has his eyes half-closed; he looks at his mother then sleeps. The mother, noticing his behaviour, says, "You're not really sleeping, naughty thing", and he smiles, going "Eh . . . eh." Then he goes back to sleep. Again he looks at her with half-closed eyes and smiles. Then he sleeps without moving and his mother says, "As long as he doesn't close his eyes properly he can stay like that the whole day."

Mrs Harris asks Romana if the baby was eating when she arrived, and if the mother seemed a little depressed—was this unusual? She wondered whether Simone had noticed his mother's depression and because of this withdrew his attention from her. The mother seems to feel the baby desires something that she is not able to satisfy. Simone seems to feel that milk is not enough; he moves his mouth, puts his hand in his mouth, and the mother says, "Aren't your hands nice." Later, when the baby sucks his dummy and spits it out against his mother's mouth, putting his face and mouth close to hers, and she feels he has been sucking the dummy long enough, there is a link with the last session when he wasn't sleeping at night, "the little animal". It is as though she felt she might not be giving him enough strength. There is a lot of contact between the mother and baby; she is very solicitous and attentive towards him. She is continually asking him questions about what he wants; but finds it difficult to tolerate when, instead of sucking, the baby stops, as if the mother might have been telling him "enough". The mother seems disturbed when the baby seems to wish to play with the nipple—then she says "enough"; she prefers to hold him cheek to cheek.[2]

MH: There seems to me, you might say, a kind of sexual feeling between her and this little boy baby and the breast.

With the baby himself, and his attitude to you—how he looks and looks at you. . . . Now where does he first do this . . . it is after she says "Stop" when he is playing at the breast, and puts her cheek to his cheek, and then he notices you, and watches you. I am wondering whether he attributes to you what is coming between him and his close, exploratory relationship to the breast—as if you are, you might say, his rival, a daddy who might say "no, stop".

> ## The mother, the breast, and the guest

Q: I have the impression that often when the baby pays attention to Romana, the mother tries to divert his attention back to her.

MH: I would think so; a bit like his own hands when he isn't feeding at the breast but puts his hands in his mouth, and she says, "How good your hands are"; his hands are rivals to her breast.

RN: In a previous session, she took up a doll to distract him from me.

MH: I'm just wondering about this feeding at the breast . . . in this observation he is very very close to her, continually turning to his mother and caressing her, but there does seem to be something about the breast that he turns away from. I mean, he puts his hands in his mouth, and you said you'd noticed before how he would put his mouth over the nipple, somehow exploring it, but not sucking from it. I would think it is something specifically about the *nipple* that he is trying to work out: the nipple as representing both what gives him the breast, but also what takes it away. The nipple in this way is a kind of intruder between him and the close, face-to-face absolute contact with breast. There is a link between this intruder that takes away the breast, and you who take away something of mother's attention, and maybe the baby's feeling about daddy with mummy in the night-time. The mother seems to feel that there is something coming between them—that the baby wants something, or is upset about something; as if again she finds it difficult to conceive that this may be a kind of *necessary* upset, and that he is maybe having to *work out* something that he is experiencing. This would be connected with something that she seems to feel, not theoretically, but much more through her maternal and tender qualities—that she wants to give this baby *everything* that he needs. She would like to give him total attention. That would somehow relate to her feeling of jealousy when he is interested in you, or in his hands instead of her.

Then she takes him out. It is interesting; she has taken him out, and she comes in keeping him cheek-to-cheek. That would seem to mean absolutely fused, the two of them together. Then it would seem that, being securely fused to her, he becomes friendly towards you: he warbles, he smiles, and seems to call you. As if he is confident, at one with mummy, so he can be interested in you.

RN: Yes . . . he looks at me most of all when he is in his mother's arms. If he is lying down, or in bed, he looks at me very little.

MH: Being close to mother, at one with mother, he can then be friendly to you. I'm just wondering whether in the warbling and smiling, there is any element that you might pick up as *triumph*. "I've got mummy—I've got her total attention now."

RN: I think yes, in this period here, though things have changed a little bit.

MH: Because it would seem to me that when he is on his mother's lap, stretching his arms and smiling, and the mother says, "Little devil, who's a little devil?", it is as if she is somehow identified with him as being this clever little devil who has acquired mummy for himself and pushed daddy out of the way. He has succeeded in getting mummy so he can be friendly to daddy, or the equivalent of daddy as the observer, because he has got his mummy. He looks at you and smiles, and belches again, and then rubs his open mouth against mother's face, and then he seems to complain . . . and looks at the floor near you . . . then, puts his finger in his mouth, and kicks.

Comings and goings of the object

I am wondering whether he splits off into you the mummy who isn't holding him—the mummy who is away; because when he looks at your lap, that is the place where he *sits* with his mummy, often. So when he looks at *your* lap, it is as if he is working out something to do with the empty lap, as if you represent the mummy he is *not* with, who comes and goes and disappears. You see he has looked at you very hard, and you have been visiting every week, so I would think that he does recognize you. And it does look as if he is puzzling out something about you—he also looks at the floor by your feet, as if that might have something to do with your coming and going.

RN: Yes, his mother told me this week that he loves to look at people's feet; in fact he was in his mother's arms and she had her feet like this, and he was looking hard at them.

MH: So it has begun to dawn on him that the feet take people away, and bring them back. So I would think he is at this moment very preoccupied with the comings and goings of his object.

RN: He is about four months now.

MH: Already, with this looking down at the ground, and his preoccupation with the nipple, it looks as if he is beginning to think about coming, and going away. He recognizes her; but there is also the fact that she goes away. So . . . mother says, do you want the dummy; and he watches several points of the room, but he is unquiet. He looks at Romana, seems to smile at her, still looks at her, and then suddenly drops his head. Then he watches for a long time, putting his hand near his mouth. So, I would think here he is trying to work out something to do with different parts of the room (which after all he knows very well), working out something about his world through the points of the room . . . and when he suddenly drops his head, it is as if a thought had suddenly entered his mind, that he would like to *put away* from him.

Again with his hand near his mouth, and his mouth near the mother's mouth, there is a kind of coming close to, and clinging to the mother, against this *thought* which has visited him, which is I think to do maybe with rivals, or with his mummy being taken away from him. The mother does seem to sense there is something that is distressing him, but again, to somehow feel that it is *her fault*. She seems a bit over-anxious about anything is upsetting him. So— she puts her cheek against his cheek, rocking him and trying to soothe him. Then, when he is sucking the dummy and she is caressing him, it is interesting when she says, "Before it was the sun, or so it seemed to me"—what did she mean by that? As if the sun was distressing him?

RN: It is a part of the country where there is a lot of fog, and she often says to me, "There's no sun"; she likes the heat, the sun. Where she lived as a child it was hot and sunny.

MH: That would again seem to be a bit in line with this slight cloud of depression that she feels about not being able somehow to give *total* satisfaction to this baby.

The bottle, and a distance from the mother

Eighth observation of Simone, age three months seven days

RN (*reads*): The door is opened by the girl who is looking after Simone while his mother is back at work at the school. The baby is in the pram in the hall. The baby's feeding routine has changed. According to the mother, the baby was not eating enough, and he cried continuously for two days; he was very disturbed. "Now he is calmer because he eats," she said; "For ten days he has slept well even during the day, and this has never happened before." The baby sucks quietly and intermittently on the dummy in his sleep. His arms are bent upwards by his head. After ten minutes he jerks, brings his hands to his face, stirs, and wakes up. He looks at his mother, and smiles. "What are you doing," she says, "you've spat out the dummy, you know." In two weeks he has put on 700 grams. "You've had a sleep, so you're smiling." The baby shakes his legs and smiles at his mother. She prods him gently: "Smile, you rascal!" He turns towards me, looks at me for a moment, then suddenly looks away.

The baby looks at the bees, and smiles, but smiles more at his mother who is winding up the toy. He watches very attentively while she does this. His hands are tightly clenched on his jacket; his gaze and gurgles directed towards his mother. "It's finished, the bees have stopped singing." The baby moves, makes noises, looks at the bees, looks at me, shakes his legs, looks at me, turns towards the bees and smiles, looks at the light, goes "Oh . . . eh", then looks toward me again and smiles. He puts his hands on his tummy and goes "Eh . . . eh." He seems restless, goes "Eh . . . eh" again, shakes his legs and arms. "The bees always come down, they fall down all around you," says his mother. He looks at her and his smile seems happy. "Is it better if I take them away, or do you want to see them again?", she asks. She hangs the game so it dangles above his face, and sets it going; then she leaves.

The mother goes out; Simone follows her with his eyes. He looks at me with surprise; he appears decidedly unhappy. The mother returns: "Aren't the bees still going round? Are you tired of being there?" She takes his hand and kisses it. Now the baby is definitely whimpering. The mother sits next to him and picks him up from his cot: "All gone . . . you're a little rascal, never wanting to stay put." From his mother's arms he looks at me and gives a big smile. He gives me a long look. "Look at these bees, see their colours?", says the mother. He looks at me, makes some noises, looks at the bees, smiles at me several times, goes "Eh . . . eh." He kicks his legs, smiles, appears restless. He puts his finger in his mouth, looks at me and makes sounds. The mother says, "Where are you going? Stand up nicely!" He looks restlessly at me; he becomes happier when his mother holds him standing on her knee. He moans and she says, "Tell me, what do you want?" She shows him a bee; the baby continues to moan. He seems on the point of crying. He opens his mouth and presses it against his mother's face. The mother puts him in the pram and he breaks out crying, then he calms down a little but is not completely quiet.

MH: Yes, that is interesting—the anxiety about the mother going back to work. Now, by the time of the next observation, she has already gone back to work? ("Yes.") Because when she says he hadn't been eating enough, and now he is quiet because he is having sufficient food, does she mean he is on the bottle now? ("Yes.") You see, one feels that probably the impetus to put him on the bottle had been because of her going back to work, and her worry that he wasn't going to get enough.

RN: Though she only works a few hours in the morning; by midday she is always at home.

> The mother's uncertainty

MH: So she's not so long away, but there is the anxiety that he might have wanted the breast while she was away, so now he is put on the bottle. It is interesting that it takes him a little bit longer to be friendly to Romana this time. He is friendly, he is interested; but very much related to his mother—to the little bees that he has had from the beginning, to the chandelier. . . . She seems to be a little more uncertain now about whether these bees are, for him, good objects or bad objects. After she's been out, and he seems a little unquiet, she says, "The bees are falling down, they are falling down on you", almost as if she is voicing a kind of nightmare that she feels he might have about the bees while she is out. Because, before she goes out again, she wonders, "Is it better that I take away the bees, or should I wind them up again?"

This time, when the mother goes out, he seems to be a bit upset when he looks at you. This is also the time that, even when the mother is with him towards the end and gives him a little bee, he goes on crying; and when she puts him in the pram he bursts out crying as if he is more upset about some *distance* between him and the mother—after all, he has lost the breast, he has now got a bottle . . . It is only when she takes him into her arms again that he seems quieter, though still a bit upset. It is as if he feels he has lost some kind of closeness to his mother.

The significance of the dummy for Simone's mother

Ninth observation of Simone, age three and a half months

RN (*reads*): Simone is in his mother's arms when she opens the door. He looks at me for a long time extremely attentively. Then she holds him in the rocking chair, turned towards me, with his arms outstretched, while she speaks to me about a mutual friend who is unwell and possibly pregnant. Simone is calm and looks at me with a serious expression, not smiling. He looks at his mother's lap, then at me, attentively. With his hand in front of his mouth he looks at me and smacks his lips. He looks around, breathes heavily. His mother says "boo" to him; he smiles at her and she says, "Are you a bit sleepy, yet? . . . Simone, you're eating your hand all up." She holds him up next to her face: "Help—you're eating me." He puts his fist in his mouth, looking at his mother, sucks on his fist, looking above his mother's head. "You're eating your hand up!"

I say something, and on hearing my voice, he smiles slightly. The mother rocks back and forth in the chair. She dries the baby's mouth with a tissue. He looks round at her when she says *"ciao"*. He looks around him with arms outstretched. He looks at me, goes "Eh." He changes position frequently in his mother's arms. He coughs. "What are you doing?", she asks. He sticks out his tongue a little. "You know you're eating me, don't you?" The mother gets up and puts the dummy in his mouth. He looks at me fixedly. He does not seem to want the dummy. The mother turns on the light. "I am putting you down for a bit", she says; "I'll wind the bees up for you." She is kneeling next to him. He looks at her, turning his head round, with his hand in his mouth. Then she goes out.

Simone fastens his hands on the dummy. He loses it; he puts his hands in his mouth. He is restless, moans. The mother comes back in; he looks at her. When she approaches she makes cooing noises, and he smiles contentedly. "Look at this nice bees," she says, and he is almost able to touch it with his hands. The mother goes out, comes back in, and pops the dummy covered in honey in his mouth. With the dummy in his mouth, he smiles, turning towards his mother, who is crouching next to the cot. He makes sounds continuously, moving the dummy with his hands and looking up over his head. The bees stop. He turns towards me and looks at me.

The mother goes out into the kitchen. Now Simone puts his first finger into his mouth and sucks strongly. He looks towards the window, is quiet for a few moments, and then starts moaning, putting his finger in his mouth again. He looks at the window, moans, stretching out his arms. The mother hears him and says, "Who is crying now? Do you want your dummy again, or do you want to have a little sleep?" She picks him up. Lying on his mother's knees, he stares at me. Then he is stood up against his mother, cheek to cheek, and again stares at me. Then he sits in his mother's arms, face towards me; then stands, stretching and flexing his arms in front of him and making noises. He is restless. The mother rocks him in her arms. He becomes still, sitting with arms outstretched, and looks around.

The mother goes out to let in her sister-in-law. The aunt comes into the room and offers the baby a rattle that makes a noise as it is taken out of its box. She goes out again, and the baby looks at her thoughtfully, and casually takes the toy and puts it to his mouth. The mother stops him and tells him he has a dummy to put in his mouth. The aunt has come back in and sits in the rocking chair; he notices her and smiles. She talks to him, shows him a picture of a baby in a newspaper; Simone looks interestedly. He looks at his aunt, then in front and around him. The aunt talks to him and he laughs heartily. Every so often, but much less than before, the baby looks towards me.

MH: A main point of interest in this is the mother's attitude to the dummy. Because the dummy seems to be in a sense an object that she does regard as part of *her* gift to the baby, as if in her mind it is linked with the breast, and this is what he should have instead of the breast—this dummy with the honey on it. It doesn't seem to be a rival. Whereas his hands do seem to be rivals; she does seem to feel his hands are not a good thing—are linked with dirt, or unconsciously with masturbation.

Comment: Having his own thing . . .

MH: Having his own thing, you see, and doing it independently actually *is* masturbating, getting pleasure by himself. But you see there was also this anxiety about *playing* with the breast, instead of actually feeding from it.

When she picks him up and puts him near her and says: "Help, you're eating me", and then later on "You know you're eating me", she seems to actually *like* that—it doesn't seem to worry her.

RN: She likes it, and the child loves to come near her with his mouth open, as he used to with the breast.

MH: As if in a way this pleasurable contact is acceptable to her, this eating of the face, and it had already started with the breast. It is an almost exploratory contact with the face. In a way it was more difficult for her to allow this with the breast.

> Some other baby

Now where is the point where you felt he was watching his mother's lap . . . because I think it is interesting that after this, the aunt comes in with this picture of a baby, and the baby watches this picture with intensity. I am wondering whether there is some idea that *some other baby* has taken this breast from him. He looks at you, and he looks at the picture, as if he is trying to figure out something about where it has gone. Who is at the breast now?

Notes

1. The observation numbers refer to their order in this book. The observations recorded here represent a selection from those originally undertaken by RN.
2. This paragraph is taken from a transcription in Italian since a section of the tape is missing.

CHAPTER TWO

The pattern of normal development: the end of breastfeeding

Weaning is accompanied by the emergence of particularly painful feelings in the baby, which bring out infantile elements in the surrounding adults that in turn disturb the baby. This is shown in the account of a visit of a friend of the family. The experience of the loss of the breast induces feelings of rage in the baby that result in aggressive behaviour. The intensity of feeling is such that to spare his mother he attacks instead an inflatable toy cow. To relieve his violent feelings Simone seeks an alliance with an older child. Of particular interest is the twelfth session, in which Simone shows how, through evolving representations of the breast, he internalizes the object.

The end of breastfeeding and the underlying feelings of the adults surrounding the child

Tenth observation of Simone, age six months, thirteen days

RN (*reads*): Simone is on the patio in his pushchair with his mother, looking at the small children playing in the garden. He looks at me intently, putting his hand in his mouth and stretching out his arms. He rubs his fingers and looks intently at a male friend I met in the garden and who is speaking to me. He takes hold of a little bell, brings it to his mouth, kicks his legs.

Inside the house, Simone is put in the kitchen in his pushchair, putting his hands to his mouth and smiling happily at the family friend who came in with me and who plays "peek-a-boo" with him, saying to me, "You know his parents don't give him enough to eat because the paediatrician says he likes thin babies!" Simone gurgles and looks smiling at me, then concentrates on making tinkling noises with his bell.

With his dummy in his mouth, he looks at the friend, while his mother, at the sink, talks to him. Simone, on his back in the pushchair, looks up towards his face: "I'll buy you a lovely cow who will make plenty of milk for you—*gniaf gniaf!*" Simone sucks the dummy, looks at me where I sit in front of the friend, then at his mother. The friend picks him up and bounces him on his knee. "*Pim pum potto questo bimbo passerotto*" ("this baby, little sparrow"). Simone looks at me, then at his mother standing in front of him. While playing, the handle of the bell seems perhaps to have caught him in the eye, and he breaks out crying. His mother picks him up; Simone goes "Ehh . . .", looks intently at the friend, who is now writing at the table. The mother sits down holding the baby, who is still looking at her friend. Then he concentrates his attention on me, meanwhile sucking the little bell anxiously and biting it. He jerks his legs. The mother goes to the sink to clean the bell, and Simone turns towards me, holding out his arms and making little joyous sounds.

The mother prepares a little pot of apple purée for Simone, which he eats willingly, looking now at me and now at the friend writing. He goes "Eh . . . eh". His right arm is under his mother's, his left arm stretched over the apple puree. He goes "Mmm", eats, then looks at the feeding spoon approaching his mouth. He looks again at the friend writing. The apple is finished and he looks at the empty pot. He looks at the friend, who is drinking coffee, then laughs.

Then his mother holds him standing up on her knee, jerking his legs, and he coughs with the residual cough from the whooping cough. He seizes a paper tissue from his mother's hand that had been used to wipe his face, and tries to eat it. He anxiously takes the dummy offered to him instead and puts it in his mouth. He goes "Ahh . . . ehh", and makes noises, chewing the dummy. Then he touches his mother's cheek as if to remind her [that] her face is not turned towards him.

"This dummy is nice!" she says, and he carries it with both hands to his mouth.

He now pays a lot of attention to the friend, who is reading what he has been writing. The baby looks at me, loses the dummy, stretches his arms, coughs. He puts the dummy to his mouth again with two hands, going "Ehh . . ." The dummy falls out of his mouth and on to the floor. The mother says, "I'll wash this dummy again." He grabs it, then suddenly lets go. With the edge of the dummy held firmly between his lips he looks smiling at me, then suddenly lets it fall to the ground. "Baby, what are you doing?", says his mother, as she washes it and gives it back to him. He drops it again and looks at it for a moment on the ground. "We'll leave it on the ground", says the mother.

Simone looks at the friend, who has started writing again. He grabs his mother's thumb and tries to pull it towards his mouth. "That hurts", she says, and gives him the dummy again, which he chews hard, smiling at the friend still seated at the table. He continuously pushes his body backwards into the chair.

> ## General comments on baby observation

RN: Would it be appropriate for me to recommend the name of a paediatrician to the mother?

MH: I think you could suggest somebody to her. Being the child's paediatrician yourself is different from mentioning somebody whom you know to whom the mother could go, if she wishes to do so. That is the sort of information it is quite reasonable to give.

RN: Should I give the mother any information about child development, in line with my observations?

MH: I would think it is really better not to do that. In so far as you are going there as an observer, you are trying to learn something from yourself; you may even be learning something from the child that may in fact contradict what you learned theoretically about child development before. It is not a good idea to give her information about what a child at such and such a time would be expected to be doing. It is better to listen to what the mother has to say about the child—to give her an opportunity to express her opinions, her doubts, and to help her think things out for herself. Is the mother a bit worried about the development of the baby, and wants to seek some advice—is that the problem? ("No.") It is much more important if you can get it organized so that you listen to what the mother has to *tell* you about the child—enabling the mother to really communicate to you her own observations and to think out *with* you how she is seeing the child. Everything the mother has to tell you about what she has noticed about the child in between the observations—her reflections on the way he is developing and what has been happening—is important, and it may be important to *her* that you are there and interested in her telling you this.

You can sometimes get a situation where things would seem to be going very wrong with the baby and the mother, and the mother does become very worried about it. Certainly if the mother asks you to whom she could go to discuss it professionally, it would be quite reasonable for you to advise her who would be able to do that. It is much more likely than not that in the course of your observations there will be things that you notice from looking closely—difficulties in the relationship between the baby and the mother that make you anxious, so you feel you ought to say something about it, but I don't think it helps to do so. This is, in a general way, how any relationship between a baby and its mother develops. They have their ups and downs, and work their way through the difficulties.

But this need not preclude you from joining in with the mother's *pleasure* in what the baby is doing—saying nice things and admiring the baby in the way one generally would. You can be an *enthusiastic* observer, and sympathize with the mother's anxiety. Something between a professional person and a friend—not necessarily as active as a friend might often be, but not just a professional behind a screen either.

One thing it is very important not to show in your expression is *disapproval*. If you find you are disapproving of what is going on, you need to do a bit of self-analysis and work it out inside yourself, and not inflict your criticism on the mother.

> ### Summary of Simone's story so far

RN (*reads*): To summarize what has emerged from the sessions with Simone so far: to begin with there were problems with sleeping; these ceased at one and a half months. At three months Simone's feeding changed from breast to breast and bottle, and he became extremely agitated for ten days. He had cried for two days and the paediatrician thought that the baby was getting insufficient nourishment. At four months he started to cut his teeth and showed a lot of interest in his own feet and in the feet of his mother. At five months he was weaned from the breast. At five and a half months he started to take mixed foods from the bottle that at first he spat out but the mother gently accustomed him to it and after three days he accepted it even without sugar. After weaning, when he sees the bottle he opens his arms wide and opens his mouth and when he has finished his meal he cries disconsolately. He sucks quickly and voraciously, preferring milk and milky mixtures. While feeding from the bottle he turns his head suddenly towards his mother's breast. He had gone away for the Easter holiday but had come back early because of contracting whooping cough. He had been to hospital for a check-up and the nurse was struck by the fact that the baby remained quietly in his mother's arms (he was about six months). He had been eating for two days from a little spoon, very happily according to his mother. She said he had always taken apple purée from a spoon. While he was waiting for his little spoon, I saw him holding out his arms and smiling at the plate, remaining for a while with his arms extended. From the 20th of April he was also very interested in buttons and necklaces.

MH: In this observation Simone seems to have been rather more suspicious of the friend than of you—the friend is a man? ("Yes.") He seems to recognize you to begin with as he looks at you attentively, then he puts his hand in his mouth, then he opens his arms. It is as if he connects you with the breast, mummy, feeding. Opening the arms, from what you describe, is what he does when he is offered the bottle or when his mother offers him the spoon. It is as if he links you with mummy; but it seems a bit different with the friend. He looks attentively at the friend, who then speaks to *you*. When he takes the little bell, and shakes it, and puts it into his mouth, and he kicks—that seems different from his hand; as if using the little bell to draw your attention, because you are busy talking to the friend. The friend jokily says to Simone that his parents starve him.

RN: This is because he loves to eat.

MH: When they say his paediatrician likes thin babies, did they mean you—or someone else?

RN: Someone else.

MH: It does seem from this that Simone, in the kitchen, wants to be included in the conversation. He warbles, he plays with the bell, making sounds; he looks at the mother speaking to the friend, who says they will have to buy a cow so he can have plenty to eat. It is as if the friend is trying to ally himself with the deprived baby and offer something better. Then the friend takes him and makes him jump on his knee. Simone looks at Romana, at his mother, and then—you think that he puts the handle of the bell in his eye and bursts out crying. I would think that he is a bit upset or persecuted by the friend, and feels him to be a bit intrusive when he is picked up and bounced. He feels the friend (in however good-natured a way) has done some violence to him.

Comment: He feels stupid because of the child's crying.

MH: I would think so; now, if he did first of all put the end of his toy into his eye, that seems to be an enactment of his feeling of being intruded into. It is something people like to do with little babies—treat them as if they were kittens or puppies, and play with them. This friend identifies with the baby who is not being fed enough—this starved baby; but he is not showing an interest in the child as a little human being. Sometimes babies can enjoy this being thrown up and bounced, but only after they have got over the initial intrusion. After, in his mother's arms, he looks at the friend and this time he is biting the bell; this time, there is a biting quality to the bell in his mouth.

Now, you say the mother goes to the sink to wash the little bell—why did she do that, did she think it was dirty?

RN: Maybe, because it fell down.

MH: I see. Is she still carrying the baby when she does this? ("Yes."). It is quite noticeable that when she does that, he turns with arms open towards Romana, making a joyful sound. His attitude to Romana is much more expansive and confiding than that towards this man friend.

> The persecutor who takes the breast away

Now the mother is preparing some apple, and Simone is looking towards the window—is he still in his mother's arms, or somewhere else?

RN: He is still there.

MH: He is holding his left hand towards the apple . . . he looks at you, he looks at the mother's colleague who is now writing. The apple is finished, and he looks at the empty pot. He looks at the friend, who is drinking his coffee, and he laughs. Can you describe the quality of that laugh?

RN: The friend was saying something to the baby, so it was a kind of reply.

MH: I was remembering how, as you said before, the times when he is *most* upset are the times when something is finished; he was at his most upset at the end of the breastfeed, or when the bottle is finished. As if it always means the loss of the breast. Now this time, he has finished his apple, but he looks at the friend and he laughs. I wonder if one might think of this as a manic laugh, in the sense of *laughing it off*—he doesn't care that his meal his finished, or that the friend is drinking the coffee. A manic reaction to the end of the eating, the end of the breast; and this friend who has just upset him represents some kind of daddy who has taken the breast from him—but he doesn't care. It seems to me that while he has linked Romana with his mother, he has been much more wary of this friend who has joked with him and tried to make an alliance with a baby who is being starved. I would think the friend, because of his intruding, has become a persecuting object to him. We have seen before that Simone is a very friendly, good-natured baby; he is not fretful or aggressive for long. So here this *laughing* and friendliness is a manic way of placating his persecutor—he gets over the upset very quickly and doesn't go on being suspicious.

I think it is significant that after this, on his mother's knee, he kicks and then *coughs*. I know he has had whooping cough, so he may well feel the physical need to cough from time to time. The question is, what this whooping cough might mean. I think to a child it must mean the positive physical presence of something hurtful and bad inside that chokes them and they need to cough it out. I suspect that at this moment on his mother's knee, feeling he is coughing out this internal persecutor, he is also wondering, what takes the breast away? Although we have had a lot of evidence that he seemed to adjust quite well after being changed from the breast to the bottle, and he throve better, yet he goes on feeling upset about the ending of the breastfeeding. He gets upset sometimes when having the bottle; he will come off it and go to the mother's breast and back again; so I think he is still very much dealing with losing the breast—what has taken the breast from him.

One of the baby's phantasies about what takes the breast away, of course, is *daddy*. I don't know how the ambivalence he feels towards this man friend relates to what you have observed about his relationship with his father?

RN: He always seems very affectionate with his father.

MH: That needn't preclude the other side of course—the persecuting side of daddy as the one who takes mummy away from him, taking the breast away.

Fundamentally he is a very friendly baby; and the area in which he feels deprived or persecuted is a bit split off. We see it breaking up again here; after being on mother's knee he coughs, and then takes from his mother's hand the napkin that she had used to wipe his face and tries to eat it. I would think he takes this face-cleaning to be what has wiped the food or the breast away; so he gets hold of it and tries to eat it. All this is to do with the end of breastfeeding—the separation from the breast—and trying not to let it slip away. But he gets anxious, and then he reaches out for the dummy and his mother gives him the dummy and puts that in his mouth. The dummy comes in at that moment to fill up his mouth and to put away the feeling of *losing* the breast. All this is to do with the end of the feeding, the finishing of the apple.

Now, in his making sounds and chewing the dummy, it would seem to me that he is making some sort of protest; but also, through the chewing, in some sense *attacking* and venting his aggressive feelings about the end of the feeding. It is at that point that he seizes hold of his mother's cheek, and *pulls* her to attend to him, because she—in talking (I can't remember whether to you or to the friend)—has let her attention go away from him, so he *pulls* her back. Mummy's attention has been caught by somebody else—which fundamentally, always means daddy—and he says "come back; attend to *me*". So—he has achieved mummy's attention; he is chewing on the dummy, which she notices and says is good.

> The dummy is no substitute

Now he is looking very attentively at the friend, who is reading what he has written. I don't know what was in that attention—was

there also something suspicious? He puts the dummy to his mouth
. . . when he loses it, he can pick it up himself, can he? ("No . . .")
You see, I am inclined to think that at that moment, chewing away
on the dummy, there is still the feeling that it isn't enough. There is
his mother, talking to her friend and so on, and it is no good—it is
her attention that he wants. He is a bit plagued by this man getting
her attention. The dummy isn't good enough. A more indrawn
child could just suck on the dummy and turn his attention away
from what is going on socially, outside; but Simone is a very social
child and he is not able just to shut his feelings away from what is
happening around him. For him, a dummy is no substitute for a
relationship with his actual mother. So again he drops it, she picks
it up, and he lets it fall again—he is just not contented with the
dummy.

| Controlling the persecutor |

I would think that the hard bit, that he chews on, is some kind of
attacking of this *bad* nipple, this bad person who is continually
engaging his mummy's attention; because it does go with this attentive look at the friend who is continuing to write. He strongly chews
it, smiling at the friend sitting at the table, and while chewing it, he
is also *pushing* his body back against his mother. He is, as it were,
pushing himself back into mummy, sitting inside her, taking possession of her. He is attacking the friend, through this chewing, while at
the same time smiling at him, placating him. He is indicating to the
friend that *he* is the owner, the master, of mummy. It is a way of
controlling his persecutor—by, really, *getting his teeth* into him.

Feelings of aggression and seduction

Eleventh observation of Simone, age six months, twenty days

> RN (*reads*): Simone is in the sitting room, sitting on a corner of the
> divan, next to his grandma, who has come to pick him up. He is play-
> ing with an inflatable cow and with his dummy. He looks at me inter-
> estedly. Then, from his grandma's arms, he gives me another long look,
> with his finger in his mouth, then he draws himself back, turning his

back to me, propping himself against the grandmother's shoulder. He repeats this game several times, including with his mother, who is coming and going from the room.

Grandmother says he is sleepy; the baby stretches out his hand to explore her face. "Don't scratch, will you", says his mother. He picks up the cow, holds it in one hand and hits it hard on the head. He gives it a long look and plays with its ear. He moans a little; his grandmother, holding him against her chest, promises that "mummy is coming", and takes him to look out of the window. (The mother is out on the balcony.) Now the mother shows him a rabbit made of suede, which jumps. He is very interested in it.

The aunt comes in and he immediately turns and smiles at her. She tells him Diego is coming behind her; but he does not come into the room at that point. She takes Simone into the hall to see Diego (who is downcast because he has been told off by his parents). He is in the kitchen and Simone smiles at him. Then the aunt carries him back into the sitting room and he gives me a long look. She sits in a chair opposite me and offers Simone the cow. He takes it and puts the tail in his mouth, looking in the direction of Diego, who is peeping through the open doorway, but remains in the hall. Simone holds the cow and chews its tail. Then Diego comes in. He approaches and takes hold of the cow's head, while Simone retains the tail. Diego sits down beside the aunt, who is holding Simone; she caresses him and kisses him behind the ear. Simone appears not to notice; he looks at me, then at his grandma beside me, chewing the cow's tail all the while.

The grandmother wants Simone to look at his mother, who has meanwhile sat down in the armchair next to the sister-in-law. "Look, can't you see mummy?", says grandma. Diego carries off the cow to blow more air into it. Simone, in surprise, waves his arms, then smiles at him. He repeats this and looks at the cow, which is returned to him. He is still preoccupied with the tail; he touches its back, then its head, looks at me, and bites it. Then he is given the little rabbit and drops it on the ground. He looks at it, still sucking the cow's tail. He whimpers, and the cow falls down. The aunt stands him on her knee. In this position, he observes the little rabbit as it jumps on the floor; he puts his hands together then spreads them out. The aunt turns him so he can follow the movements of the rabbit. He sees me and smiles at me, then goes back to looking at the rabbit.

The mother, next to the aunt, speaks to him but gets no response. Simone looks at me again and smiles; looks at his grandmother. Then

Diego, who is making the rabbit jump, chases it along the floor. Standing on his aunt's knee, Simone rubs his fingers along the back of the armchair. Diego is now playing hide-and-seek behind the armchair, and Simone moves so he can continue to see him. The aunt is tired of holding him in that position and passes him to the mother. Now, standing on his mother's knee, Simone smiles excitedly, kicking his legs. He stretches out his arms and laughs excitedly at Diego as he hides and reappears, going "Oh!" Diego, hiding on the floor, says "Look at me!", roaring with laughter, flinging out his arms. Simone looks at me, smiles, smiles at his grandmother, and looks at his aunt who is standing by the door offering to play with Diego.

Simone puts his fingers in his mouth, waves his arms, and watches the game intently with his arms semi-flexed and tongue between his lips. The baby takes his bib in both hands, his gaze still fixed on Diego. Then he looks at the target-board, which has been hung on the door, while the aunt and Diego play at throwing darts at a board. The grandmother says, "You want to play too, don't you?" Simone pulls his mother's sleeve out of the way so he can see them playing. Grandmother says, "He wants to play too." Simone puts his fingers in his mouth and goes "Ehh". The aunt tells Diego to go and get Simone's big teddy and give it to him. Diego does so, and Simone takes it by the ear but is still interested in watching the game of target practice.

> Scratchy feelings

MH: How old is he?
RN: Seven months.
MH [*asks for more details about the rubber cow whose tail he has been sucking*]. So, really, a kind of soft rubbery thing like a breast. I am not sure here . . . you see he is first of all with his grandmother, and he is playing this game with her, with his finger in his mouth and then leaning with his chest—but he turns his back to you, as if turning away from you and getting close to his grandmother. He is hiding from her. . . . Now, when you say he has played this with you several times, and now with his mother, you mean he is turning his back on his mother? ("Yes.") Because, later on, he doesn't *notice* his mother; you see, it seems as if here he is using his grandmother more as his mother, in a way resentful, so she becomes a better mummy than mummy. He turns his back on mummy who is busy doing other things. When he explores the grandmother's face

with his hand, and mother says, "Don't scratch" . . . now whether she is saying that because she has *observed* that he is a bit scratchy, or whether it may express some unconscious wish that he *should* scratch her face, or whether she is somehow aware that the baby is feeling a bit scratchy towards her for not paying him enough attention, I don't know.

He certainly does seem to be feeling aggressive, because after that he takes the cow and he beats its head. Then he watches it for a long time, and plays with an ear. It does look as if there, he is somehow investing the toy cow with something of his feeling towards his mummy, who is just coming in and out and not paying him anything like the amount of attention she did last time. He then actually begins to complain; and the grandmother says, "Mummy will come", but holds him more tightly to her, as if that would make it better. Which, of course, is an instinctive reaction by grown-ups if a child seems upset and wanting its mummy. You pick it up and hold it close as if you were its mummy; and sometimes that will do—the child may be able to feel you are a comforting enough object to represent its mummy—but sometimes for the child it has the meaning of being kidnapped, as it were, by not-mummy.

Now, when the mother comes in with the little rabbit that jumps, that seems to distract him and for the moment he accepts that as something good enough. But when the aunt comes in he immediately turns towards her and smiles. The aunt takes him and introduces him to Diego, whom he welcomes; but he still seems to be carrying on with that cow. Now, instead of beating the head he is biting the tail, as if these protruberances represent the nipple, which he is attacking.

This time he doesn't notice mummy. Now this is something quite unusual for him—not noticing, turning his back on his mother. So much so that the grandmother says, "Don't you recognize your mother?" Now, there may have been some note of triumph or rivalry over mummy; one senses some kind of subliminal tension between the grown-ups as to who really is the baby's mummy. It is interesting that at this point Diego takes the cow away from Simone, because you were saying that initially Diego seemed to be a bit sulky, as if he was in trouble with his parents. It is possible that at this moment he senses something within the baby—in fact it is quite likely, for he hears the grandmother say "You don't recognize your mother"—so that he comes in recommending himself as allied with the baby: these two boys against the mummy or the parents. Then begins this game of hide-and-seek with Diego and the baby, and Diego seducing the baby, getting his attention—the two boys together. Simone gets more and more excited about this game Diego is playing with the little rabbit, so, even though he is sitting on his mother's knee, he is not noticing her. The hide-and-seek seems to go from playing with the little rabbit, to Diego hiding himself—being himself the object that disappears and comes back. Then the aunt suggests the game with Diego . . . The baby is quite fascinated watching this, and the grandmother says, "You'd like to be joining in", as if he would really like to be doing what Diego is doing. That continues to be what he is most interested in; though he takes back the little bear and plays with its ear, that is a bit half-hearted, as though he is more interested in the game the big ones are playing.

| Alliance and seduction |

So, I think one of the interesting features of this observation is that you can see how it comes about that the big boy, like the older brother, can almost unconsciously tune into when the baby or the little one is feeling a bit disillusioned, or resentful, or on bad terms with mummy, and can seduce the little one into wanting to join him.

Now of course this sort of alliance between brothers—big brother and little brother, big sister and little sisters—in one way is a very important thing in the growing up of a child. But whether it is helpful developmentally does depend to some extent it is built upon some kind of fundamental friendliness between the big and the little one, comforting each other, or whether it is based on rivalry and resentment against the parents. Very interesting.

Q: [not audible]

MH: In the previous observation, the mother was very close to the baby. The baby was constantly noticing this man who was drawing her attention, and he does stay in close contact with the mother. This observation is a bit different, because grandmother has come, whose life is very much centred around the baby, and the mother does become a little pushed into the background, which is a different thing: I don't think she actually was pushed into the background by the friend.

Representations of the breast

Twelfth observation of Simone, age ten and a half months

RN (*reads*): I had not seen Simone since last June, after I had had a car accident. I was due to see him on the afternoon of the accident, so I contacted his father at the pharmacy where he works to tell him that I was in hospital and unable to come. The father said he would bring Simone to see me. When the child came, with his parents, there were a lot of people in the room. Simone showed himself to be very sociable with everyone, but seemed not to see me. I was in one of those uncomfortable trauma-style beds full of straps and metalwork, so I thought he did not recognize me. Immediately afterwards he set out with his mother to her mother's house in the Marche. His maternal grandparents have a smallholding there.

During the holidays Simone cut four teeth; now he has six. His days during the summer revolved around the following pattern: at 7.00 he took milk from a bottle with biscuits. After eating he relaxed with his eyes half closed, lying against his mother, taking hold of her, holding out a lock of her hair and playing with it. This habit began about the middle of June. After breakfast he went out for a walk in the country, either carried by her or in the pushchair, observing everything around him—people, animals, flowers, etc. At 11.00 he had yogurt and banana. If there was no sugar (as happened once) he got very angry, throwing away the little spoon, throwing everything away. Now he eats a lot, and if it is not ready on time he gets angry. After 11.00 he goes out again for another walk. At 1.15 he eats vegetable broth with meat, followed by fruit, which he likes a lot. He sits at table with the adults and wants to try everything. After the meal he has a sleep and then another walk. At 5.30 he drinks milk. At 8.30 he takes soup and cheese, still in the company of the adults. He loves to stay awake till 10 o'clock. He falls asleep in his mother's arms, then gets put to bed. Since last July, he developed a habit of placing his hand on his teddy bear while asleep. Most nights, around 3.30, he wakes up and mother goes to comfort him. She goes to make a camomile drink or puts the main light on and he tends to stay awake and play. One time this summer, when the mother was not well, he was picked up by his father. He could not be consoled and got very agitated. He calmed down only when he touched his mother, after being put in the big bed.

The mother and the aunt have both noticed that he takes hold of new objects only with the tips of his fingers; only after some time does he start using his whole hand. Around the mid-August holiday, he had a temperature of forty degrees centigrade for a couple of days, without any other signs of being ill. The doctor could not diagnose the cause.

At home, the child takes great pleasure in lights and lamps, and is very observant of his surroundings. He does not seem to have recognized Diego, Diego's father, or the other friends who came daily to see the family. However, he happily welcomed Cecilia, the girl who stays with him when her mother goes to the school. The aunt and the mother tell me that I am the only other person he greets in that way.

An account of not remembering

MH: This is very important, not recognizing you in the hospital. It is very important for him to see people in surroundings that he *does know*. You in the hospital would be different from you in his familiar surroundings at home. I was just wondering, when he had this fever in mid-August, was he away from home? ("Yes . . .") Yes, it would look as if this was related to being in different surroundings, which is something very frightening.

> **RN** (*continues reading*): I met Simone in front of the entrance to his house, in the pushchair with his aunt, who told me she was exhausted after taking him out for an hour. They went to the pharmacy where the father had changed his shoes. Simone looked at me seriously, with his head held forwards and his lip protruding. The mother, who was in the house, came out and commented on Simone's new shoes. Simone was taken in to the sitting room and stayed there with his aunt. Standing up next to his aunt, he held on to the back of the sofa, then turned suddenly towards me with a big smile. He did this several times, then he made smacking noises with his mouth and the aunt told me he was blowing kisses. He lost a shoe and tried to help his aunt put it back on for him.

MH: When Simone sees you outside in his pushchair, does he recognize you?

RN: No, he looks at me concentratedly but does not smile.

MH: That would seem to indicate that what is very important for this baby is the familiarity of his home. Did he smile at you when you were in the street?

RN: Yes, he did then.

RN (*continues reading*): The mother came in with his full bottle of milk, saying, "Look what's here." He made impatient noises. She picked him up and sat down on the sofa with him; he laid himself down on her left arm with his head on her breast, and sucked strongly, meanwhile looking up at her with his body stretched out, relaxed against his mother. He made noises while sucking. After the bottle, a dummy was immediately put in his mouth. I asked the reason, and was told, "Because otherwise, he always whines and complains, even when he is full."

Now Simone is standing against his mother's knee and he takes hold of a lock of her hair. She says, "I can see you . . . you have found a little lock of hair." He laughs, jerking his legs and looking and pointing at the lamp. He grabs his mother's cheek, looks at me and laughs, and looks at the light. His mother says, "Who has written on your hand?" The aunt replies that it was the big boy at the pharmacy a little earlier. Then Simone smacks his mother's face. "Are you punching me? I'll eat you up . . ." she says. Simone continues to hold the lock of her hair, and says, "Ehhh . . .". He turns to me and says "Eh".

The aunt says, "Simone, take the dummy out!" The mother removes it and puts it beside her on the sofa. He looks intently at it and tries playfully to get it back from his lying-down position. He takes it and hits the back of the sofa with it. Then he hits with his hand; then he makes smacking noises with his mouth. The aunt asks, "Who are you blowing kisses to?" Simone leans out and begins to play with a box of sweets from the pharmacy, smacking his lips and blowing. He takes the box of sweets, turns it around, hits it, and puts it down on the sofa. He smiles at me a lot as he bashes the box of sweets. I ask if he is used to having sweets, and the aunt says no; she tells me he never puts things into his mouth. Simone looks at me, waving his arms. The aunt says, "Blow kisses to Romana", and he carries on smacking his lips. I comment that Simone has become rich (he has changed a lot during the holidays), and the aunt says to him, "Who do you look like?" He turns towards her and she says, "Me!" He laughs a lot. He continues to play with the sweets, turning them round.

I ask the mother about his sleeping problem, and the aunt says, "I also got out of bed." He moves, jogging a picture that hangs above the sofa and knocking it against the wall, leaving it tilted. Now the sweets have fallen to the ground and Simone, on the sofa, looks round for them. The mother says to me, "You should have seen him when he came back home; he was delighted, especially by the lights."

The aunt tells me that now he loves his teddy bear, and goes out to get it. She comes back in with the bear and when Simone sees it he gurgles and cuddles it. Meanwhile, his mother places him in an armchair next to me, near the sofa.

Now Simone leans out and looks at his shoes, then he reaches out and tries to seize a little plant on the side table. The mother says, "If you touch it, it will break." The child is sometimes standing on the floor propped against his mother, sometimes sitting on her knee. He holds a leaf in his hand. "Poor thing, you've broken it off", says his mother, "no more leaf." Now he looks at his mother, with a piece of leaf in his hand; the leaf falls on to her breast. He picks it up with extreme deliberation and rumples it up. Then he turns to look at the bear and his aunt in her seat nearby. He goes to touch the half-leaf that remains on the side table, and bangs his hands on the table, keeping them on the table. Then he sits down on the floor and holds the leaf in one fist while he brushes it with the other hand. The leaf falls rumpled to the ground between his feet.

He turns towards the sound made by the aunt in the next room. She is standing at the door showing him a transparent ball with a piece of coral inside it. Simone waves his arms and laughs happily, but is still attracted to the leaf held tightly in his hand. He keeps it in his hand, while looking at another little rubber ball that his aunt is throwing towards him. He stretches out to catch it. Then he drops the leaf on the floor and plays with the aunt as she throws him the ball, laughing heartily. Then he turns round and sticks his tongue out rapidly and frequently. Then his mother says, "Who are you sticking your tongue out at, who?" The aunt gives him the rubber ball, which he puts in his mouth. Then she shows him a little rubber dog, adding, "Yes, this is a good one . . . here's the little dog." He does not look at it however, and the aunt tells me that really it is not very nice, that Simone has never taken any notice of it and shows a noticeable preference for games.

Standing on the floor, Simone turns towards his mother and smiles at her, passing the ball between his hands then putting it in his mouth. The aunt, next to him, says, "Give me your hand", and Simone holds his hand out with the ball in it. Now the ball falls down and rolls away, and the aunt gets ready to go and retrieve it. She tries to take Simone with her, holding him under the armpits, but his mother says, "He doesn't want to go."

MH: So . . . is this the beginning of your making regular observations after being away for quite a while? Because it would seem to me that all through this he is working through the problem of your

having been away, and now come back, which I think does reacti-
vate all his feelings about the weaning. Most of his play throughout
this observation is connected with the going away of the breast.
After having the bottle from his mother, he stands, he holds a lock
of her hair, he points at the chandelier; he is then hitting his mother
while holding the forelock. After he has finished with the bottle, his
mother immediately puts the dummy in his mouth, and says that
he always complains afterwards—as if saying he is never reconciled
to it finishing; however much he has, he doesn't like the end. So she
quickly stops his complaints by immediately popping the dummy
in his mouth. She seems to find it difficult to bear the projection of
his distress, anger, his upset, having to do with the going away of
the breast, the separation from the object.

She does not seem to find his hitting her in play hard to bear. He
does that while he is holding on to the lock of her hair. I would
think it is the actual distress that disturbs her: it is muted, quickly
stopped, so he cannot come out with an expression of real distress.
It is muted because afterwards the aunt says, "Take the dummy
out"; it is put on the sofa near him and he looks at it very intensely.
He takes it and shakes it and hits the back of the sofa, playing out
with the dummy something of his feeling of having the nipple
taken out of his mouth by the mother and her going away.

It is interesting that when he smacks his mouth the aunt takes it
as "kisses". You can see where the origin of kisses lies.

Q: Does the child show autistic tendencies?

MH: No, I would not think this is autistic. I think this child is
actually working at trying to manage the separation from the
breast. It is something developmental. I think the mother does find
it difficult to cope with his being really distressed—so he is quickly
given a toy, a substitute, to fill up the gap (and smother his distress).
It is the aunt who comes in with the idea of taking the dummy out.
She says that Simone never puts objects in his mouth, never takes
sweets.

RN: But it isn't true.

MH: No, she seems to mean, he shouldn't be spoilt. It would
seem that the aunt feels he ought not to be so indulged; he ought to
be able to cope with a little frustration, without having to have "the
servants" step in to help him. There is also a hint here of rivalry
with the mother. When the aunt says, "Who do you look like?", and

then answers "Me", it seems very clear that she feels *she* would like this baby.

It seems to me, when you were talking about "autistic", that you were thinking this baby might be in the situation of having too many servants. I can see that they are of a different kind from Massimo's grandparents,[1] because they are very interested in this child. They are ready to serve him; but they are also very interested in his development, particularly the mother, who does give him space to play.

So, here you have a situation that slightly invites omnipotent and despotic behaviour, as often happens with a first and only child with admiring and doting parents. But it is not only that: the child does really feel they are *interested* in what he does.

> Representations of the breast

This whole long sequence of play with the leaf is very interesting. The mother does let him work something out with this leaf. He goes from looking at his own shoes—and he has only recently learned to walk, is that right? ("Now, just after this observation.") So he is just on the verge of learning to walk. We have rather missed out on the period preceding this, but I think that almost invariably children do begin to get very interested in shoes at this point. The shoes do represent what carries the adults away—they walk away in their shoes, and they come back in their shoes.

So he goes from looking at his shoes to the leaf. I think both the shoes and the leaf represent different aspects of the nipple; because he takes that little leaf off almost as if it were linked in his mind with the dummy, and the lock of his mother's hair. He didn't pull at his mother's hair; he held on to it. But the little leaf he actually pulls off. I would think he is playing out with that leaf some phantasy of grasping and taking away this nipple. It is not just that he is aggressively seizing it; he is also looking at it, as if trying to take possession by means of examining it. He is really wondering about it. He beats his hands on the little table, as he beat the sofa, and as he beat his mother. This leaf on the table represents the breast, and he is working out his angry feelings about this object that he cannot take away with him, that he cannot take entirely into his possession.

Now he also seems to be working out something about the relationship between his aunt and his mother. The leaf falls on his mother's breast, and he takes it and crumbles it; then he looks at the bear that his aunt has brought in. It seems to me that throughout this observation there is some competition about what she can offer Simone and whose baby Simone is really allowed to be. As if he is making some comparison between what mummy offers—what he feels about mummy—and what the aunt offers and what he feels about her.

The rival mummy

The aunt quite clearly does interrupt and cut into this play, with her little transparent plastic ball to engage his attention. Earlier, when she brought in the bear, he was pleased to have it but it did not entirely engage his attention; he still had something to work through, with the leaf, that was much more directly related to mummy. It seems to me that the aunt can't quite bear this preoccupation with the leaf, so in she comes with another distraction—the ball. Although he laughs at the ball, it is still not enough to take him away from the leaf, so the aunt comes up with another one—a rubber ball. Now he does leave the leaf for that, because the rubber ball is more like the dummy, and he has had little rubber objects before, hasn't he? ("Yes.")

This is a slightly unusual observation; I don't remember others previously where the aunt has been so much in the position of a rival mummy. Now, when Simone turns and puts his tongue out quickly and frequently and the mother asks, "Who are you sticking out your tongue at—who?" (in Italian, "making ugly tongues") the mother seems to be expressing her disagreement with the aunt about the baby.

Internalizing the object

Q: [about Simone's interest in the lamp]
MH: The lamp . . . now that goes back to the beginning. You said that when he came back after being away on the holiday, and after having the fever, the mother told you that he looked at the light. ("Yes, at his home.") I can't remember if earlier on he was a baby

that used to look at the lamp? ("I don't remember him doing so.") Because you do very often notice children looking at the lamp or source of light; it is something that is stable and stays in one place. It can be a focus for attention that gives some sort of security. The light doesn't walk away in the way that the mother does. It seems that when he returns from holiday, he looks at the lamp in this way, as something that is always there. It is a fixed point, after all these changes and different surroundings that seem to have quite disturbed him.

Another change he has had to cope with has been Romana's being away for such a long time. Also when he did see her again, she was in a very different situation, in the hospital. I think in this observation you don't quite get the full impact of whatever he is working out in relation to Romana's absence, because there is this constant rivalry and interference or demand for attention by the aunt, with her toys and so on.

Maybe at that point when he is holding the hair and looking at the light, the hair may represent the nipple—the switch—that turns the light on and off. As if the light could be associated also with seeing mummy. It is like this little boy William I was talking about yesterday, whose first word was "sitch" (switch).[2]

The aunt comes up with one toy after another, as if to provide him with something much more fascinating than mummy could provide him with; but he is never seduced away for more than a moment. So he puts his mouth to the little ball, and the aunt says, "Give me your hand", almost as if she is a rival big sister who can't stand this little baby's preoccupation with mummy's breast. Her attempt to seduce him is a pretty total failure, and when the aunt tries to take him under the armpit to follow the ball, the mother says "No, he doesn't want to come". He is very definitely orientated and fixed on working something out with his mother, and will not be seduced away.

This separation has led him to try to get a clearer idea, a wider picture . . . he has always been interested in where he comes from and where you are—these two places—but it is as if his conception of the world has widened, and he is trying to get some picture of where you went to. There is some idea in the session with the table between you, of being able to be together with you but with some space between you: he can be in contact with you even though it is not in physical contact, clinging to you or sitting in your lap. One has the impression of his beginning to internalize an object that can be with him and hold him internally, and that allows him to be more free from the external object. He can be away from his mother; he can play with other children.

The lost breast and the nipple lifeline

Thirteenth observation of Simone, age eleven months

> **RN** (*reads*): I find Simone in his pushchair in the courtyard, surrounded by four girls around nine or ten years of age. He is playing with a furry tail, putting it over his face and laughing a lot. He sees me and smiles. His mother comes out and says, "Simone, let's go in, your milk is ready." He holds out his arms, says *ciao* to the other children, and goes into the house with his mother.

MH: This is interesting: Simone at eleven months, with the four little girls, waving them goodbye as his mother calls them. We get a picture here of what a little charmer he is going to be. He has been surrounded by a great deal of love and attention and appreciation. He is the little king baby in his carriage with the four attendants.

> **RN** (*continues reading*): In the kitchen he stretches out on his mother's body and sucks vigorously at the bottle. We sit round the kitchen table. Mother and baby are to my right, in front of the window. After finishing, he looks at the empty bottle, then at me, and cries; the mother offers him the dummy, which at first he refuses. "He only wants it if it's got sugar", she says. Standing on his mother's knee he looks at the window and at my jumper. Mother asks, "Can you hear the train?" But he is drawn to me. He takes hold of a lock of her hair (her "forelock"). "I can see you", she says.

MH: It is interesting how intensely he takes the bottle; then when it is empty, he cries. His mother immediately gives him the dummy, and he rejects it, but not totally—he wants it with sugar. Do you know how she knew that? ("No.") We have seen this picture before—how it is very difficult for the mother to leave this baby with any feeling of distress. As soon as he is upset, the dummy goes in the mouth to plug up his distress—not just the dummy, the sugar-dummy. We're seeing here what one very often sees with mothers who love their child very tenderly, and who find it difficult to leave him with feelings of separation, of not immediately having what he needs—so fostering over-dependence on people, on social relations. The other interesting thing is, when he empties the bottle and cries, he looks at Romana. I don't know if you can describe the quality of that look?

RN: Desperation, really . . .

MH: Almost as if what he is not able to face is the emptying of the breast, the disappearance of the breast, the weaning. Now when he stands on his mother's knees and looks at the window, and then looks at your *sweater*, it is almost as if he is looking at your sweater to see where the breast has *gone*. The mother is trying to distract him, and says, "Hear the train", but he is drawn to you as if he is still reaching towards your sweater. He is preoccupied with this empty bottle, this disappeared breast.

Q: Last time the aunt came in and tried to distract him . . .

MH: So, at that moment, do you think she was distracting him towards the train so he shouldn't continue being drawn to Romana? ("Yes.") Now he grabs his mother's forelock . . . this he has done before, keeping a hold of her, claiming her as his own, so she shouldn't go. Somewhere he is not reconciled to the disappearance of the breast; he is holding on to a forelock–nipple. I don't remember when this started—did he hold his mother's hair when he was feeding?

RN: It began at seven months—after he had been weaned.

RN (*continues reading*): He goes "Muk-muh-muh" rhythmically. His mother repeats the sound, then imitates a horse: "Is this a little horse?" But Simone goes on making the first sound, holding on to her forelock and pulling it with his other hand. A noise is heard on the stairs; "There are the children coming down to play", she says. Simone grabs her hair and pulls it. He takes her forelock and tries to pull a hair from it. The mother immediately says, "You can't have it!", then, "Look who I can see." Simone looks around and takes out the dummy. "Who are you going to give it to?" The dummy falls to the ground. "Now the cat will get it", she says. A whistle is heard; it is a helicopter. "What's that whistle?" Simone looks up towards the window. We go out on to the terrace. Simone looks very interested. It disappears, and mother says,

"It's gone away, call it back, we can't see it any more, call it back." He cries, grumpy and frowning, and moos loudly to call it. Then he cries. In his mother's arms, he looks up and waves his arms about, wailing loudly. (This happened once before with a helicopter and he made a big scene.) Another train goes by outside. The mother says to him, "There's the little train, see how nice it is." But he doesn't stop crying. Standing on his feet he yells and seems on the point of crying. His mother picks him up and he continues to make mooing noises, looking fiercely around him. He quietens down when the mother points out the train beginning to move again. She carries him back in, saying, "We'll turn on the lights." She turns on the kitchen light and puts him in the high chair, saying he can have his toys—some transparent plastic bottles, a little plate, and two empty boxes of cigarettes.

MH: His mother seems to be playing a kind of game with him about the forelock, when she says, "I can see you, can I?" What does she mean by that? . . . is she joking, saying "I can see what you're up to"?

RN: I don't know . . . yes, maybe.

MH: Later, when he tries to pull out one hair, she seems to be saying, "I can see you, wanting to pull out my hair, or what's inside my hair"—something like that. Then he takes the dummy out of his mouth, and she says, "Who are you going to give it to?" It looks as if, almost unconsciously, she is saying "I can see you plucking the nipple out of me, and who are you going to give it to now?" I think that does express something of her anxiety about how the baby, having got all he can get out of the breast, will then take it to charm other people with it. I'm not sure if she may even have felt a little jealous of those four girls at the beginning who were entertaining him in his baby-carriage. She is very much trying to engage his attention, actively trying to interest and entertain him. Now, when the helicopter disappears, mother says, "It's gone away, call it back, we can never see it again, call it back." He moans, knits his brows, and makes a kind of bellow to call it back. It looks as if what she says chimes in with the feelings that Simone isn't quite allowed to have, or letting himself have, of sadness and maybe anger to do with the lost breast. We get a hint of how difficult it is for her to let him feel sadness and anger—almost as if she feels he may turn against her, and get it from somebody else. It reminds me of the mother of a child who was about to start psychotherapy—a child very much loved and doted on since birth—and mother's worry was, supposing he doesn't like the psychotherapy, he will never *forgive me* for giving him this bad experience; she wanted an undertaking that he was going to have nothing but a happy time in his therapy. One could look at the mother's statement about "it's gone away—call it back" from a slightly different angle. She is also expressing something of her own feelings about being mother to Simone and feeding him: about her own difficulty in allowing that now to be in the past. She has a hankering back to the past when the baby was always dependent on her.

RN (*continues reading*): I am sitting beside him to his right. He smiles at me, squirms around in the high chair going backwards and forwards. He puts the bottle tops on the little red plate, looks at them, puts one in his mouth and chews it. One bottle-cap remains on the table, the others fall to the ground. He smiles at me, then bangs his little plate, turning it over. He puts the cap to his mouth. The mother goes in and out of the kitchen; he goes "Baa baa" and she responds in the same way. Simone bangs his plate on the table, takes a cigarette box, and puts it on the left next to another one. He notices an elaborate pen-cap in front of me on the table, looks at me, and reaches out for it. He examines it attentively, holding it up and down, looking at the loop of string that dangles from it. He holds it in two hands, bangs it noisily on his plate, looking at it and at me, laughing. He plays with the string and goes back to banging his plate. The mother picks up her knitting from the table and begins to work on it. Simone drops the plate on the ground, looks at me, the mother, the ground. The mother says, "Where's the little plate?" He continues to play with the pen-cap, holding it high and low, looks at his mother, and makes a smacking sound with his lips. "Who are you blowing kisses to?", says his mother. Then Simone puts the pen-cap in his mouth, looking at his mother, waves his arms, goes "Eh", and rocks himself forwards and backwards. He stops when he hears a noise. It is his aunt, calling from the garden. She enters, and seeing Simone playing with the pen-cap, asks, "What's new?" The mother replies, "It's Romana's, that he's stolen." He puts the cap to his mouth. They talk about school. The aunt comes closer and says "Let me see what you've got there—that's nice." Simone stretches out his arm, holding the pen-cap, and shakes his head. The aunt insists, and he gives her a piece of plastic wrapping that was on the table. Simone continues to chew and play with the pen-cap. The aunt insists, holding out her hand. He turns away grumbling with a severe expression. Then he bangs the pen-cap on the table. The aunt says, "Will you give it to me?" and he holds out his hand, firmly grasping the cap, but without giving it to her. He sucks it again.

MH: That's very interesting; shall we stop there? He's had something before then—a bottle-top . . . He seems to go from the cap of the bottle, to getting the cap of Romana's pen, as if the one from Mummy isn't quite right, and maybe Romana has *the* one. The impression is that by this time she does actually feel quite rivalrous towards you, as she does towards the aunt, who comes in presently. It is very difficult for her to let the baby take an interest in some other woman—as if she does somehow feel slighted or deserted. With the mother's continual talking to and involvement with the baby, one gets the impression that you are in the position of an outsider who is watching this very close love relationship; you're not quite included in it, in the way that you were when he was a much smaller baby. Now it seems he is very much her little boy, her sweetheart, her possession—but one who is devastatingly attractive to other women. He is also clearly *interested* in other women! He looks for Romana's cap and pen, and you give him the cap; he examines it with attention; shakes it up and down to see the cord from which it is hanging; and brusquely lifts it. He does seem to be developing a feeling that he has the *right* to have what these admirers round about him have. The way that he stretches the cord and hits the plate with it, knocks the little plate to the floor and looks at his mother and you.

He didn't seem to be upset at that point, when he looked at you? **RN:** No.

MH: Did he look as if he were cross, or was it in a defiant way?

RN: I don't think so. He looked as if he expected me to pick it up for him.

MH: He then goes shaking the pen-cap up and down, hits it on the table quite roughly—showing who is master, you might say.

Now this is interesting. He looks at his mother, and sends her a kiss! I don't know how that was, but it comes over with a slightly perfunctory air, as if he is pleasing or placating her. When she says, "Who are you sending the kisses to?", was the kiss in your direction at all? ("No.") She doesn't take it as an expression of tenderness or affection to which she might respond; it is as if she feels herself to be a recipient of favours, and one among many. Then in comes the aunt—is it she who says, "There's a new thing"?

RN: Yes, referring to the pen-cap.

MH: It is as if she is saying "Will you show me your little penis?" It has something of that quality—flirting with the little boy.

RN (*continues reading*): A woman comes to visit with her baby of sixteen months, called Alessandro. The aunt takes Alessandro in her arms and sits down next to Simone. He turns and goes "Ehh?", then holds out his arms to be picked up. He looks as if he is going to cry, then he smiles, but strangely, at Alessandro. He stretches out his hand and takes Alessandro's hand, and pulls and shakes it. "See how Alessandro's walking", says the aunt. Simone leans against the baby, looks at him, but then busies himself with the pen-cap again, fiddling with it then throwing it to the ground. He also throws down one of the cigarette packets. He plays with a piece of the wrapping tissue. He leans towards Alessandro, who looks up. "It's down", says Alessandro. The aunt takes the bottle-cap and gives it to Simone, who puts it in his mouth. He drops the plastic wrapping on the ground. Alessandro leans over, takes the wrapping, and offers it to me. I give it to Simone, who smiles at me with excessive gratitude. The cap is dropped again. Alessandro picks it up and throws it to Simone. He takes it and throws it up and it drops down again. Alessandro throws the cap again to Simone, who lets it fall. The children repeat this several times and Simone laughs. Alessandro goes and takes a cigarette box, which he gives to Simone, who bangs it on the table and pushes it towards me. Simone smiles, so does Alessandro; they look at each other. Simone suddenly turns to the table and puts his hands down on it. He makes funny noises; his face is wet with sweat and he seems highly delighted. He touches a button of his shirt and looks at it. He looks at Alessandro and smiles at him. Alessandro walks to the aunt. Simone looks and smiles at the aunt. He looks at the light. The aunt says to Simone, "Do you want to get down?" Alessandro's mother picks him up and the babies look[[Q2]] at each other, sitting opposite each other at the table. Simone smiles, looks at his hands. His mother passes by and he stretches out his arms, crying to be picked up. The mother lifts him down and helps him to walk. Simone keeps one hand in his mouth and holds on to her arm to get her to pick him up.

MH: Fascinating—shall we stop there? You can see how immediately his nose is put out of joint, when Alessandro comes in and the aunt picks up the other baby. He is *going* to cry; then he smiles, but strangely, at Alessandro; he holds out his hand, takes his hand and pulls and shakes it. You can see that he really struggles with his feelings. It is as if he felt like crying, then said to himself, I mustn't be a baby in front of this bigger boy. Instead of regarding [him] as a rival baby, he puts out his hand as if to say, let's be boys together. Yet he is not quite sure—because when he gets the hand, he *pulls* it like he had been pulling the hair earlier, almost as if threatened by being overwhelmed by this desperate baby feeling, wanting to have the nipple to hold on to still.

A lifeline to the nipple

Now Alessandro, I take it, is walking . . . Simone throws the pen down, and the cigarette boxes, then he stoops down . . . When he threw the cap and the cigarette boxes down, did he look as if he was going to do something with them, after throwing them on the ground?

RN: I had the impression it was a communication between the children.

MH: He seems to be throwing down the gauntlet, to see what Alessandro might do. Alessandro picks it up and gives it to you, then you give it to Simone and he smiles with *excessive* gratitude. It is as if he were *risking* something when he threw that down—something that belonged to him. Then it becomes a game, when Alessandro picks it up and gives it to Simone: throwing it down, and having it returned. It has something of the meaning of a lifeline—the nipple that the baby is holding on to. He felt first of all threatened when the aunt picked up the baby; then he decided to throw away this nipple object and see if he could make a relationship with this big boy. What then develops is really quite a charming game between the two of them. He is pleased to be able to take part in this game, that can help to overcome some of his baby anxieties. He is very happy; then he fingers the button on his shirt and looks at it, almost as if to say, "I didn't need to hang on to that nipple cap she gave me—I've got one on *me*, on *my* shirt". He's got a little penis himself! He looks at Alessandro and smiles at him, as if to say, there they are, boys—buddies—together. When the aunt helps Alessandro to walk, he looks at him smiling, feeling quite happy about it.

RN (*continues reading*): Now the children are in Simone's room. He is sitting with his legs out wide in the middle of the room. Alessandro crawls rapidly round the room. The two mothers are there, sitting opposite each other, and the aunt. Simone laughs excitedly, waving his arms when his mother shows him a large transparent ball and throws it to him. Simone cannot catch the ball and it slips away. I throw it to him; the ball slips away; Alessandro goes nimbly after it. Simone watches; the aunt holds out some little boxes to him and he grasps them. Alessandro comes up and takes the boxes from Simone's hands. Simone does the same to Alessandro, who moves towards his mother and puts a large plastic fork in his mouth, one of Simone's toys. At a certain point, Alessandro throws a little plastic box in Simone's face. Simone turns crying towards his mother, who picks him up and sits him on the floor next to her. Then Alessandro goes quickly up to him. Simone is frightened and hides. The mother says, "He's not coming to get you, you know!" Then Simone puts a box to his mouth and plays with it. Alessandro, from behind, gives him a rather heavy hug round the neck. After a moment of surprise, Simone turns again to his mother to be hugged, moaning even more disconsolately. "Be friends with Alessandro", she says, and brings the children together, but after that they seemed to have lost interest in each other.

MH: It doesn't last very long, actually—as one might expect with two such little children. Let's think how it begins to go wrong. This big transparent ball comes, and Alessandro can get it, and Simone is left very much as the baby who can't. It seems Alessandro can't stand the aunt giving Simone the small boxes instead of the ball—he comes and takes the box from him. Alessandro's ambivalence breaks down in the direction of hostility, grabbing things from the baby, and Simone feels terribly hurt. When he turns to his mother in that depressed way, to be hugged, he feels more *hurt* than anything else. It is a fascinating observation. One can see how this is basically a pretty friendly little boy.

Mother returns to work—the new sweetheart

Fourteenth observation of Simone, age twelve and a half months

RN (*reads*): The baby is on the bed in the bedroom being changed by the mother. He kicks his legs and smiles at me. The father, sitting on the rocking chair, says to me, "Have you seen the new little bed?" Simone, now in his father's arms in the chair, gives a scream—the mother has put his shoes on crookedly. He quietens when they are put right, then cries and seems irritable. His father talks about his birthday celebration yesterday. Simone now walks holding hands with his father, plays with the rocking chair, and wants to be put in it. He pushes himself forwards and back. The father says "*Clo clo*" to the baby's movements. Then Simone is lifted into his bed. He holds on to the edge, then falls and is upset. The father says, "Show how you give kisses to Cecilia—only to Cecilia." He is put on the ground. Holding on, he bangs his hand on the bookcase. The father says, "Nobody is holding you." He leans over and rummages in the toy box. The mother comes in carrying a little wind-up bird that was a present from another child. Simone takes a plate out of the toy box and looks at his father, who gives him the little bird that the mother had brought in. He takes it and looks at it. He is sitting on the ground. Then he starts looking through the toy box. Then, still sitting, he gets interested in the bird. He turns, looks at me, smiles, leans forward, and plays with the bird, which he holds in his hand and tries to wind it up. The father places a little mat under him and he grabs it. He has the idea of getting something from the box, and takes out a little dog. He then lets it fall to the ground. He climbs on to his father's knee.

Cecilia enters. Simone goes to meet her, holding his father's hand. He smiles, makes a noise, then turns to his toy box. He turns to me. The father says, "Pippo." He runs through the room, holding on to Cecilia. Cecilia leaves him in his father's arms and he cries desperately, going "*Na . . . waa*". Cecilia picks him up and takes him to his little bed, where he has learnt to unscrew the nuts and insists on doing this. Simone shows pleasure in being with Cecilia, and imitates her. She says to him, "No no—look at Ceci's gloves. No, no." (The mother tells me that for around two months Simone has loved to put one thing inside another, and vice versa; if he does not succeed, he gets enraged to the point of crying.) He repeats "No no", laughing and holding Cecilia's hands. Picked up again by his father, he cries; he wants Cecilia.

The mother comes back in and offers him the furry tail—but he wants Cecilia. They try to distract him, showing him the drawer underneath his little bed. He puts some keys in it, closes the drawer, and laughs. His father says, "Where are the keys? Here they are." Then he turns to me and adds, "He hides everything: he looks into your face, puts the object behind his back, then you have to ask him 'where is it?' and he brings out his hand to show you what he'd been hiding."

Now Simone walks holding his father's hand and crying "*Mh*". He goes towards the electric plug. Father says, "There, you're walking by yourself", and Simone takes a few steps on his own. The father leaves to go back to work. Simone cries. The mother says, "He wants to go with you." She picks Simone up and rocks him backwards and forwards, sitting on the bed. She says to him, "Where is Little Red Riding Hood? She's gone to find her grandmother. Where is grandmother?"

MH: It sounds as though the mother is feeling a little bit desperate at the end of his passionate crying. It seems to me that Cecilia for the moment has become his sweetheart; as if there is some kind of problem about mother and father being together, but Cecilia is *his* sweetheart. The question is how much that relates to mother going back to work and being away a good part of the day. They laugh about him, saying [that] two months ago he was always putting one thing into another, and vice versa. How long has she been back at work? ("Since September.") It is as if her going to school has very much stirred up his oedipal feelings, his curiosity about where she *is* in the day—a bit like the night now. Before, in the day, he always kept his eyes on her; but now she is out for long periods. And when she was there, she was *very much* there. So it would look as though one of the things she dreaded has come about: his feeling of mummy being his exclusive possession, that he could go in and out of whenever he liked, has been split off and lodged with Cecilia. It is interesting about the father saying that now he hides everything, and puts things behind his back. There is Mummy hiding herself from him during the day, and mummy and daddy's secret hidden relationship; it is as if he is saying "I can hide things too". Hiding behind the back indicates some phantasy about what he hides in his bottom, behind his back; so I wonder what is the situation regarding his defecating at the moment? She doesn't say anything about that? ("No.") I wouldn't be surprised if he were constipated, perhaps. It is an area where a child can hang on to his own possessions, and exhibit defiance—his refusal to have *this* taken away, at any rate.

The other thing—about things going into each other—you can see in his looking for the electric plug. You put things together—the plug goes in there and the light goes on. His difficulties in sleeping at night are very much connected with his phantasies about his parents' intercourse. His father, who we don't usually see, seems to have entered into this in order to try to encourage Simone to be that much more grownup—"Tell her about your new bed"; "You're standing by yourself".

Q: [about the mother's feelings]

MH: I was referring to Simone himself, with his passion for Cecilia. With mother away, the connection between mummy and daddy is now more inescapable for Simone. They said that, when in his cot, he would unscrew the bolts. So there is this wish to separate, pull apart mummy and daddy—the oedipal jealousy of the parents' togetherness. He is transferring to Cecilia the former sweetheart relationship he had with mummy. In a certain way the preparation for mother being away a good deal of the time was not a gradual one. Whenever she was around she was always very much in evidence. I was thinking of that last observation when he blew her a kiss, as if to say "I know you want me to notice you". So it is a very big change for him now mother is away a lot of the day. He is very used to having someone who regards him as their little sweetheart. It looks as if he feels Cecilia is a better bet than his mother at the moment.

The only baby

Fifteenth observation of Simone, age one year, five months

RN (*reads*): I met Simone's aunt outside the house and we went in together. Simone was ill; he had a fever and was in his mother's arms. When he saw me he smiled broadly and passed from his mother's arms to those of his aunt. We sat down round the kitchen table. The father said, "Have you got earache?" Simone motioned "no", and pointed to his forehead. Father and mother seem worried. Simone, in his aunt's arms, held an egg in his hand and observed attentively what was being carried to the table. He was put down on the big seat at the head of the table beneath the window; broke the egg, and ate some bits of the chocolate inside, holding his hand open and murmuring. He looked around, making incomprehensible sounds. When he was not understood, he cried (he seemed to want the dummy, but with sugar on it). Then he stretched his hand out over the table and played with his father's watch, making "brrr" noises with a plastic box in front of him.

The mother gave him a small empty feeding bottle, and Simone put some pieces of bread inside it and shook it.

The father, who was sitting at table on his left, said he needed to see the doctor, and he laughed, playing with his father's hand. The father asked for a kiss, and Simone leaned towards him and touched his nose. Simone shook the bottle in his hand; then his hands reach towards his mother's hand (she is seated on his right). Father says, "Where is Cecilia? And uncle Piero? And Ceci—how does Ceci's *motorino* (moped) go?"

The parents each hold out a hand to Simone and he pulls them alternately, laughing. However, he seems anxious. Then the mother says, "Do you want to write?" and gives him a pencil; he motions no with his head, but then draws. Mother comments, "Only scribbling."

Meanwhile, the mother gives her husband a cigar, and Simone holds out his hand; the father gives him a cellophane wrapper. Mother shows Simone the drawings that he has done for him (the cat, the little goose, etc.). Simone is now picked up by his mother, who is standing; he puts his head on her breast and looks at me. She sits with the baby in her arms; he holds the dummy in his mouth, lowers his eyelids, moves his mouth, his arms meeting under his mother's. The aunt calls "Simone", and he shakes his head. The father calls "Pippo" to him, and he turns; meanwhile, the mother is telling me that these days he cries when he is being undressed.

Now the child sucks the dummy, looking in front of him. The father asks, "Is he very hot? Have you touched Pippo?" Simone raises himself up, stretches himself out again, and gazes at me fixedly with lowered eyelids. He turns to look at the aunt who is sitting near me. He closes his eyes and goes to sleep, with his mouth open and the dummy outside his lips. Now he sleeps, and the dummy falls out of his open mouth.

MH: So, does the father call him Pippo—is that the father's name for him?

RN: No not really—it is a joke that he sometimes calls him Pippo, sometimes Arturo, but not all the time.

MH: Now, when the aunt calls "Simone", is she trying to draw his attention away from his mother? Yes . . . so again, it is a situation where all the grown-ups are competing for Simone's attention. To go back to that (the business of the sugar)—how did he actually make himself understood—that he wanted the dummy to be dipped in sugar? I see, by a process of elimination, they came to the right answer. I was just wondering who it was who finally understood what he wanted—was it the mother, the aunt, or the father? You can't remember which?

RN: Probably the mother.

MH: Today, when Simone has a fever and is not very well, it is as if in a sense they all felt they needed the assurance of his feeling awake and responsive. He certainly does seem to feel that he owes something to all his audience. When he comes in, he smiles at you, and goes to the aunt—as if to satisfy both of you with a greeting. It does look as if he is not feeling well, but he very clearly knows where: when his father asks about his ear, and he points to his forehead, you can see he knows very well where the pain is. He is also very precise in his mind about what he wants: he wants the *ciuccio* in sugar and the other things don't do. You could say he plays a bit with the chocolate egg, and he plays with the bread inside the bottle, but in the end it is the sugar dummy that he sucks on for comfort and goes to sleep with.

It is interesting that, although he is not feeling well, he is quite friendly and responsive to almost everything that is asked of him. His mother gives him a pencil to write with and he doesn't really want it, but then he seems to realize that she wants him to write, so he makes a few scribbles. He also seems to want to take in what is going on around him—his father takes a cigar, so he reaches out to share in it, so it has a cellophane cover. It seems to me that there is quite an identification with his father. Writing with the pencil is to please his mother, but is also in response to an identification with his father. Again, he responds to father calling him "Pippo", as if he and father have some sort of collusion—as if only his father knows this special name for him.

I wonder whether, when the mother says he gets upset these days when he is being undressed, this is to do with some feeling of humiliation, when he wants to be a big boy like daddy. I think he does feel an alliance with father—as father's companion and little man—but at the same time he feels the pressure from all the women in his life, who do really think of him as their little sweetheart.

Yes—he is *the only baby* in that family, and the only little baby. The mother is pregnant again—but at this point he does not know

... One can well see, for this child who is the light of all their little circle, how undoubtedly he will have his nose put out of joint by the arrival of another baby.

The relationship with the father

Sixteenth observation of Simone, age one year, five and a half months

RN (*reads*): When I arrive I find Simone at table in his usual place, and he smiles at me a lot. Then he cries because his aunt has not put forward satisfactory toys. He agrees, however, to play with some little plastic animals and is very engaging towards his aunt. In front of her she has some nuts as well as the animals; now he tries to take a big piece of the salami (*coppa*) on the table. When he is given a piece he seems to both want it and not want it. He goes back to wanting the *coppa* and takes it, shaking it in front of him, and demands the knife. The aunt, who is sitting on his left, says no and makes a gesture that Simone imitates. The mother wants the *coppa*, he turns towards her and protests with a grimace.

MH: When his mother wants the *coppa*, is it Simone's little piece that she wants, or the big one?
RN: The big one.
MH: I see.

RN (*continues reading*): The aunt tells him that now he's got dirty hands and he must leave the *coppa* alone; he says no. With difficulty on his part, he relinquishes it; the mother wraps up the *coppa* again in its plastic film. Then Simone hits the *coppa* with his hand, ignoring his mother; he unwraps it and hits it with his hand, which is holding a piece of bread. Now he hits the arm of a family friend who is sitting on his right. He seizes the *coppa* again, out of its wrapping, and flings it on the table.

He yells, because the aunt leaves out to go to work, and stretches out his arms. His father, seated on his left, tries to distract him, showing him two little plastic oxen. He quietens a bit, but continues to cry. His parents comment that Simone is very light-fingered and will grab things if they are not looking. Mother says, "What a mess, Simone", and goes to pick him up and take him to be changed. The child bursts out in tears. She tells him she won't change him after all, and he calms down and gets down from the high chair.

On the ground, he runs to me, calling my name. He plays jokingly with his father, who says, "What's up, Simone? Why were you in such a rage?" He tries to get up on the seat beside me. The mother says, "No, you mustn't get up." Now Simone goes and sits in the little seat by the window. The mother, standing beside him, talks to him; and to everything she says, he yells "No!" (she was telling him to take a different seat, etc.). Simone appears happy on the little seat, making contented noises, raising himself up, looking at me. He plays at sitting down and getting up, calls me and looks at me. He is picked up by his father, and looks at me from his father's arms. He climbs up with difficulty to take something from the sideboard (standing on his father's knee), then stretches out his hands towards the coffee, which has been served in the meantime by the mother. The mother gives him the dummy with sugar, while he remains in his father's arms, playing with his hair and turning round to look at me. He gets down and comes straight to me.

Then he stands on tiptoe, and touches his hair. His father beckons to him with a book and he looks at the pictures with interest, touching them with his finger, turning the pages. He looks at me, and points, shouting, at a picture of bells, wanting me to look at it. He goes "Don do do do . . .". Then he takes a pen and writes on the open book on his father's lap. His father talks about birthdays, referring also to the time of Simone's birth, and says that was perhaps the only one that he remembered well. He says to the child, "Yes, when you were born you caused your mother a lot of trouble", and Simone looks at his mother. Simone goes back to the little seat, plays with a book and pen, goes "To to to . . .", gets up on to the seat and sits down. Then he encircles his head with a large piece of plastic cord, gets up, and sits down again. He tries to pull the seat under the table, but his mother persuades him to stay sitting, and he plays the get-up and sit-down game.

MH: When he puts that plastic string round his head, what is it—a little circlet? ("No, it's big, heavy.") I am just wondering what that has to do with his interest in his father's hair. Does his father have very thick hair—what is it like?

RN: Not especially . . .

MH: It may be that he is making himself look a bit more like daddy, in identification with his father. Towards the end, after touching his father's hair, he leans forward and looks at Romana;

and then he stands up and touches *his* hair, as if there is some kind of comparison between himself and his father, asking: what is it that makes daddy so interesting to women?

At that point, he accepts his father's drawing his attention to the pictures, and he does look at them; but he uses the book, again, to *catch* Romana's attention. He takes the pen as if to say "I too have a pen-penis and can make interesting marks". So there is very much an impulsion to identify with daddy, but also there is a competition—to *be* daddy.

> Fear of losing his role in the family

Q: [about his crying on being changed]

MH: I would think it is as if being changed means being a baby, and takes some of his more important grown-up status from him; he feels humiliated by being a baby with a wet nappy. Right from the beginning there seems to be this dissatisfaction with his lot as the small child: being given the little piece of *coppa* isn't enough—he wants the knife that cuts it, he wants the big piece. It is humiliating when his aunt says his hands are dirty, and his mother says his bottom is dirty and he needs his nappy changed. You can see there the defiance and resentment against these grown-ups who are stopping him from being the *big one*.

> The king baby

With all his charm, there is also something a bit tyrannical beneath the surface—such as his wanting to have everybody with him when he wishes. He cries when the aunt goes away; he comes towards you to catch your attention, then later on when father suggests he writes, he does it in order to hold your attention.

I think you get a good indication of how, later on, when he has a sibling, it is going to be very difficult for him to take his place as one of the children, instead of remaining this king-baby who is everybody's sweetheart. It is interesting that the father says at this point, remembering Simone's birth, "He gave his mother a lot of trouble"—as if somewhere at the back of his mind there is the possibility of another child giving as much trouble as Simone. What a difficulty such a child will have—he has a major problem ahead, with the loss of his identity as the light of everybody's life. It has already started, with the mother's preoccupation with her own health and with the baby inside her; he must already feel the removal of some of her attention.[3] You can see how the *father*, and his relationship with him, is going to be of particular importance.

How the new baby is made

Seventeenth observation of Simone, age one year ten months

RN (*reads*): I have not seen Simone for two and a half months. He has been with his mother in the country, in the Marche; they spend their holidays with his grandparents on his mother's side as well as with grandma on his father's side. His father usually joins them for a few days, but recently, he stayed two weeks with them.

The entrance door is open and I enter without ringing the bell. I meet Simone in the anteroom. He is in his mother's arms and they are coming out of the bathroom; he has no pants on. He looks at me and says "*cacca*!" (pooh). I ask him if he made himself dirty, and his mother nods. Mrs P puts Simone down. He goes into his room very quickly and comes out again almost immediately, carrying a big boat. He brings it to me to look at, saying: "boat", then he goes to fetch another one. "Boat", he exclaims, while he shows it to me. He returns to his room and comes out gain holding a toy pig: "Mana [Romana], pig!" he says and shows me the animal. He seems very happy.

I enter the room after Simone. He is still wearing his vest and pyjama top. He says to me, "Look!" and pretends to run a race: "Mana, race!" He takes a stick and pretends to fire. Then he cries out, "Look, grandpa shoots!" Mrs P comes in and encourages him to put on his pants, but he does not want them. Then she goes out and he follows her, calling out "Mammina". Simone goes out and in several times calling "Mammina", who is in the bathroom.

Simone comes up to me and says, "Mana, look!" and then says again, "Mana, *ciao*." His mother tries to persuade him to put on his pants, but he answers "No". Now, his mother takes him up, puts him on his bed and dresses him. In the meantime, she tells me that Simone still wakes up during the night around half past two or three o'clock, and at a certain point the parents have to bring him in to their bed. Mrs P, who is seated on the bed near me, tells me that now, however, the problem with sleep has diminished considerably. There were two or three nights, however, when Simone was wide awake; the mother says disapprovingly that "the people who live upstairs [the flat above them] always give him all sorts of things to eat" and so she is unable to regulate his meals. Meanwhile, Simone is on his knees on the bed. He points to some pictures hanging on the wall. "Grandpa shoots pretty girl", he says. His mother says, "There, another grandpa!", and in the meantime makes him get down off the bed. "Bed", he moans, and climbs up on it again. Mrs P encourages him to take down the small pictures so he can see them, but "without breaking them".

Father comes in. Simone runs into the hall to meet him and immediately says to me, "Mana". Mrs P comes in and Simone shows him the toy horse that is lying on the floor. Father asks, "Did you tell Romana that you have seen the sea?" "No", Simone replies. Shortly afterwards the child calls out "Babbino!" (Daddy) and wants to hold his father's hand, but the father cannot give it him because his hands are dirty (he has been in the cellar bottling some wine). Simone goes into the kitchen with his father.

Meanwhile, Mrs P who remains in the room, tells me about her new pregnancy (she is expecting her baby in March). She seems weaker or more tired than during her first pregnancy. She tells me that during the summer she suffered from a prolonged tachycardia and she had to consult a specialist about it. Now she is still worried about this illness as she had a similar incident while Simone was being delivered. Mrs P discovered she was pregnant after this episode of tachycardia.

Mr P comes in followed by his son, who is holding a tablespoon in his mouth. Mother says to Simone, "Tell Romana what you have eaten", and he answers: "Sugar—sugar . . ." Mother tells Simone again, "Tell Romana what Pippo did to you", and the child tells me the story. While they were visiting an aunt in the country, her cat, Pippo, came in stealthily to where Simone was, and quite secretly stole his dummy and ran away with it. Simone realized that his dummy was missing when they arrived home, but then it was too late and they could not do anything about it. The first night, the child woke up and cried desperately. For two or three nights, each time Simone asked desperately for his dummy, they gave him some sugar. Little by little he was able to give up his teat altogether.

Simone goes out with his father, then he runs in saying, "Mana", and shows me a book on cats. "Is it Pippo?" I ask him, pointing to a picture of a cat. "No", he answers quickly. Then he turns over the pages slowly, pausing every now and then to let me look at the different pictures. He lingers especially when he comes across a picture of a kitten peeping out between the legs of a dog. Mother brings in some coffee and Simone wants a piece of sugar. She takes it off the tray and he cries to have some. Mrs P asks, "How many sweets can you eat?" and, crying, he answers "One." His mother goes on, saying, "You have already eaten one and that is enough." Then, crying, he begs, "*in braccia!*" ("pick me up!"). After that, he gets distracted and plays with a plastic mouse that is on a toy cart. His mother, smiling, comments on him and he seems happy.

Meanwhile, Mrs P, who is sitting in the rocking chair, tells me all about her visit to the cardiologist this summer. At the same time, Simone is playing with a toy chair on the floor around his mother's feet. Now he is playing behind her chair. She gets up and asks Simone to move a bit further away. Then she goes on talking and he moans from behind her chair. Mrs P notices what Simone has done and asks, "You dropped the little screw—did you pick it up?" "Yes", Simone replies, and his mother calls him "a liar". The child goes to bring the small pictures that are on the bed, and puts them on the toy cart. Then he drags the toy tortoise behind him, goes towards the table and takes the empty tray. He puts it on the floor and asks for "sugar, sugar". Then he turns the tray round on the floor and his mother takes it away from him. Simone goes to get some toys and calls out their names: the pliers, the ball, and so on. His mother tells me about their return home from the country. "He noticed a lot during the first two days. Now Simone is much better, he is bigger and can control himself."

The child shows me the pliers. "Mana," he exclaims, "red!" They are green, however. Then a train goes by outside, and mother asks, "Can you hear the train?" Now, Mrs P tries to repair his torch. He takes it, unscrews the small lamp and puts the torch on the bed near me. "Bravo", he says, and applauds himself. He goes back to his drawer (which is underneath the bed), then screws back the small lamp and says to me, "I've put it in its right place." "Pliers", he says. He takes a plastic hammer and hammers the torch. His mother tries to dissuade him, saying that he will break it that way. Then she takes the torch away, saying it is broken and must be thrown in the bin. He begins to cry and, running after her, sobs "Pick me up!" Mother picks him up and kisses him. Simone hugs her affectionately, and she remarks, "Why are you hugging me so much this morning?"

I am sitting near the bee toy, and Simone wants his mother to wind it up. The bees go round and the music starts ("Für Elise"). He stands up and tries to catch them in his hands as they go round. His mother asks him, "Which is the most beautiful? . . . they are all beautiful." He laughs and then asks, "Ugly?" "No," retorts his mother, "they are all beauti-ful." Simone goes on, "Beautiful, beautiful, fat . . ." Mrs P asks him, "Have you seen that fat one? It is the queen." He is very fond of bees; he smacks his lips saying, "*Bona, buona*" (good). Then he takes up a toy car. "Car!" he exclaims, and brings it near me, then he opens its doors and says, "Brr . . . brr . . .". He hammers on his bed. "Gusta, mummy, Gusta!" he says (his name for his Aunt Augusta). Then he adds, "Bees, I want to press the button", and begins to cry. His mother lets him press the button, showing him that it is quite difficult.

How the new baby is made

MH: That is a very interesting observation. It is fairly clear that Simone is absolutely preoccupied with the new baby and with how the new baby is made—starting off, you might say, with exhibiting his own little penis. When he meets you and says "*cacca*", does he say it in a somewhat shamed way?

RN: No, he sounds triumphant.

MH: So he is really drawing attention to his little bare bottom and his penis. Then he goes out and fetches you a boat, and then another boat—as if recommending himself with this penis he is showing you. It is interesting, because you say you haven't seen him for two and a half months, and yet he comes out and sponta-neously welcomes you.

The baby's sexuality—seducing a new mummy

The boat and the pig—are they new toys that he got in the holiday and that he is bringing to show you?

RN: I don't know.

MH: I wonder whether the pig suggests some kind of identifi-cation with his grandfather and his farm, the shooting, and so on. When he says "look" and pretends to run a race—"Mana, race"—and takes the gun and shoots, I wonder whether he is expressing both some kind of identification with grandfather and his shooting-gun penis, and some kind of competition with him, and showing this to Romana. Because "Mana" is not so unlike "Mammina": as if you represent a kind of mummy that he is attempting to seduce with his own potency, his own little penis, saying he is really worth you paying attention to him. The mother seems to come in as a mummy who says, "Put on your trousers and hide your little penis", somehow reducing his seductiveness, and he doesn't want that. When she goes out again, he then gets quite anxious, feeling he has upset her, and wants to go and find her. When he comes back near you and says "Mana, look", what is it he is showing you?

RN: The same thing.

MH: So it is again as if he is presenting his little penis to you, as if you are interested even though his mummy is not. He is quite emphatic that he doesn't want his pants on, but his mother insists, and he accepts it when she does actually put him on the bed and put his pants on. Now as she puts his pants on, quite evidently unconsciously aware that he has been displaying his little penis to you, she then talks about his waking up in the night. Then she says it is because the people upstairs give him all the wrong things to eat. It is as if to say, *they* are the ones who excite his sexuality—it is not me and my husband and the prospect of the new baby; that's got nothing to do with it. It's those people upstairs who take this interest in him and give him ideas that make him wake in the night. It is as if she is saying, *she* can't help it if other people seduce him and get him all excited; *she* can't regulate his meals.

Now, it is interesting when he is on his knees on the bed and says, "Grandpa shoots pretty girl". You can see the connection between the gun-penis and the pretty girl! He does want to stay on the bed, though his mother wants him to get off it. So . . . when father comes in, he immediately goes to tell father that you have come. Father asks if he has told you he has seen the sea, and he says, "No". Shortly afterwards he calls "Babbino" and wants to hold his father' s hand.

Comment: [about the appropriateness of Simone's use of language]

MH: Before, they were worried about his language, weren't they . . . in a sense this is a child who has hardly needed to speak, in order to make his feelings known. He has always been surrounded by women who answered all his questions. Now the mother talks about the baby and about her tachycardia. She seems to be worried about it; could the tachycardia be connected with anything at all serious?

RN: I don't believe so.

MH: On we go to this interesting business about the sugar becoming a replacement for the dummy, *ciuccio*. Is this actually a true story, or is it meant to be a fairy tale that the parents have told him because they want to wean him from his dummy? ("Yes.") You see, I think this is a bit of an indication of how difficult it is for this mother to frustrate this little boy: to definitely set limits, and encourage him to grow up. A story comes in—it is the cat that did it, not anybody else, not her. One can well imagine that the child will take that as being really the baby inside her who has taken it away from him.

I think one of the problems of these parents as a couple, and particularly of the mother, is of being parents who can set limits and take responsibility for ways in which they are bound inevitably to be objects of frustration to the child. It is a situation that often comes about with parents who are in too great an identification with the child or the baby, and not able clearly to differentiate themselves from him. This is something that does make it that much harder than it otherwise would be when the next baby comes along, because the child feels so terribly displaced from his position of being the little prince at the centre of everybody's life. He has not had that much experience beforehand of working out with the parents some of the frustrations of being a child among adults. So, when the next child comes along, there is profound disillusion. He is cast down from his omnipotent position, as well as having to cope with feelings of jealousy.

> Sweetening the child's difficult feelings

It is interesting that they replace the dummy with sugar, something sweet—very much trying to sweeten the baby. Then he brings Romana a book of cats to look at, and you think he is trying to tell you about Pippo. It is interesting that the page he stops at shows a little kitten peeping through a dog's legs, as if this kitten is the wretched little baby that daddy's penis has put in. So that's the culprit! He wants more sweets, and the mother says how many can you eat? He answers "one", and she says "well you've already had one, and that's enough". I suppose he must know numbers by now, and can probably count one, two—he probably knows "two"

("Yes."). I wonder, when he says "one", whether he is repeating what his mother has said—that he is only allowed to have one sweet; or whether he is also saying that there *is* only one sweet for him, one mummy, one breast; and also, that mummy should only have *one* baby. I just wonder what is the significance of that "one". When his mother said, "You've already had one", it seems to come home to him that he can't be the baby again, and he asks her to hold him in her arms.

Then, when he gets on to playing with the plastic mouse in the toy cart, he seems to be taking his feelings about the baby being inside the mummy, and investigating them there. Then he seems to gradually, in his play, get round and *behind* his mother, and she asks him to move a little away. Is that because he is moving too close to her, or is hearing what she is talking about?

RN: She doesn't know what he is doing with the screw.

MH: It looks as if what he is doing, which is something to do with unscrewing, is something dangerous, something naughty, pulling apart the parents, but also the mummy and the baby. As if getting behind mummy means somehow getting in and taking apart the baby and the mummy. You might say he is trying to unscrew whatever is keeping this baby inside mummy; if he can unscrew the place where the baby is kept, then it might crawl out. Now, whether that relates right back to the beginning of the situation when he has done *cacca* in his pants, and had his pants taken off, and whether the doing of that *cacca* had the significance of shitting the baby out of this pregnant mummy that he has inside him . . . This might throw some light on what you thought was his triumphant air. He was not just showing off his little penis, but also feeling triumphant at having attacked and shitted out the baby.

Then he turns round the tray on the floor and his mother takes it away from him . . . I wonder what he was doing with the tray that his mother didn't like? . . . So that again would be to do with taking something away from where it belongs, on the table: taking it away and treating it badly. Because the next thing he does, bringing the toys and naming them, as if they represent himself or parts of himself, suggests he is showing off his performance and all the things he can now do—he can now talk and so on—as if he is again recommending himself to you. Like a grown-up, he has got all these things, these attributes. It is interesting that he picks up the pliers, in particular, and calls them "red". Now maybe he really doesn't know the names of the colours; or maybe it is that he is seeing them as red, because he sees them as something that repairs, like a nipple or a penis. . . . He is trying to repair the torch with them. They seem to represent something that can take things apart and then put them together, and put them in the right place. Almost as if he is trying to say to you, as mummy, "What do you want with daddy? I've got these pliers and I can take things apart and put them together in the right place . . . I can put a baby inside you." But then, later, his mother calls his bluff and breaks his heart by saying that the torch is "broken"—he is someone who breaks things, not someone who puts them together. He is quite heartbroken and has to be picked up, and be the baby in her arms again.

> An ugly part

It is interesting how she experiences him as being in a destructive, pulling-to-pieces mood. One would be inclined to think that her anxiety about that is that much greater in so far as she is not able openly to admit to herself that her pregnancy is bound to be hurtful to him, to arouse jealous and hostile feelings. She is doing everything she can to avoid that; but at the same time she is a little bit persecuted by feeling he might be doing something to undermine it. Because when she says, "Why is it you embrace me so much this morning?", she shows she is aware of his need for affection and reassurance, but she can't quite let herself think a bit further to see that this is to do with his very ambivalent feelings about the baby and the fact that she is seeing Romana and talking to her about her pregnancy. It does sound from this that she has not as yet openly admitted the fact of her pregnancy to Simone.

When Simone asks for the game of the bees, a toy that hung over his cot when he was a newborn infant, it suggests his wish to find that intimate primitive contact with his mother again. When his mother says, "Which is the most beautiful? They are *all* beautiful", it is as though she is saying Simone is beautiful, and a new baby is also beautiful. Simone laughs and says "ugly", and she says no— they are *all* beautiful. I would think that is something to do with his perhaps wondering if he is ugly, because he knows somewhere there is a part of him that does feel very ugly, and that wishes she would accept him as ugly, but she says no—you're all beautiful. Then he says "beautiful, beautiful—*fat*"; and she connects that with the queen bee. One would think that must have something to do with *her* bigness—she must be showing a bit fatter now?

RN: Not yet.

MH: He is feeling in some ways shut out from his mother, as if she has betrayed him. When aunt Augusta comes in, she is a mummy-person who doesn't upset him by having daddy's baby—an idealizing mummy who lets him be her little sweetheart, her little husband.

The little chair—the new place in the family

Eighteenth observation of Simone, age one year eleven months

RN (*reads*): As I enter the house I hear Simone crying desperately, because his father, who was with him, had hidden himself. He carries on crying bitterly, because he wants to go out. "Out", he sobs. His mother, who is in the kitchen with his aunt, does not want him to go out, because he has a cough. Simone sits down at the head of the table near his father; meanwhile he calms down when they give him some sugar in a teaspoon. We are all seated round the table and coffee is served. Mrs P tells me how she has broken the news to Simone about the prospect of his baby sister; she told him one day in summer after he had been naughty. "No", he had retorted, and added that he would throw her in the washbasin. At the same time, the lady who lives upstairs and who looks after him when his mother is out (he calls her "Aunty Nana"), told him she would take his little sister with her "and not him", upon which he screamed.

Simone was out while Mrs P was telling me all this. Now he comes in holding a teddy bear on his head. Father says to him, "Tell Romana that you can ride the tricycle." The child goes out of the kitchen and comes in again dragging the tricycle, and shows it to me. He gets on it and rides towards his aunt, who is over by the window; then he looks out and shakes the handlebar. He wants his aunt to sit on the back seat, behind him. They tell him to sit there himself, but he keeps insisting. Eventually, they persuade him to put his teddy bear on the back seat. Simone goes out and comes in again with a triumphant air, carrying the teddy bear, the little wooden Pinocchio, and the fireman. He goes back into the corridor, leaves the tricycle there, and returns carrying the teddy bear across his shoulders. Then he puts it in my arms to look at. His aunt explains to me that he is copying his father, who carries him on his shoulders. Now Simone wants his aunt to take his place on the tricycle while he sits on the back seat. His aunt tries to please him for a bit. He goes out, comes in again, approaches me, and makes a few comments such as "I am sitting"; then goes towards the window. Mrs P, who is still sitting at the table, remarks on the beauty of Simone's new gym shoes and adds that he would later give them to a poor boy. "No", says Simone, as he passes by me on his tricycle. I remark that his shoes are really beautiful, like those of an adult. The child smiles proudly; then his aunt points out that they are ridiculous because they are "for adults in miniature". She laughs, and Simone, who is riding forwards and backwards, laughs too. Mrs P tells me that Diego's parents are expecting a baby too, in May. Meanwhile, Simone has gone out with his father to fetch a big box for his mother. He comes in again, comes close to me and tells me that he has been in the cellar where the "bino-vino" (wine) is. His mother tells him to put away his toys, but he answers "No".

Simone goes out of the kitchen and returns with a plastic tractor. He goes forwards and backwards singing. His father encourages him to take the digger-bucket and put it in the tractor-trailer, then something goes wrong and he begins to scream. His aunt comments while his father tries to help him, and eventually he calms down. The child chatters as he sits in front of the digger and the tractor. Then he makes his father understand that he wants to climb on his back. His aunt tells me that sometimes Simone calls his father "Gigina", and this annoys him. I ask them to explain this nickname. They say that probably the child wants to pay his father back for saying that he behaves like a girl. Then his mother asks him, "Is it true that you will have two baby sisters?" He appears not to understand her question, and answers twice, referring to the tractor. "You see", says Mrs P to me. Then his aunt picks up the conversation about the baby sister again: "Where are you going to put her?", she asks, and he points to the driver's seat on the tractor, next to him. His parents then speak to me about uncle Robert, who lives in the Marche; he is a farmer and uses a tractor in his fields. The aunt asks Simone, "Where is the tractor's engine?" and, excitedly, he replies, "Here it is!"

Meanwhile, I ask Mrs P how she is feeling about her tachycardia. Simone calls me again. Father comments on the forthcoming birth of the baby sister, and tells Simone that "we shall all be together". The aunt resumes the conversation about the tractor and asks, "You have never been on the tractor with uncle Robert, have you?" "No", Simone replies. He plays with the digger on the floor and grasps my foot with it, deliberately. Father says, "Simone knows about Uncle Robert's tractor and about the one in 'Little Walter'." I extract myself from the digger while Mr P and the aunt talk about some friends. Simone comes close to me and bites my knee. "Oh, no", his father cries out, and adds that today the child is quite nervous. He was behaving like that, he says, because "we were talking amongst ourselves".

Mother says to Simone, "Go and bring your book to show it to Romana." He comes near to me and says, "Mana, look", and then comes back with his mother and his book. Mrs P wants him to sit on her lap, but he says "picciolina, picciolina" (little chair), and goes to get it, putting it between his mother and me. He opens his book (which mother tells me he is very fond of and does not tear) and says, "Sun, Mana, milk . . ." Then he looks at me and says, "Get the book of the duckling—Pepperino." He sits down again, picks up the comic about Mickey Mouse and says, "Duckling, here it is!", then he puts the comic on the table, goes into the bedroom, and comes back running, saying it is raining.

Now Mrs P wants to put him to bed. He begins to cry, and flings himself into his father's arms. "Gigi," (short for Louis) "babbino", he cries, "babbino!" "Then I will put your little sister in your bed", says his mother. "No, it is too big", he answers.

The pain of displacement

MH: This is a way to recommend a little sister to an older child! The little sister will have his bed, the little sister will have his place with the grown-ups—if he doesn't behave himself! It is an indication of the difficulty the parents have in really being able to accept and identify with the *pain* of the child at his displacement. If they were able to really feel it, that would threaten their own unworked-through childish pains and jealousies that cannot be borne or admitted. It is not at all an unusual attitude. You can see how very near to feeling desperate the child is, despite being surrounded by affectionate interest: there is a whole area here that is not recognized by the parents or by anyone. In this desperate crying and need to go out, and his fear that his father will not take him out, you can see his fear of losing his father as an ally who can take him away from these claustrophobic feelings of jealousy and infantile dependency that he feels when he is close to mummy.

Now, the mother told you that she broke the news about her pregnancy to him one day in the summer when he was naughty. The implication would be that he's a naughty boy, but he won't be her only child because she is going to have another one to *replace* him. So he immediately retorts, "Well I'll flush *her* down the wash-basin!" The mother's unthinking behaviour is because she doesn't know how else to talk about it—other than in those infantile terms. In this way she more or less confirms the conviction that every child has that the new baby is going to throw him out—the new baby is coming because he is unsatisfactory, he is no good. So the child's fears of displacement are used as a kind of weapon to make him be submissive and behave himself. In one way it seems terribly surprising that a mother who is so tenderly attached to her little boy should behave in this way. But it is not so unusual; and I would think it is a measure of the extent to which the mother's tender relationship with the baby has some degree of narcissistic identification in it: seeing the baby as a child-part of herself. It goes together with her problem of being able to admit that the child has nasty parts of himself, painful feelings; and in *the very nature of things*, he must have complicated bad or destructive feelings. She as a mother is not going to be able to prevent him from having those feelings.

Put it this way: the mother who desires so much to be a perfect mummy to the child, to prevent him from having any pain, is in a sense not grown-up. She is still the little girl who feels that mummies should be able to give children *everything*. That is not an adult view of the world—to feel that there is or should be an ideal mummy who can make it easy and painless. It is just not real. This terrific tenderness, yet over-indulgence, towards the child, which does not allow his nastier feelings to be seen, is liable to lead on later to a hurt or resentful feeling in the mother's heart that says, "I gave him *everything*—and this is what he does to me!" when he starts being nasty. Undoubtedly Simone will start to have nasty feelings when this next baby comes. It is bound to lead to a struggle with the child later on, unless the child gets so intimidated that he is *squashed* into behaving nicely, rather than allowed to be himself.

> Infantile conflicts in the parents

But, of course, parents can become educated through their children. This may happen with Simone's mother together with the father. But, at the moment, these occasional threats that the new baby will take his place unless he behaves himself are a bit shocking.

Then father comes in and says, "Tell Romana you can ride the tricycle." So father is showing him off, encouraging him—saying he's a little man like me. It is interesting that he is behaving like a little man, with auntie sitting on the seat behind him—

Comment: Like the sister.

MH: Like the sister, yes. One can see an increased identification with his father—such as when he carries the teddy bear on his shoulder, like his father carries him. This identification with the father is one way out of being caught in this very jealous, claustrophobic, displaced situation with his mother. To go on to this rather extraordinary remark of Simone's father—about how beautiful his new gym shoes are, and he should give them to a poor boy—how did he say that?

RN: To provoke him.

MH: It would almost seem that the father's need to provoke him is to project his *own* feelings about being the poor boy—as if in some way the prospect of the new baby has made the father feel a poor displaced baby. Also, the mother is not feeling too well herself, so she is probably less interested in him sexually, and therefore he feels a bit displaced.

This kind of thing does throw light on how so many marriages do break up on the birth of a child, or the second child, in so far as the birth does stir up infantile areas in both parents, and the father suffering from little-boy displacement goes off to find somebody else. I am not suggesting there is any indication of this here; but if one looks carefully at these infant observations one can recognize the kind of infantile conflicts that are thrown up by births and pregnancies. And how difficult it can be for parents to *grow into* being parents, rather than remaining children in identification with their own children.

It is interesting about those shoes: when Romana remarks how beautiful they are and the child is proud, then the aunt says, "They're ridiculous—they are for adults in miniature." It is as if she is saying they're ridiculous because it just leads him to think he is a little grown-up. It is interesting that *she* should do this, because in certain ways she has sometimes treated Simone as if he were a miniature adult—as if he were the little penis that she is in love with. There is a hint of some little-girl rivalry in relation to Simone and the father being boys together.

So now we hear that Diego's parents are expecting a baby. So Diego is going to be jealous as well. It is interesting when Simone comes and says he has been to the wine cellar with daddy—as if he feels that is some grown-up place where he has been allowed to go with daddy.

Then there is this interesting bit where he is laughing at the father and calling him a little girl. There are hints that the father is not entirely happy about this new pregnancy; he feels a little put out. Now it may be Simone senses this, calling his father "Gigina", silly little girl, equating him with the little sister. Girlish is equated with babyish, on seeing his father behaving in a babyish way. Men are tough—they can do things, they don't have babyish emotions. If you're upset, that means you're babyish, you're a girl. He is already—you might say—in *training* to become a male chauvinist pig!

This part is very interesting—father commenting on the future birth of the baby sister—and he tells Simone "we shall be united together". Mummy can have her little girl, but you and I will be men together, and we won't mind—we won't cry. You get an indication there of how children, particularly little boys, can be encouraged to split off their more tender feelings of jealousy and turn to toughness, despising these mummies and babies. It is a way of trying to split off their femininity—I don't mean homosexuality, but femininity in the sense of feelings, softness. It is a quick way out of his baby feelings of dependence on the mother, rather than acknowledging them, staying with them, working through them, to make them part of himself. One can see how very important it is for the mother to be able to recognize and support the child's tender attachment to her, while at the same time noticing he feels painfully jealous and attacking towards her. It seems to me that Simone is a child of very rich emotionality, a very passionate child, and it is clear that his mother also is very fond of him. But I think it is going to be quite a problem for him to retain this. It is not that the parents are entirely imperceptive; when Simone comes and bites Romana's knee, the father says "No". He says the child behaves like that because he is nervous and we are talking among ourselves; he feels left out. But to remember that, and behave accordingly, is another matter.

> The small chair

It is quite clear that he is making efforts himself to find his own place. When the mother says "Bring your book" and he comes back and doesn't want to sit on his mother's lap, although she offers it. Instead he says "small chair"; this is his attempt to find his place, not with the grown-ups on their big chairs, and not with the baby on mummy's lap, but on a *small chair*. In his book, he is showing everything he has learned, and then—the duckling . . . This seems to suggest something like, *you* [Romana] should be his girlfriend. Then he comes back saying, "It's raining" . . . what does that mean, I wonder. Is the rain like the depression he is trying to cope with, underneath. He seems to collapse when his mother wants him to go to bed; and when she threatens "I'll put your little sister in your bed", he says, "It's too big", meaning, *"That's my place; it fits me"*.

You can see here how frightened his mother is of his being defiant and turning against her. She is almost trying to discipline him, by threatening not to love him and to put the baby sister in his place. There seems to be no way of his really getting out and escaping from his feelings of depression—which I think is probably true, with this child. I would be surprised if he managed to cut off and harden himself, in the way that some children can, by turning away from the mother. I would think that he has basically got a very tender and loving and responsive nature; and he hasn't found a way out by becoming just a tough little boy who despises little girls. I think he probably can't escape from it. How he is going to work with it, though, I don't quite know. It is possible that he could become an over-good little brother, like another mummy to the baby. I would imagine that he is a child where, sooner or later, the baby would touch his heart. I think this little boy's femininity and emotionality is pretty strong. We will have to see how he deals with it. He is a child who has a good disposition—a rich, feeling disposition; but he has been brought up to be very dependent upon being loved, being admired. I think maybe that over-dependence on being admired, and pleasing the people round about him, could stultify his growth into a stronger type of independence which would make use of the full range of his personality. He is over-dependent on pleasing his *external* objects.

It would be very interesting and instructive to follow him, and the whole family, through the birth of the next baby. There is a whole family observation here.

Notes

1. Another child who had been discussed.
2. This was her first grandson, Gawain Williams.
3. The mother is not yet pregnant. However, at the time of this supervision, her pregnancy was well established, and Mrs Harris was informed of it.

CHAPTER THREE

The story of the birth of the next sibling

A round two years old Simone learns that his mother is expecting another baby. This produces in the life of the child a change that one could define as "catastrophic" (in the terms of Bion). Emotions of peculiar intensity trigger multiple attempts to find ways of tolerating the pain. We see him exploring various identifications, both masculine and feminine—with his farmer grandfather and his hat, cows and the birth of piglets, and his shotgun. He identifies with the mother who has a baby in her tummy. Mrs Harris brings out very clearly how Simone's curiosity about the baby stimulates his epistemophilic instinct. The importance of stories at critical moments of a child's life is very evident: how they allow the emotional experience to come to life in a poetic and imaginative way that can contain intense and baffling emotions.

Feminine and masculine qualities

Nineteenth observation of Simone, age two years, one month, and ten days

RN (*reads*): I call at Mrs P's house on the 4th December in the morning, but there is no one at home. I go to find the father in his pharmacy; he tells me he is worried about his son because of the coming baby. Lately, Simone has often "telephoned" his grandfather in the country and asked him how the piglets are, and if the calf is born. (The other day, he had heard his mother talking to her father on the phone about a cow that was due to calve.) Ten days ago, Simone had again had difficult problems during the night. Yesterday, when he heard his parents talking about the new baby, he said spontaneously that he would have put him in his tummy. Last night, Simone slept in his parents' bed. At one point, early in the morning, the mother asked her husband to touch her tummy to feel the baby's movements. When the father moved to do this, he jostled against Simone, who immediately transferred himself from the bottom of the bed where he was, to a position in between his father and mother.

For some months now he has been fixated on his hair, perhaps since he saw his grandfather wearing a cap, a *beret*, and demanded that his grandmother make him a *beret* also.

Meanwhile, Simone comes in from the back of the pharmacy with his mother. He is holding a pair of pliers that his uncle Piero has given him. Simone sits down at his father's desk and "writes", then he turns his attention to various small funnels and pharmaceutical instruments, and goes towards the shelves where these are kept. He approaches the cloak-stand, and wants the assistant to hand him some of the hats on it so he can try them on.

I arrange with Mrs P to see Simone the next day.

MH: He has found his way into the parents' bedroom and wants to be *in on* what is happening—to be involved in the parents' intercourse and what is growing inside mummy. There also seems to be a terrific identification with his grandfather (through the cap on his head), who has the cows and the pigs. We can see how it can be a bit of a relief to a child to have not only a father but a grandfather to identify with. The father sleeps with mummy, and that evokes painful feelings of jealousy in relation to him. It also seems as if he identifies with his mother, because he says he would put the baby inside him—is that his *own* tummy? ("Yes.") I remember Simone is a baby who has always been very close both to his mother and his father, and had very close attention not only from his parents but also from the aunt. So it is quite a difficult situation for him to find they have been thinking about another baby, who will push him out from his position at the centre of the family.

The child'd identifications

There is also his uncle Piero . . . so Simone puts himself with the men of the family, as if the pliers were a penis-like object; the cap on the head also represents something similar. In wanting to try on the hats on the cloak-stand, he is trying to identify with the various different men. The forthcoming birth of a baby sibling is very much a spur to him to try to grow up and be a man like daddy. But there is also having to cope with his envy of mummy, who has a baby in her tummy, because he would also like to have a baby in his tummy. He seems to me to be developing into a little boy who has quite strong feminine as well as masculine qualities, identifying strongly with each of his parents. Identifying with the different qualities of the other men he is fond of—his uncle, his grandfather—helps him to achieve an *introjective* identification, rather than feeling that he actually has to *be* daddy, projecting himself into him and displacing him in relation to the mummy. It helps to take the *heat* out of his jealousy of daddy, the feeling that the only way to be a man is to *be daddy*. A child can have a despairing feeling that there is only one man that his mummy likes—and that is daddy—therefore if he is not daddy, it is no good. But if there are other daddy-like people in his life, then he can feel that some day he also may become *a man*. So, for Simone it is important, with the new baby coming, that he strengthens his relationship with these other men who are fond of him and important in his life. When it is unbearable for him to think about daddy in bed with mummy and interested in the baby inside mummy, Simone can turn his attention to grandpa on the farm, who has a cow with a little calf—that is not quite so unbearable. He can take an interest in the approaching birth of the piglets even when he cannot bear to think about the approaching birth of the baby. He is a child who lives in a pretty rich, intimate social milieu.

There is some phantasy here that grandma made the cap for grandpa, and so really it is mummy who gives daddy his penis, or makes him a man; so grandma ought to do this for him. I think that touches on some kind of omnipotent phantasy of the little infant— the phantasy that really, everything comes from mummy, and in fact, mummy made daddy. It is almost the opposite of the equivalent omnipotent phantasy that Eve was created from Adam. But I guess the Bible was written by men.

The value of fairy tales

Twentieth observation of Simone, age two years, one month, and ten days

RN (*reads*): I enter the house, meet the mother in the hall and hear Simone calling me from his parents' bedroom: he is in the big bed with his father. He tells me "the thieves ran away".

I go into the kitchen with his mother; meanwhile Simone gets up, comes into the kitchen and wants to look at his book of fairy tales. He sits at the table and, while turning the pages, says to me, "The thieves ran away . . . Pippo, the hat, the smelly piglets, the magic fish . . ." The father comes in and explains to me, in relation to the frequent repetition of the phrase "the thieves ran away", that Simone hates all violent people. He sits down at the table next to his son. Simone says, "Look, I'll show you the bad man!" He is excited. Father tells me the book of fairy tales was bought only the day before. He says that in the past few days Simone has also become very keen on gloves, since he saw Diego wearing some. The father tries to help Simone turn the pages, telling him the story at the same time. Simone is annoyed, and says, "The magic fish, the little horses, Pippo feeding the hens . . .", etc. Then he tells his mother, who has come close to him, to "move a bit", and carries on recounting "the farmer, like grandpa . . . the piglets have stolen everything." The mother asks, "What have the little rabbits got in their mouth?", and he replies, "Sweets", then "Look, Romana—the hayloft!" Then he starts to tell the story of Berto the Tractor.

Mother shows him Pippo's shoes; he says, "They're broken", and wants to show me the runaway thieves and the crown that he calls a cap. Then he adds, "I'll read you this", and takes another book. The father suggests a different one and remarks that it is torn. Simone shows it to me and the mother says she will repair it. Simone goes to get the first book and father brings him another one. Simone says, "Paperino (Donald Duck)—*tore*" (*investigatore*—detective), and his father corrects him. Simone continues, saying that Paperino the detective was working while Topolino (Mickey Mouse) was trying to collect the nuts the thief had put in a hole. "Who were the thieves?" asks the father: "Chip and Chop." Simone is angry with his father for interrupting, and motions him away. The mother comments on the illustrations that appear as Simone turns the pages: "What are Chip and Chop's feet like? They're blue . . .", but he goes on ahead and takes up the first book, turning to the story of the magic fish. Mother says Simone likes that book best because it is new. The child tells the story as he turns the pages: "The *peccatore* (*pescatore*—fisherman) was eating when he heard a terrible noise, the fish came, the *pesciolino picciolino* (*piccolino*)—small fish came with the small mouth, the seagulls come; look, a thief with a hat!" Mother says, "It's finished', and he repeats, "It's finished."

Then Simone wants his mother to draw a picture of the captain on a sheet of paper, and after that he looks for his hat. He doesn't want his own pen and asks me for one. His mother puts a cushion on his chair and he says, "Let's do a captain, a hen, a wolf captain." Then he asks me if I would like a cushion, too. The mother offers him milk and biscuits but he wants neither of them. He says to his mother, "Are we going?", and she replies, "Nowhere." He makes a messy scribble on some paper and calls "Mummy, Gigi!" [his father's name]. He offers me the milk his mother had put on the table and asks, "Do you like it?" He wants me to give him my pen again (he had given it back to me) and says, "Let's draw the magic fish."

I ask where aunt Augusta is, and the mother says she has gone to the theatre. Simone repeats this. The mother remembers a phrase from a song that aunt Augusta often recites to Simone and the child loves, about Pinco Pallino and his father's bicycle. He chants `"Paperino, Paperino" and jumps up on his chair. He asks, "Is this milk?", and mother says, "Do you want some?" He repeats, "Is it milk?", and watches me with curiosity as I take a drink and eat a biscuit. "Are you eating, Romana?", he asks. Meanwhile, his mother offers him some orange juice, but he does not want that either; he takes a biscuit but it is clear he is not hungry. He holds his pen in his mouth and says, "My cigarette is burning!" His mother makes a comment, and he looks inside my empty glass of milk and asks, "Do you want some more?"

The father comes in. Simone wants him to pick him up, and in exchange the father asks for a big kiss and says, "Who is the most beautiful in the world?" The child urges his father to sit down, and after that wants him to tell him the whole of the first story again—the story of Pippo the fisherman and the magic fish. "Pippo is changed into a farmer," says his father, "then into a rich sea captain, then into a king, then at last he becomes a fisherman again, because people are only really happy when they can be themselves." Then Simone wants the story of Chicco and Checca and father goes out to fetch the book. The child puts the "cigarette" back in his mouth and talks about his grandfather, who puts on his cap and goes out shooting. Mother tells him to put on his shoes and come down from the table. "Right now!" (*insomma*) she exclaims, and he repeats "Right now!" She tells him that *she* is the one who says "Right now". Simone is still in his father's arms. He wants his cap but he does not want to come down—"*in braccino!*", he says ("Pick me up"). He demands his cap, which his mother points out is the red one that he wore at the seaside in the sun. "What do you want this for?", she asks, laughing because she sees he is hiding it. Simone laughs too. His mother says that sometimes he has his cap on all day at home.

MH: That is a lovely observation, where it seems both the mother and the father are somehow following Simone in his phantasies. The central thing is his preoccupation with the thief, and how the thief runs away. You get evidence later on in the observation that the thief is both himself—wanting to steal daddy's cap or daddy's penis or daddy's position—and also, the thief is this baby inside mummy who is swallowing up what really belongs to *him*.

You get some idea from this of how helpful it is to a little child to have these fairy stories that can put into a mythical form and *express for him* the complicated intense emotions that he has about this baby inside mummy, and the whole threat to his position in the family. We could go through this almost line by line and look at what these figures symbolize for the child . . . how the smelly piglets represent both some dirty, messy infant part of himself, but also the new baby, smelly and greedy; the magic fish in the water is the penis or the baby inside mummy; the little rabbits with sweets in their mouth are like the new baby who is going to take the food from him. You get a clue here of how the cap on the head is linked with the king's crown—giving added point to his obsession with caps: it means being the king, the boss.

There is also identification with the mummy—as when he gives Romana the milk and asks how she likes it.

Now it is very nice to see the way his father tells the story of Pippo the fisherman—how Pippo is changed into a rich man, then into a king, and then eventually back into a fisherman, because "we are only happy when we are ourselves". Oh, this is written in the story . . . then it is the father who *picks this out* in telling the story. It expresses for the child his attempts at projecting himself into, being, these different characters. In a sense it gives permission to the child to *imagine* that he is daddy, and then to come back to where and who he really is. In a situation where the child feels threatened by his anxiety about being displaced by the new baby, that very threat can be something that does stimulate him to try to *imagine what it is* to become a mummy, to become a daddy—what it is like to be this baby inside. A threatening situation can be a spur to expansion, to development, to growth.

The epistemophilic instinct

Twenty-first observation of Simone, age two years, one and a half months

RN (*reads*): I find Simone in the kitchen, in his chair, at the head of the table. His mother says, "He wants the *panettone*, he is hungry—I will cook his dinner." Sitting down, he continues to ask for "*panettone* . . ." While his mother is cooking, he stares at me and wrinkles his nose. Meanwhile, she offers him some cream cheese. He says "no" at first, then accepts it. He collects the crumbs of cheese then puts a pencil in his mouth (a "pipe") and looks at me, wrinkling his nose. His mother bends over towards him, and he thrusts the pencil in her mouth, saying, "You must smoke!" She suggests writing with it: "I saw a cat . . ." she begins. At first Simone laughs, but then he becomes restless and demands "another *panettone*", looking at me and crying. His mother sits close to him and asks, "Shall I read you a story—which one?" He says, "Paperino" (Donald Duck).

As she turns the pages of the book, she encourages him to name the animals. "A little mouth", he says, pointing to the elephant's trunk. "Read, read!" She talks about Topolino (Micky Mouse). "The thief!" he cries. "Why was Topolino upset," she asks, "don't you remember?" Simone does not answer; he is absorbed in his book. Mother sits close to him and puts his dinner in front of him. "Read!" says Simone, and she begins the story of Topolino, who was upset because Chip and Chop wanted to steal the hazel nuts. "Who were the nuts for?", she asks. "For Topolino", he says. "No," she says, "for the circus animals"; and then, "What does Topolino do? He is telephoning—", and Simone replies, "—Paperino", and so on. She cuts up the meat in front of him, as he holds up the book and says "Read it!" She speaks about the stories as she feeds him, and he eats slowly while pointing to the pictures. She asks him questions about the characters in the book and he replies.

She tells me that Simone has not been feeling well lately; he has not eaten his soup at all. She continues to read the story while he points to the pictures and repeats "Read, read!" The story tells how Paperino (Donald Duck) prepares a trap during the night to catch the thieves. They come along and unintentionally release the trap, which makes a small bell ring, but Paperino does not hear because he is fast asleep. While this is being related, Simone fails to swallow a piece of meat, and spits it on to his plate. Mother carries on with the story, but Simone taps her angrily on the arm demanding, "Tell me about the magic fish!" She feeds him, and he says, "Read!" "I will", she says, as she cuts more meat and tries again to feed him. He looks at a picture of a soldier with a plumed hat, and mother tells him that Pippo's hat is more beautiful because it is made of straw. She carries on making comments in this way. Simone speaks about the "thief who ran away", and she says, "I made an unlucky mistake when I read you that story!" She continues to cut his meat and feed him. He eats, but his eyes are fixed on the book. Every now and then he gives me a very serious look.

Then he says, "Mummy, I want the tortoise that talks", pointing to his ear. "No, it's the shell . . ." she says, "I'll go and get it—but first you must eat." She comes back with the shell, saying "Uh". Simone takes the shell in his hand and puts it to his ear, and then wants me to listen to it too. "Can you hear it, Romana?", he asks, stretching out his hand with the shell. I pretend I am holding the shell and putting it to my ear, and say "uh . . ." He laughs and plays with the shell, while his mother tells him a story about it. He puts it close to his ear, then hits the story book with it. His mother offers him some soft cheese but he refuses it, so she puts out some Parmesan cheese instead and he points to this with his finger. With one hand he holds the shell to his ear, and with the other he eats the cheese. "Is the cheese hard?", asks his mother. "Shall I cut it up for you?" Simone looks at me and says "my plate". Holding his cheese in his hands and eating it, he watches his mother as she does the washing up. Then he takes a notebook from where his mother had put it on a shelf, and places it on the plate in front of him. The doorbell rings and the mother leans out of the porch; shortly afterwards the father comes in holding a comic, which he shows to Simone.

"You're back Daddy, from work . . .", says Simone, and jumps into his arms.

The father kisses him and says he will show him the little shoes he has for him. He takes off his jacket and Simone wants him to take off his shoes, too. Father wants to show me "St Lucy's little donkey", but Simone is not particularly interested in it; he wants me to move a bit so he can get a large kitchen knife that is behind me, and cut something with it. His mother objects, "Only grown-ups can use the big kitchen knife", and father adds, "Before you've noticed how sharp it is you will have cut yourself." Simone insists on having the knife. He sits on my chair, as in the meantime I have got up. Then his father picks him up, but Simone keeps moaning, wanting something. I ask if he is not feeling well, and the mother tells me that on Monday he had a fever and she wondered if he had a sore throat, but perhaps he was teething. He had no temperature on Tuesday, but only started eating again yesterday evening. The father offers something to Simone that he does not want, and he begins to cry and goes to his room, followed by his father.

The aunt comes in, saying she has got home early because her pupils have gone to play *mongolfiera* (a game they are learning in preparation for Christmas). She follows Simone into his room; he seems quite happy, laughing and rolling on his bed. Father wants him to tell him what he has been doing that morning. He had been out shopping with his mother, who bought a pair of trousers for his father, and aunt Nana, who bought trousers for uncle Piero. Simone repeats to me what his father had said. He goes to the little table and takes a stick of lip-salve, saying to his aunt, "Put on some lipstick!" His aunt pretends to put some on and invites him to do the same, but he says "no". The father remarks that only ladies use lipstick, but the aunt says that lip-salve can be used by anyone who has sore lips.

Simone takes down a small picture from over his bed: "The little Eskimo", he says, then he touches the puppets that are lying on the table, then jumps on to his bed and kicks around. Father goes out, and the aunt comments on Simone's new shoes. He laughs. She says they seem a bit heavy. Then, since she is sitting next to him on the bed, she asks, "Show me, how do the Eskimos kiss each other?" He puts his face and nose close to hers and says, "Like this!" He stands up on his bed and takes a picture off the wall, but the nail comes off, too. The aunt comments on it. Simone takes his toy camera and pretends to take photographs, but he cannot do it so the aunt offers to teach him. He wants to load it, but cannot manage it. He says it "doesn't move" and puts it back again.

The aunt asks Simone if he has been on his bicycle that morning. He stands up on his bed and talks about the illustrations in some little pictures on the wall. His mother comes in, picks him up and says, "We went to see some very small babies last night" (a friend had had a baby and they went to the hospital to see her). "Who was crying?", asks his mother; "a tiny baby called Daniela", she continues. Simone seems quite indifferent and continues to jump around in his mother's arms. "Gently", she tells him. Then Simone asks me, "Romana, do you want the lipstick?" His aunt asks him, "Do you put it on, sometimes?" and he says "no", meanwhile getting back on to his bed. The aunt asks him again, "Who puts it on, then? Mummy, aunty . . .", and continues, "Did you go to G in the mini-car?" "Sihii" (si—yes), he anwers. "You're a fibber," she said; "you went in the Fiat 500."

Meanwhile, the child laughs and continues to jump up and down on the bed. The mother says, "I am going to look for the bicycle; do you know what aunty's children have done? They let a huge balloon go up high in the sky, then it came down on a road in the village. A man found it and gave it back to them."

Simone continues to jump happily, singing softly to himself. Mother is preparing lunch for us all in the kitchen. He asks her if his dinner is ready, but when asked to come and look, he doesn't want to. The noise of an engine is heard outside. Immediately Simone says it is Ceci. "It's Ceci," confirms the mother; "she's got the car. Go and see; it's sunny out today." "There's thick fog," says Simone, "thick", he repeats. He goes to the window then resumes his jumping on the bed.

The aunt invites him to play with a big cat, speaking in a cat-like voice and calling it "the talking cat". Simone wants to give the cat a piece of bread, then he takes his pyjamas from the bed, puts them on the cat's back. He tells his aunt, "Let's play together now with my pyjamas!" The aunt comments, then suggests he ask his mother if lunch is ready. He replies, "Covered up!", and puts the pyjamas against the wall, then throws them on the floor. The aunt asks him who has thrown his pyjamas on the floor; and at first he does not reply, then he says, "You!" She says, "Who are you going to say that to?", but he continues to insist it was not him.

Simone leaves the room and goes to fetch his tricycle. He comes back in accompanied by his father. The child comes to greet me, saying, "Ciao" (hallo), then goes off again with his father. "Mamina," (Mummy!), he calls, "what are you doing?" Coming back in, he says, "Aunty, shopping—you and the man" (referring to me). I ask him if I am a man; he answers "no", and stomps around the room rather noisily. The aunt talks about Santa Lucia, but he does not seem to take it in. Meanwhile, his mother urges him to "do the shopping". Then Simone finds his aunt in the hall and asks her to take down a hat from the cloak-stand for him.

MH: In this lovely session, we can see how Simone has discovered the ability to think and talk very quickly. In the first part, when he is here with his mother, there seems to be this double demand—for *panettone* to eat, and for the story to listen to. It is as if he is hungry both for food, and for understanding.

> Curiosity about the baby

We maybe get a clue a bit later on as to the reason for this *intense* demand he is making of his mother—when we hear about his having been taken to see the new little baby in the hospital the day before. This would stir up all his own baby feelings of wanting to be fed, but also, his *curiosity* about this baby and where it came from; this I think is evinced by his demand for a story—"read me a story". The story he wants to have is to do with this baby.

I think you can see that curiosity a bit later in the session, when he asks for the shell and is listening to the sounds inside it. That is a bit like the times when his father was listening to the sounds of the baby inside the mother's tummy. You can really see the basis of all curiosity here—it is what Mrs Klein calls the "epistemophilic instinct"—and how this is related fundamentally to curiosity about the mystery of birth and the mystery of conception and inter-course—how babies are born. The child feels that the answer to this mystery lies inside the mother's body. Of course, some children can turn away from this, overcome by feelings of resentment and anxi-ety, and cut off the feelings—they do *not want to know*. They are threatened by the painfulness of the uncertainty, and the painful-ness of the jealousy. But Simone's curiosity is intensely stimulated. You see this in the whole of the first part—where he keeps saying "Another *panettone*", and then "Read, read!"

The main story seems to be to do with the thief who has stolen the nuts that are meant for the little animals. And the mother seems to intuitively feel that this is a very important story for him, because she examines him on how he remembers it. One aspect of "Simone the thief" is wanting to steal the food that the mummy has for this little baby inside. His demand to be continually fed—more stories, more *panettone*—is also in a certain way this thief part of him operating, demanding *all* the food, *all* the stories from mummy.

Now, let's see, when the father comes in . . . as I have said, the "tortoise that talks" is really very interesting—the baby inside the mummy talking, the noise inside the shell. You can see when his father comes in, his obsession with the baby inside mummy wanting to be fed, seems to change over to wanting to acquire daddy's penis—the kitchen knife. He *insists* on having this knife, just as before he insisted on being fed or having a story. The interesting thing is that shortly after that, the aunt comes in, and that seems to relieve the situation; she follows Simone to his room, and he seems very happy now—he laughs while he rolls over on his bed, as if he feels a bit released from this obsession with daddy's penis or what is inside mummy. It is a less intense, less desperate situation for him when it is opened out by the aunt coming in. He can play at the aunt being his girlfriend—"put on your lipstick"; and when she offers it to him he says "no", as if to say, "I don't want to *be* you, I want you as my girlfriend". The aunt joins in this game with him when she asks, "How do the Eskimos kiss each other?"

It is after that, that the mother says he has been to see this baby the night before, and we have a clue as to why he has been so desperate about what's inside mummy. I didn't quite understand this bit about the pyjamas . . . he takes the pyjamas and says, "Let's play all together with my pyjamas." It almost looks as if at that moment he is putting his pyjamas on to the cat, as if the cat was the little baby between himself and the aunt, as was a little earlier the picture of the Eskimo in the game about the girlfriend; it then becomes this pussy cat. He then puts his pyjamas away, on the wall, and says "covered". It seems to be connected with some kind of sexual game with the auntie; throwing away the pyjamas to come closer with his penis, because after that he comes in with the tricycle. When he comes back into the room with the tricycle, that is when he talks about Romana as a man—"auntie and the man"—as if they were a couple. He says the two of you are "shopping"—meaning, shopping for a baby.

> The child's theories about sexuality

Comment: [about the big bed, and making a baby]

MH: I agree, I think it is to do with making the jump from being the baby, to being the daddy who goes shopping with the mummy to get the baby. How many weeks is it now till the baby is due to be born? . . . in March—so it is very soon. And this observation was December. He is certainly absolutely fascinated and occupied with his theories about how this baby got there—being daddy who goes shopping for the baby, wanting to be the mummy who gets the baby inside. He is quite obsessed with the whole situation. Very interesting.

Comment: [about the pencil in her mouth]

MH: I would think what is arising with his increased desire that has to do with the threat of the new baby and his curiosity as to how the baby got there, and daddy's penis, is maybe some kind of confusion about heightened sexual feelings in his own penis, and the nipple. It is a sexualization of the eating, with an increased desire. A confusion between nipple and penis, and mouth and mummy's vagina, or the place where he feels the baby is put in. You find this confusion between orifices—oral and genital, penis and nipple, oral conception—in fairy stories. All these myths contain the child's theories about the nature of his world and how babies are born. You can see in Simone his heightened sexuality and desire, and how it is quite difficult for him to manage, but his family do listen to it and go along with it. With other children, and even with him at certain times, there can be a retreat from this curiosity—a whining and not wanting to know. But here, he very definitely is *wanting to know* and is expressing his theories.

> How to put order into confused emotions

No amount of explaining "the facts" of how babies are born can ever answer that curiosity. It is something that has to be expressed in emotional forms and *lived through* so the child can know and manage his own feelings better. It is important, when children ask, to tell them "the facts" as truthfully as possible—not to avoid them or circle around them. But the facts are not enough.

Q: [about how emotions are thought]

MH: Yes, absolutely. The emotion is the thing that gives the meaning; and the thought is a way of organizing that meaning and giving form to it.

And this is a situation where the child's emotion is really *accepted*. It is clear the mother *enjoys* responding to him; and the aunt very much enjoys taking part in the games that he initiates. The father also enjoys it, though he worries about how the child is feeling.

Q: [about Simone's role-playing]

MH: Yes, it is all right for Simone to pretend he is this, that, or the other; but you always have to return to *yourself*.

One day it will be his turn

Twenty-second observation of Simone, age two years, three and a half months

RN (*reads*): I find Simone with his mother at his aunt's flat; the boiler has been out of order for about ten days, and the family have been spending most of the day there, from about 9 a.m. until after the evening meal. Simone is wearing his favourite jockey cap with the word "Oregon" on it in capitals; he is also wearing his aunt's after-ski boots, that she has put on him. His aunt is at church for the Sunday mass.

Simone's mother is rather pale. Her baby is due at the end of March, but she tells me that she does not dare to speak to Simone about it because his aunt Nana has been rather hard on him. One afternoon, when she had to go to the hospital, Simone had gone to his aunt Nana; and she told him that when his mother brought his baby sister home from hospital, she (aunty) would not have him to stay with her any longer. After this episode, which happened about the end of January, Simone had started to stammer. Simone watches us while his mother is relating all this, quite briefly, as the details have already been given me over the phone by her husband.

The television is on. "Look!", says Simone to me; he is holding a pen refill as if it were a cigarette. The mother talks to me about the central heating problem: "Trr . . . trr", Simone says, imitating the sound of the electric drill, and the mother points out that that morning they had heard the sound of the drill and the hammer. She is seated in the sitting room, copying out a recipe for spaghetti. Simone, next to her, plays with a tin that drops on the floor. "You must pick it up", says mother. "No", he answers; then he finds a rubber and asks, "Does it write?" "No, it rubs out", his mother replies, and he rubs on the small table. He opens a drawer in the desk and looks for various things, naming them as he does so. He chants, "Where are you", and takes out some typewritten papers. His mother says, "If aunty could see you . . . those papers are in French, give them to me!" Simone gives them to her while he sings: "One day in September, *osti*,[1] da . . . da . . . da, la la!" (I think he is imitating Diego, a ten-year-old boy, the son of their friends.) He turns over the papers, pretending to stamp them with the velvet-covered record-cleaner. "I'm going to school", he says. "What are you doing?", asks his mother. "I'm learning to read . . . no, look at that cap!", and he points to some boys on the television who are playing baseball and wearing caps like his. "Those are all aunty's", says his mother, referring to the papers. "Bring them all here!" Simone sings, "When I read my recipe, you colonel who writes so well . . ."; and he dances over to his mother and gives her the papers. "Pick those up from the floor," she says, "there are lots of them." He pretends to stamp on them while he sings, "One day when it is my turn (*un giorno di turno*) my recipe from the colonel . . ." (his father takes turns/shifts in his pharmacy). I ask him who is the "colonel", and he answers, "He's in the story about Colonel Tac who has got lots of hats." His mother says she doesn't know what he is referring to—probably it is to do with one of the many cartoons on television that he's been watching lately. Meanwhile, the child says the cap is like Diego's, singing, "*Il giorno di turno*, Diego . . . the recipe . . . the colonel." The mother tells me that he often seems lost in his own thoughts, but then he takes up things that he has in fact heard.

Simone takes the record-cleaning pad and brushes it lightly against his mother's legs. "How soft it is!", mother exclaims. He pretends to stamp on his aunt's papers, saying, "I must do my homework on the days when it's my turn", then he plays with the record-cleaner again; he brushes it against his mother's legs, across her chest, and on her face, while she talks to him. Simone wants to pass the pad over her eyes too, but she says, "The dust's coming in", and then kisses him. He starts again on "I must do my homework", with the mother replying, "What did the teacher say to you, did you do well?" He repeats, "*Un giorno di turno*" as he goes several times into the hall, where he puts some of the aunt's papers into the shoe cupboard. The mother remarks, "So that his aunty can't find them any more."

The mother goes into the kitchen to make coffee; he goes with her and I hear him calling her "aunty". "Aha, I'm aunty, am I, Simu!", she exclaims, and entreats him to put the papers back where they belong, "otherwise aunty will cry". Simone goes back into the hall and his mother asks him what he is doing; "A little job", he replies, as he takes the papers out of the shoe cupboard and puts them in the sitting room. He goes "Clok, clok", imitating the donkey; then he is attracted by a group of boys whom he sees on television wearing jockey-caps/base-ball caps. After that, he switches on a powerful lamp, and then screams, because the light is too strong for him.

The mother, who has meanwhile come back into the sitting room, speaks to me about the warehouse in the country where they are preparing for the Carnival. Simone interrupts with "All the children at Fano . . ." His mother laughs and tells me that Simone evidently remembers the shed at Fano where the allegorical Carnival floats are kept during the winter. "The lorries, the tractors . . .", he carries on, while his mother enlarges on his description: "A man on the lorries, the children, the streamers", etc. Simone joins in with, "I go on the tractor too—the tractor with cars on it . . . but the little cars aren't in the oratory, they have been moved." I ask who has moved them, and he answers "Minella the policeman." He follows his mother into the kitchen.

Simone comes back into the sitting room carrying a plastic hammer in his hand, and asks his mother for a handkerchief. He takes it and puts it under his sweater, and then hits the sofa with the hammer. He watches the television, where the boys with the caps are still playing baseball. He approaches me and leaves the handkerchief on my lap. He goes to his mother in the kitchen: "Come here, Rita!", he calls. She comes back into the sitting room and puts a cup of coffee on the table. He complains and says the papers "are mine!" His mother says, "No one will touch them", and moves the child away from the little table. Simone wants to cover the papers with my handkerchief.

The doorbell rings. Mother calls out, "Look, who's there?" Before his aunt comes in, Simone calls in a loud voice, "I've found your papers!" He leaves the handkerchief next to me and goes to open the door. Meanwhile, the mother tells me about her problems in leaving Simone when she has to go to the hospital at Treviglio. The child and his aunt come in; he seems to be listening attentively to what we are saying. The mother tells the aunt about the papers, saying, "Most probably Simone has put them in a very good place; I think they are in the shoe cupboard." Then, turning to me, she says, "I found the lentils in the bathroom." Simone says, "Look, I'll put them in the shoe cupboard for you", and he follows his aunt quite happily. She talks to him and tells him that, at church, Diego served as an altar boy. We could hear the child talking in the kitchen with his aunt; meanwhile, the mother told me more about the business with aunt Nana (previously mentioned).

Simone, still in the kitchen with his aunt, asks for a meatball, but she tells him it is not time yet. So he comes into the sitting room carrying a plastic bag containing her pupils' schoolwork. The mother says, "Has aunty seen you?" Simone replies that he wants the gloves. The aunt comes in and says "Hands off Cuba!", and takes back her bag. Simone laughs and follows her out; he is carried back by her, holding the gloves. His mother asks him, "Whose gloves are they?" Simone says, "Mine." The aunt says, "Once upon a time there was a man who was called *Tutto Mio* (all mine)—who can that be?" She asks again, "Do you know who that is?", this time pointing to a piece of wire that Simone has taken, putting the top section in his mouth; "It's the lead from my tape recorder." Then she shows him a magazine which has many pictures of boots in it. "Are aunty's shoes there?", he asks. She talks about the shoes, then Simone goes into the kitchen and she follows.

He comes back pulling a trailer with some cars and an aeroplane loaded on it, and saying, "A little lorry . . . this is *l'ospedalissimo* (the "most" hospital)." His mother says that for some time, since Simone hurt his forehead a month ago, he hasn't wanted to hear about the hospital. "What did the nurse say to you?", she asks Simone. "Darling [*gioia*]", he answers, and continues to say "*ospedalissimo*" while he tries to pack all his toys on to the lorry. Then he shouts and screams, seeming very upset because they won't fit in properly. His mother intervenes and then his aunt helps him, saying, "Look, like this", and he is happy. She suggests he makes a garage. She plays the part of the parking attendant and asks if he has a ticket; he says "no", so his mother gives him some money.

> ### The mystery of grown-up things

MH: This is a very detailed and fascinating observation. You can see the way this little boy is struggling with the meaning of his experience about this forthcoming baby: how he does seem to shift in the intensity of his feelings between his mother and his aunty. One of the main themes here is in this little song that he sings—"one day when it is my turn" . . . which could mean, one day when it is his turn to be a mummy or a daddy and to have a baby. Quite clearly, at the moment he feels a little in the shadows; but *one day* it will be his turn, and he will be the important person in the family. In certain ways he is a little uncertain as to what is the star part—is it to wear the boots of the aunt–mummy who is going to have the baby, or is it to be the daddy? Interestingly he starts off here wearing his aunt's boots, and he is very interested in his aunt's papers and in what she writes. It is almost as if his mother's unseen baby, that he cannot view yet, has opened up his mind to the mystery of all the fascinating things that occupy grown-ups. This aunt has all these papers and activities; and he feels "I must do my homework; and some day I will have my turn"—there is an awful lot to learn, but if you learn it, then some day you will play this star part.

It is evident he has been rather naughty, because the aunt has threatened that when the baby comes, she won't have him to stay any longer; so I suppose he has behaved himself badly with her?

RN: [*comment—inaudible*]

MH: I see, it isn't really a threat, she is just teasing. In England somebody might say, "When this baby comes he is going to put your nose out of joint"—a kind of castration meaning. I see he has begun to stammer. Did he actually stammer in this observation with you?

RN: No, not here.

MH: It is something very amazing that even in a family like this, who are very fond of this child, the idea of the new baby does, none the less, stir up depths of infantile emotions in the grown-ups that they try to project on to the child.

Now Simone's curiosity and desire to investigate and master things is immensely stirred by this. He takes this rubber and asks, "Does it write?" and his mother says, "No, it rubs out." That is interesting because he probably already knows that it doesn't write . . . ("Yes.") Then he rubs out on the table. So I tend to think he is really dealing with his thoughts about this baby who has just been written-in to the family. He would like to rub it out. Then when he comes to the drawers of the desk and searches and sings softly "Where are you?", again he is preoccupied with the baby and where exactly it is, and shows his interest in finding it. But instead of the baby, he finds his aunt's typewritten papers—papers that have been written on, that he sees as the equivalent of mummy's baby: this is aunty's baby. Then he is singing, imitating Diego the big boy; he plays at being big and at school.

> There are mental babies also

You can see the link in the child's mind between the production of a baby, and what is expressed by writing and talking about something. You get this equation over and again in analytic work with children—where your thoughts are for the child, your mental babies, your creations. Simone won't be able to read anything as yet, but he has got the idea that what is written on these pages is something the grown-ups are very interested in. He says ,"When I read my recipe, from the Colonel that *writes so well.*" So again, "When it is my turn"—when he is a big boy like Diego, when he is a daddy, and, like the colonel he can *write so well* and make all kinds of recipes . . . It is as if he can see himself being able one day to play many parts, wear many caps. Later, there is his preoccupation with the place where all the carnival costumes are kept.

After singing this song about "my turn" and the recipe from the Colonel, he then strokes his mother's face with this piece of velvet, as if making love to her—he touches her legs, her chest, her face . . . he is gently caressing.

The house spaces and the mother's body

After this he gets on to stowing away the papers: he puts the papers into the shoe cupboard, hiding them from aunty. Later the mother says they have found lentils in the bathroom, as if he is using places throughout the house to represent the mother's body and the places where you might cook up some nice baby—he really is obsessed with the *recipes* of the colonel. *What* substance do you take, and *where* do you put it inside the mummy, so that it really will grow into a baby.

You could say that at the moment he is already wearing different hats—he is experimenting with being different characters. When he says he is "doing a little job", taking papers and putting them in the sitting room, he says "clok clok clok", as if he is being a donkey. He is making use of different phantasies to express his preoccupation with what sort of things come together to make a baby, and where that baby can grow. There are all the carnival costumes, lorries and tractors . . . as if he has a picture of the mother's body containing inside it an infinite variety of objects to be explored.

After that he follows his mother into the kitchen with a plastic hammer in one hand, and he asks for a handkerchief and puts that under his sweater; then he hits the sofa with the hammer. That is a

representation of being both daddy and mummy in intercourse—
the handkerchief is the breast, and with daddy's hammer he bangs
the baby in.

Then he watches the big boys with the baseball, to see how they
do it; then he comes into the kitchen and says "Come, Rita".

A new moment of desperation

When she comes into the sitting room and complains about the
papers, he says firmly "that's mine", as if at the moment he is really
laying claim to possession of everything. Of course, he knows very
well that they're not his, and when his aunt comes in he says virtu-
ously, "I have found your papers"—not that he's been taking them
away and hiding them. He wants his aunty's glove—"they're all
mine". At the moment, his more direct passionate attachment
seems to be to his aunt, with all her paper babies, more than to his
mother, perhaps splitting it off as if to spare her from his too insistent clinging and demands. That moment of desperation at the end
is interesting, when he feels he cannot get the toys back in the lorry,
as if he feels he has attacked his mother and cannot put things back
together again inside her. That is a little hint of the panic that underlies all his attempts to work it out—the panic that his life is going
to fall to pieces.

A point of "catastrophic change"

Twenty-third observation of Simone, age two years,
three months, twenty-two days

> **RN** (*reads*): Simone is still staying at his aunt's. He is in the sitting room,
> on the sofa with his father, taking down several of his aunt's books
> from the shelf and putting them on the sofa. Meanwhile, he talks about
> Diego: "Gigi, put them up", referring to the books he is heaping up
> next to his father. The child opens one of the books and says, "There is
> nothing in this one" (it has no pictures and is closely printed). His
> father tells him that Mr Bianchi has another Disney fairytale for him.
> Simone carries on with his activity, talking as if to himself; "Poetry", he
> says. "Whose books are those?", asks the father. "Aunty's", Simone
> replies.

The aunt comes in; mother leaves the kitchen and also comes into the sitting room, saying to her, "Don't be angry!" She adds that when Simone wants to do something, he always says "I must", as if someone had ordered him to do it. Simone says, "Romana, fairytale!" Aunt Augusta tells him to be careful handling the books, and he carries on. By now the pile of books is enormous. The mother and father ask him to put them back, saying, "There's no more room!" Meanwhile, Simone talks about "a fountain, where they press a button; the children go into the pool and there are no more fish!" The parents ask what fountain he is talking about; the father thinks he is remembering his bath from that morning; but then, on reconsideration, thinks he is probably talking about the communal fountain in the town.

Simone comes towards me with a piece of paper in his hand. I am on the sofa next to his aunt. He places the paper on my foot and pretends to take my measurements, saying, "Three." Then he goes to his aunt, who asks him, "Is it bigger or smaller?" "Smaller", Simone answers. She explains to me why Simone is doing it; he has seen his grandmother, who is a dressmaker, taking measurements. She also tells me that last summer, after watching his grandmother take his parents' measurements, Simone had become extremely upset, and shouted that Gigi and Rita belonged to him.

The child, who is evidently listening, comes near me and says, "I am jealous!", and continues to measure my foot. Aunt Augusta carries on telling me about what happened that time last summer. Although grandmother wanted to make Simone a shirt too, he refused to let her take his measurements; he said that granny was "ugly"; and then, to her, "You—don't touch my daddy!" When the grandmother replied, "He's my son!", Simone became even more enraged.

Then Simone says he wants his baby sister to be as big as Kelly, who is five years old. The aunt says, "Look, here comes Diego", and Simone gets excited. Diego is holding a paper *bomba*[2] and shows it to Simone's father, who is sitting on a sofa. He gives his father a paper "tongue" (*lingua delle donne*) and the father puts it in his mouth and blows it out, showing Simone how it works as he does so, and Simone laughs.

Then the father turns and speaks to Diego's mother, who has just come in. He is still on the sofa and talks to Diego, next to him, about the paper "bombs" they have at Carnival. Simone goes up to them and calls out, "Imbecile!", then switches on the lamp by the sofa where I am sitting. Diego cavorts in front of Simone, and tells him about the carnival costume he is going to wear that day. He asks him for a kiss; then goes to embrace Simone's father. Simone approaches them, and says laughingly to his father, "Don't be an imbecile", then embraces him.

Diego's father comes in and talks about food (he is of solid, sturdy build); while Simone's father grumbles that his son follows him everywhere, even into the bathroom. Simone and Diego, who had gone out, now come back in—Simone holding a rubber hammer, while Diego holds the *lingua delle donne*. The aunt takes the maraccas and asks Simone what they are called. Diego leaves the paper toy on the sofa and says to me, "Romana, let me know when you are going to have your coffee!"

Simone's parents are sitting next to each other on the sofa and the mother is holding her husband's head between her hands and looking into his eye to find out why it is hurting him. Simone sees them and cries, saying, "No, Gigi!" Mother explains that he does that because he is afraid she is hurting his father. Simone moans, and wants his father to show him some films. "Another time, when Romana comes", promises the father. Simone is holding a video, but his father takes it away, and the child cries desperately. The father embraces him closely. "What a noise!", exclaims his aunt, "Shall I smack your bottom with the hammer?" "No", Simone answers in a serious tone. He wants his cap back, which he had taken off when Diego came and placed on the television set. His father puts on the cap for a few seconds, remarking, "I am a young chap." Simone takes it from him; the father speaks of the ogre in the story and how Simone is afraid of him, saying that this is quite normal.

Simone takes up the book, sits down near his father, and opens it. Father begins the story of the seven brothers who were very poor. Simone becomes absorbed in the tale, and comments with gestures on what his father is reading to him. As soon as he comes to the picture of the ogre, who has a big belly, he becomes suddenly distressed. (I say that the ogre has a belly like that of Diego's father, and Simone bursts out laughing.) Simone's father talks again about his fear of this story, and how it is not very nice for children. Meanwhile, the child says, "Read, read, go on, go on!"

The mother comes in and asks if Simone is hungry. He says he isn't, and asks for a drink of juice. Mother tells him there is no juice but there are *pennine* (small pen-shaped pasta). But Simone wants the book. He sits at table and cries, "Read!", clapping his hands and screaming that he wants the book. "Where did you go yesterday evening?", asks the mother; "We went to see the building where Simone was born", and she also says that when they passed a supermarket, Simone had said, "Diego lives here."

Overview of the different phantasies

MH: He is able to *express his feelings* extremely well; and to get enormous relief from having stories read to him that do express in an artistic form the phantasies and feelings he is having about the baby. His interest in stories and books is quite marked, as with this pile of books; he feels there is so much in them that he wants to learn. There are his own phantasies too, like the fountain where you press a button, representing the breast that he had as a baby; then, he says, the children can go into this pool because there are no fish there any longer—the babies are going to be out, and the children are going to be in!

It is interesting how his jealousy of the grandmother comes in: his mummy and daddy are *his* children—Rita and Gigi—not granny's. His father isn't *allowed* to kiss his cousin . . . "Don't be an imbecile!", he says to his father.

If we jump to that bit about the ogre with the fat belly—was it you, Romana, who said the ogre resembled Diego's father? Simone was clearly quite upset by this picture, because (I would think) that is the kind of monster he sees as his mummy, with the fat belly. Again you can see this undercurrent of anxiety—that everything is going to fall to pieces and he is going to lose everything. When his father takes from him this little video film, he breaks down and cries desperately, as if it symbolizes *everything* that he fears will be taken from him.

You can really see from these observations how the birth of the next baby is a point of terrific change in a family—what Bion would call *catastrophic change*. It has all kinds of possibilities, but also there are deep and terrible anxieties attached to it for the child.

Birth of the next sibling

Twenty-fourth observation of Simone, age two years, four months, and three weeks

RN (*reads*): I enter the house and find Simone seated at table with his father and mother in the kitchen. He looks at me sadly and silently and does not speak. His father is next to him on the left, holding a book with the story of Aladdin's lamp in it. (I excuse myself for a few minutes to go to the toilet; when I come back it seems to me that Simone has been watching my steps.) When I rejoin them, father is reading the story, with some emphasis. The child plays with some rosary beads and now and then looks at me, or comments on the story; meanwhile, father is feeding him. After a while the mother joins them and sits next to him. The story presents the opportunity of talking about the zoo, where had been the day before. The father talks about the animals, in particular the ostrich. Simone says it had a large mouth, and father nods, then talks about the children's games, in which Simone had taken part.

The mother is on her son's right and is cutting up his meat. The father continues the story, and I notice that Aladdin is Mickey Mouse. Mrs P explains that in this series of books, the people in the story are given the form of various Disney characters.

The father goes out for a moment and mother says to Simone, "Do you hear aunty Nana calling uncle Piero to dinner, why aren't you eating?" Simone plays with his beads at the table and takes a spoonful that she offers. Father comes back with a load of Simone's storybooks. Pointing to one of the characters, mother asks, "Who's that?" "The wood-pecker", he replies. Then she says, "Why is it tied up?", referring to another picture of a puppy. Mr P begins to read out one of the stories. Simone holds the book in front of him and looks carefully at the pictures, while his mother tries to feed him. He carries on playing with the beads.

MH: Could you just remind us, Romana, where we are in relation to the next baby?

RN: She was born on the 14th March. [The observation took place on the 20th March.]

MH: So the baby was born just four days before . . . and Simone has seen the baby, in the hospital.

RN (*continues reading*): While his father talks about Red the Foxcub, mother feeds Simone his pasta and he smiles happily and seems to enjoy his meal. After some cream cheese is put on his pasta, he says "read", and eats the pasta himself, commenting on some sentences in a story about a farm. He stops chewing frequently with his mouth full to look at the pictures in the book. "Look at it swimming . . . look what's here—a tortoise . . . little birds", says his father. Simone stops eating and leans over the plate to look at the book with his fork in his hand. "Look, he's gone out with the shotgun", says father. The child continues to eat his pasta while looking at the book. He looks at his pasta, the book, his father and the corridor where his mother has just gone. They talk about Old Sniffer (a dog) who dreams about foxes. Mother comes back, and offers Simone a drink; he takes it. Father asks his wife about their baby, and she replies that she is awake and quiet. Simone leans over the storybook while his father goes on reading.

Somebody knocks at the door. It is Kelly, a five-year-old girl, carrying some *polenta* (semolina). Simone looks at her attentively but says nothing. Then he drinks his fruit juice greedily. His parents remark that it is the first time he has drunk his orange juice since his mother went into hospital to have the baby. Meanwhile, Simone keeps his eye on the corridor, which he can see beyond the open kitchen door.

Now his father has got to a crucial part in the story and Simone becomes absorbed in it: Toby the puppy wants to save Red the foxcub, that the hunter wants to kill. Shortly after he becomes more cheerful and is distracted by Kelly's polenta, saying he "wants all of it!" "Not all," responds his mother; "see how hot it is." Then Simone covers his eyes with his hand and looks at me through his fingers for quite a long time; then he says to his mother, "Come on, mash it up for me!" "It's not potato, you know", she says. Simone blows on the polenta, then makes his father blow on the piece he is giving him. Suddenly Simone looks at me and says, "Listen, Romana", turning towards the passageway behind me.

I turn round and see the mother coming in carrying her newborn baby. "*Ciccia* (chubby, plump thing), she's just woken up!" He seems excited and his father says, "Let's read the story to your baby sister too." Simone pushes the table. The mother sits down next to Simone on his right, holding Francesca, who is sleeping peacefully. Simone drinks from his glass while leaning over her. His mother says, "Look, she's almost bald", and he asks, "Why?" She replies, "You were like that too, and now you've got curly hair." The baby carries on sleeping. Mrs P tells me that as soon as Simone saw Francesca with her dummy, he told her that later on, Pippo would take it away from her. He is still excited; he has an apple in his hand and wants some water. "Rita!" he cries. Then he dips the apple in the water and eats it. I ask his mother why he is doing that, and she tells me that she often dips her biscuits in milk before eating them.

MH: Now who is Pippo . . .?

RN: The cat . . . whom the parents told Simone had taken his dummy.

MH: Ah yes, I remember.

RN (*continues reading*): Now the baby starts to whimper, and mother asks Simone, "Why is your little sister crying?" He tries to imitate the baby and utters a true and lifelike "Moo". "What a loud voice this baby has!", I say. He laughs and jumps excitedly; father asks him not to be silly, and mother tells me that lately he hasn't wanted to be washed or changed in the mornings. Meanwhile, Simone gets himself all wet with his glass of water and mother threatens to take it away. He moans at his father and wants to be picked up. Father takes him to go and open the chest of drawers. He talks about *grappa* (brandy) and the mother tells me that the people upstairs drink grappa after lunch.

Then the father gets up and asks if the hen has laid an egg for Simone and his sister. The mother says the egg is for Simone; her husband looks and finds a little chocolate egg in a box, together with a hen made of sugar. Simone is pleased, and father says, "You wouldn't have had the egg now, if you'd eaten the hen." Simone goes out of the kitchen then comes back in wearing his cap and holding a bicycle chain-lock (a locked wire loop): "Look, Romana." After him his father comes back into the kitchen, and listens to the almost correct explanation Simone is giving me about the use of the bicycle lock. Then the mother asks Simone if he went on the bike the day before; "Yes", he answers, and she laughs, because it is not true.

After that Simone tells me he is a bricklayer. Then father and son go off into Simone's room to play. After a few moments they can be heard quarrelling, and Simone cries desperately. Mr P comes back into the kitchen and explains what happened: he was playing with Simone, who had the plastic pliers that his mother had given him when he went to see her in hospital. Father asked Simone to lend them to him, but Simone refused ("these days he wants everything to himself, he is completely selfish"). So his father told him he would go and get his real pliers. This was the point at which Simone burst out crying. Simone is still crying, sitting against the wall in the hallway. I approach him and he gets up and goes into the room in front of me; I sit in the rocking chair. He goes back into the hall and his parents go to him. He says he wants the real pliers, and mother looks for them but cannot find them. He calms down, holding the toy pliers, the set of spanners, and the bicycle lock.

Now we are all in Simone's room. Mrs P, holding the baby, and her husband sit down on the bed; Simone is looking for something in his toy box. His mother, who is watching, calls out, "Look, there is the *codine*" (the little fox-tail, a real one). He says, however, he is looking for a bomb. Mother says, "Look at the baby animals!" Meanwhile, Mr P asks my advice about Francesca's jaundice; and immediately afterwards, Simone seeks my advice about a piece of material he has found enclosed in a plastic case in his toy box. Then he takes the fox-tail and rubs it gently against the baby's face, saying, "Let's tickle her!" He picks up the plastic telephone and puts it next to his father on the bed. The father says he is telephoning his grandpa. But Simone says, "Your mummy!" "She is your grandma, grandma Giuseppina!", says his father. Then he pretends to shave a duck, that is drawn on a small blackboard. He takes a small shoe from his toy box and brings it to me saying, "Look, Romana!" Mother explains, "They were yours, Simone, but they don't fit you any more." The child goes up to his mother, who is still holding the baby, and asks, "Shall we put it on here?", and he lifts up the blanket to try the shoe on his sister's foot. His mother asks, "Who's this?", and Simone replies, "My baby sister."

He seems restless; he plays at building, repairing something with the spanner. His father moves towards the baby and mother notices that Simone stops immediately to look, and then resumes playing; but he is careless now and throws some tins on the floor. She asks him where a certain triangle is that his aunt had made for him. "Diego took it away", he answers. Mother says he always blames Diego when he does something wrong. His box is empty now, and he pretends to wet the rocking chair where I am sitting and then his little bed. "Oh, what are you doing—you're wetting everything", bewails his mother, and he goes up to her and says, "Don't cry." He carries on pretending to wet things, including the duckling—pretending to bring water from a cardboard box, saying it is a fountain where children go to drink. Then he "washes" his pedal car.

He turns his toys out on the floor, then concentrates on watching his father, who is adjusting the steering wheel of his red plastic car. Father makes a cardboard box into a wagon for the cows. Then the mother asks him if he will take Francesca while she gets lunch ready for aunty. Simone wants his mother either to give the baby to him or to put her in the cardboard wagon—to "put her in the wheat"—and mother says she is too little. So Simone suggests she should be taken into the kitchen and "shown the wine bottles".

As I get ready to leave, I notice that Simone is grumbling at his father because he is holding Francesca. He wants to put the baby in the cardboard box, which is now in use as the car's trailer. Mother manages to appease Simone only when she pretends to put the baby in the trailer.

The parents' unease and the child's suspicion

MH: You can see that in this observation, Simone is very uneasy, and it seems to me that both the parents are also somewhat uneasy with him, and trying hard to keep him happy. For quite a while, there is no *feel* of where the baby is at all—both parents are absolutely concentrated on Simone. He does have his eye on his "court"—on his parents and on Romana, when she goes to the toilet and he watches where she is going, as if he is all the time a bit suspicious that somebody might disappear—to go and have a look at that baby!

It is interesting when he picks out, from his visit to the zoo, the ostrich with its *long beak*. Do you have in Italian the story of the stork bringing the new baby? ("Yes.") I wonder what he means later on, when his mother points out the woodpecker and he asks, "Why is it all tied up?"

RN: It is the puppy that's tied up.

MH: It is as if Simone is enjoying both parents being occupied with telling him a story while he is eating, and he exercises a bit of tyrannical power when he orders his father to "read!" He will eat; and he will be read to—he wants both parents.

Am I right in interpreting the first part of this observation as being very uneasy, with both the parents fully occupied in trying to entertain Simone? They don't seem to talk to you about anything else; they are making a great effort to make him feel he is at the centre of things.

RN: Yes, and during the first days Simone did not want anyone apart from his mother to hold the baby.

MH: When she does come back, and mentions that the baby is awake, Simone ostentatiously ignores that, and leans over the book to make sure they concentrate on going on with the story. You can see his anxiety that he is going to lose not only his mother, but everybody else as well—the fear that the baby might assume the centre of the stage, whereas he has been centre stage throughout his entire little life up until now.

Greed and conflicting feelings

MH: Who is this little girl Kelly, who comes in with the polenta? **RN**: She is a neighbour, the daughter of the relative who is going to look after Simone when his mother returns to work. **MH**: He looks at her, but doesn't seem to greet her; he is drinking his orange juice but looking at the corridor, as if keeping an eye out for when the baby might appear. He says a bit later, "Can you hear, Romana?" The parents' anxiety about Simone's eating becomes clearer when they say this is the first time he has drunk his orange juice since his mother went to hospital—as if he had been on a bit of a hunger strike, and needs to be entertained in order to eat. But here, he is drinking it all; and when he gets absorbed in the story, his interest passes to the polenta, and he wants it—he "wants it all". That again is an expression of his underlying grievous feeling that he wants *all* of mummy and daddy and everybody else; he doesn't want to have to share with this new baby at all. So his mother has to do further things to this polenta: she has to mash it for him—though I take it, it is already mashed and ready to eat? ("Yes.")

When the baby comes in he makes a valiant effort to be grown-up about it—he calls her chubby or plump and tells you she has just woken up. When his mother points out the baby is nearly bald, he asks "why?"—do you feel there was some anxiety that she was in some way incomplete, or damaged? ("Yes.") This is a very typical worry of the older child—that there is something wrong with the baby—and has to do with his own aggressive and jealous feelings.

Problems in expressing emotion

MH: It is fairly clear that Simone is having great difficulty in managing his emotions altogether. This *excitement* when the baby comes in is an indication of the emotions that he is not able to express for himself—his anxiety that there is something wrong with the baby; his feelings of jealousy about the baby having the dummy/breast; when he says the cat will take the dummy away from her it is really himself, not wanting the baby to have the breast. He calls his mummy "Rita", as if he were the daddy, ordering her to attend to him. We have actually seen him do this before;

but at the moment, particularly, he is unsure about his identity: he has been displaced as the baby, and he has to be a grown-up, so he doesn't say "Mummy", he says "Rita".

I suspect it is an effort on his part to be mummy's husband, as if to say: the baby is to be looked after by Mummy, and Mummy only—exercising a kind of control over the baby. On the other hand it is also saying that he can't quite stop Mummy from looking after the baby, but nobody else is to do so—they must centre around him. He is undergoing the acute struggle that every child of good feeling does have: on the one hand they would like the baby to be wiped out, on the other hand they are terrified lest anything bad should happen to the baby. In some way or another he must try to accommodate that baby in his life, without being subjected to *overwhelming* jealousy.

> An identity crisis

Now, here comes his sister crying . . . at that moment he really identifies with the baby, and he cries too, in a lifelike way.

And here, the mother is talking about his not wanting to be washed and changed in the morning—as if he doesn't like that reminder that he is a little child. But, after the baby crying, he seems to become increasingly restless, as if he doesn't quite know where to put himself; he wants his father to pick him up and hug him; he wants to get in to the chest of drawers; he wants to get at the grappa—but that is very much a grown-up thing, for Daddy. Father here undoubtedly senses Simone's unease, and tries to console him by showing him the special egg that the hen has laid for him.

He goes into the kitchen, and then comes back dressed in "big boy garb"—the cap and the bicycle loop. Again in that little sequence you can see the child's unease with himself, not quite knowing where and what he is—should he be a little child that needs to be picked up and hugged by Daddy, or a big grown-up man like the people upstairs who drink grappa, or a big boy with a cap who rides a bicycle. This indicates something of the acute identity crisis an older child has when the next baby is born, and they are displaced from their previous position in the family. You can sense the urgency with which they try to find some kind of comfortable position to contain their identity. In all this he sees

Romana as *there for him*, watching him all the time; and what he does is a way of *showing* things to her, as well as demanding things from his parents. Probably seeing you at the hospital, when you came to see the new baby, increased his suspicion that you too might be unfaithful to him, and come to watch this baby instead of him; so he looks to make sure you are watching him.

The bicycle loop is really to keep the bicycle from being stolen. That would link with the cat stealing the dummy. As if he is saying, he has got the chain that will stop the bicycle being stolen, even if he has had his position as the baby at the breast stolen from him. He is going to be the bicycle-rider, the little boy, and he is not going to have *that* stolen from him.

> The parents' difficulty in tolerating the child's intensity of feeling

I don't understand this bit—when the mother asks if he was on the bike yesterday, and he says yes and she laughs . . . is he able to ride the bicycle? ("No.") It is all a bit sad, because she is more or less implying that though he *thinks* he is like Daddy, he isn't. And later on this bitter crying with his father seems to be to do with his feeling that he is being bought off with the plastic pliers. He feels he is being *patronized*, with Daddy just pretending to give him the real thing; he is really being treated as just a baby. There is here a hint of infantile competitiveness on the part of the father, as if he feels he needs to put Simone in his place, implying "Who are you to think you can repair things and do things for Mummy?" You get an idea here of how quickly sensitive and intelligent children like this one pick up any hint of patronage or humouring on the part of their parents. They do need the *intensity* of their feelings to be taken pretty seriously. Simone says, in relation to the baby in mummy's arms and the small animals, he wants to "find a bomb".

> Simone confronts his difficulties

Then you see his resentment about his father talking to Romana, since he immediately engages Romana's attention after that. In a way, he feels that if he could just be this baby's daddy, he would feel all right towards it; when he takes this fox-tail and rubs it against the baby's face, saying, "Let's tickle her", it is as if he and mummy are *being parents* together. Later, when he plays with the toy telephone, he refuses his father's idea that he is telephoning his grandpa, and tells his father he is phoning "Your mother!", as if he were a grown-up. Now, when he gets on to this bit about shaving the duck . . . I would think again, this is some kind of identification with the daddy, who shaves. Then he takes these small shoes and tries them on the baby, as if to say, "These were mine when I was a baby—she has them now I am a big man, a daddy". His mother wonders, and he tells her "She is my little sister", very much trying to be grown-up, giving his former place to her; then he goes to try the spanner again—the daddy-tools. But his position of being big brother pretending to be daddy is disturbed when father *actually* comes to join mother and the baby; he feels thrown out of that identification. He throws the tins down on the floor, as if he is trying to get rid of the bad feelings. When the mother asks him about the triangle, he says, "Diego has taken it away"; we have seen before, Diego is for him the bad little boy who *takes* things—the rival.

Then he gets on to this pretend wetting. He doesn't at the moment actually wet his pants; instead he plays at wetting everything around him, pretending that really he is *washing*, not weeing—that he has the fountain/breast that feeds and washes the children. His hostility is hidden under that pretence.

Later he has this difficulty with the triangle of mother, father, and baby; he does not want his father to hold the baby while mother gets ready to feed. So I would think that the father is very central to this observation. He is the rival, the one who interferes with Simone's attempt to cope with the arrival of the new baby by pretending that he *is* his daddy. He feels he could let mummy have this baby and look after if, if she would only accept *him* as its daddy. But that is exploded when mummy and daddy come together.

The "imbecile" infantile self that damages its objects

Twenty-fifth observation of Simone, age two years, five months

RN (*reads*): I go to Simone's house at lunch time; the entire family is at table, including Mrs P's mother, who has arrived recently from the

Marche. Simone looks at me a lot; his mother is seated on his right and helps him to eat. He still shows slight signs of stammering, and just now there is a problem with the kitchen knife. "Who uses the knife?", asks the mother, and Simone replies, "But I am big now!" Father asks him why he didn't come to see him at the pharmacy, and Simone says, "It was closed"; father says he could have come earlier when it was open, and the child replies, "I would have touched the cash-till!" "You know you mustn't touch everything!", Mother and father exclaim together.

Mrs P tries to get Simone to eat an artichoke. "I can't because it upsets me!", he says. "Where?" asks his father. "In my big tummy", he replies. Then his aunt offers him more of the casserole and he accepts willingly. He looks at me and asks, "Do you want to eat, Romana?" I thank him and say I have already eaten. "Then you must have a drink", he says. At that moment the baby is heard crying. Aunt Augusta gets up and brings in the baby. Simone is exultant, then silent. He gives Francesca a smacking kiss and (encouraged by aunty) waves hallo. The mother takes Francesca, who is sleeping. The father says that later on he would secretly give Simone some of his grandfather's white wine. Simone laughs and (referring to the orange juice he is drinking) says it is disgusting, then adds, "with the potato". Mother gives the baby, still sleeping, to her sister-in-law. Father asks what Simone calls Francesca; "*Ciccina*" (chubby thing), answers the child immediately. Then father asks why he hadn't been to Bianchi's that morning; it appears that he met some people after Mass and after that seems to have forgotten about it. Father explains to me that he is allowed to go to Bianchi's every day to get a book of fairytales; this is after calling out each morning that he needs urgently to do a pooh.

Meanwhile, the family talk about problems of holidays, school, etc. Simone thrusts his fork in his glass to mash the orange peel and potato together. He is upset and argues with his father because he wants the knife. The father, irritated, says, "Stop pulling my sleeve!", and Simone starts crying, saying he wants "to go to daddy to dry my tears". He smiles when his daddy picks him up. Then he takes the tape measure and measures the high chair. He chants "*lonza, lonzetta*" (the loin, the loin), and the aunt explains to me that he loves to measure like that, singing meanwhile.

Now the family talk about food and how foods are named in different dialects. Meanwhile the baby has been taken back to bed, and father tells me his view that the "delivery is fundamental" (in forming the baby's character); "This time everything went very well, and the baby is very good."

Simone sits on his tractor, and after a little while calls me and says he is going to fetch the screwdriver. He says Francesca is crying (which is not true); his aunt suggests they go and have a look. Mrs P says that yesterday he told his baby sister, "Don't cry . . . you can stay with me." Simone comes to me and wants me to go to his room to see his car; he says it has "broken down and won't go, it's lost a screw". I sit down on the rocking chair and Simone says to me, "I'll show you this imbecile" (*il deficiente*), and, while speaking, he hits *Braccio di Ferro* (Iron Arms—a big rag doll) and knocks it to the ground. Then he says the cat next to it (a large soft toy) is also "*deficiente*", hits it, and knocks it on the floor. "Aren't they your friends?", the aunt remonstrates. "No", he replies, seeming very angry. She invites him to make friends again, saying, "They didn't do it on purpose you know . . . now they've fallen into the puddle and hurt themselves." Then Simone, quite excited, hugs his teddy bear and calls out, "Grandpa'. He goes back to *Braccio di Ferro* and calls it "*deficiente*'. I ask his aunt how he came to know this word, and she explains that her brother (his father) used it once when he was angry in the car. Straight away Simone intervenes and tells me all about the incident. Then he says he's going to mummy, and goes out.

He comes back into the room saying, "I'll put you in the pond . . . I'll do you a nice picture, this is the wheel . . . that's enough now, I'm tired . . . *deficienti, deficienti!*' (imbeciles, imbeciles!). The aunt remonstrates again, "Poor things, look how good they're being now!", but he says he will squash them with the "*pan*". She explains that when Simone doesn't know a word, he invents it. Simone says, "Come on, I'll cut you all to pieces." "Why?", she asks. "Because they're crushing my little car . . . I'm cross because they put themselves in the pond." The aunt replies, "But it was you who put them there", and he says, "And after I'll put them in the cupboard", and opens the cupboard door.

Mother comes in and he tells her that his car isn't working. "What should we do about it, do you think?", she asks, and he replies, "The mechanic has gone away, he is down that road over there, but I am going to find Bob, the one with those disgusting animals . . . then Bob will show me the hens." The mother explains he is referring to a story in a book that her husband bought him, but she does not know that story herself. Simone goes on, "My name is Bob . . . I am Vincent", and he takes up his toy box. He says he is going to Bob's, to the "spacemen", to Vincent, to his grandfather's. He seems rather excited. He takes the book, saying he is going to see Bob, and his aunt says no, he's mistaken—that is not the book about Bob. Simone insists that it is, and in fact he is right. Then he wants her to read it to him. He turns towards me and explains the story; then he turns towards his aunt and very soon he is absorbed in the book.

Meanwhile his mother tells me that she is the only person whom Simone will accept should hold Francesca; he absolutely does not want his father, aunt, or grandma to hold her at any time.

> Greed

MH: In this observation you can see how Simone immediately presents himself as a big person: he wants the kitchen knife—his is big now. And there are hints here that father is a little bit hurt by being ignored—Simone didn't come to see him at the pharmacy. It is interesting how he manages to alarm his parents, by saying he kept away so he wouldn't steal from the cashbox! They immediately say, "But you mustn't . . .!" It's also interesting that he shows he is aware of his greed—saying that he won't eat an artichoke "because of my big tummy"—he is restraining himself.

Comment: Perhaps he didn't like the artichoke.

MH: Yes, that may well be so; but there is also some defence against his greed, which I would think at the moment is very strong. Later on he deals with this by being the grown-up, the breast, and offering food to Romana—"*You* must take this".

Comment: The wine and the juice . . .

MH: Yes, that is part of the pretending, that this is the *real thing*. You can see his attempt to be delighted when his aunt brings in the baby, but then his jealously comes out, and he smacks her. Now, when his father says he hasn't been to Bianchi—who is Bianchi?

RN: The bookshop, where he is allowed to go as a reward for going to the toilet.

MH: I see . . . that's why suddenly he needs to go to the toilet, as if to say he is controlling it. It would seem that he wants not just the licence to buy his own books; he wants to have *the knife* of daddy, whatever that knife means. As if it represents the accolade that he is really grownup and can be trusted with dangerous things. Now, what does it mean when he takes a tape measure to the high chair and says "loin"?

RN: He is referring to that part of the pig.[3]

MH: So that might link with the knife too, as if he is able to take and cut up his own food.

Now father starts to talk about the delivery, which was a good one this time—as if to say, this baby is going to be *marvellous*. He is already somehow idealizing this baby that has come about in the right way, while expressing some sort of disappointment or disquiet about Simone. It seems to me that Simone does register this, and once again tries to get the grown-up screwdriver, and says, "Francesca's crying"—i.e., she is not such a marvellous baby as you think!

Wanting his "stupid" part to be recognized

After that he goes to Romana, and asks her to look at his car, which has "broken down", as if he is coming to ask her what is wrong with him and how to mend it. Now, when he says "I'll show you the imbecile", I would think he wants to show Romana the stupid or deficient part of himself, that is linked with his damaged object—to show her what damages his relationships. I think this is related to what his father said about his unsatisfactory delivery. He feels very hurt about that, and wants to get rid of this stupid, unsatisfactory part of himself that causes damage. It seems to be related to the incident when his father used *"deficiente"* in the car. His view is that his *omnipotence* is in fact stupid, and stops him from learning. There is a mixture in his mind between feeling that he wants to get rid of his omnipotence, and a projection into the grown-ups, who "crush" his little car, his little or infantile self. He says, "I'll cut you all to pieces"—they are crushing his little car. There is some kind of recognition on his part of ways in which the grown-ups have encouraged him in this—encouraged him to grow faster and to be bigger than he really can be.

The child's own place in the family

It is very difficult for parents who adore their child—especially perhaps a first child—not to encourage a kind of *precocity* that makes the child feel bigger and more important than he is. I think it is always a terrific struggle for the first or adored child to *find their own place* in the family, when confronted by with the arrival of the next baby. Later, he wants his mother, too, to know that his car is out of order, and that he needs help. You can maybe think of this car as representing his internal containment, his feeling about his own size and identity, which is all "out of joint".[4] His life is in disarray at the moment; he needs help to put things together in a different way from before.

What is so very healthy and developmental in this child is his capacity to express through his play and phantasy precisely what his emotional state is. One doesn't feel it is stuck in any pathological position; he is fighting and struggling to develop the whole time, and pushing mainly forward.

The story of Genesis according to Melanie Klein

A session with Martha Harris and Donald Meltzer

Introduction

Donald Meltzer: This morning we have planned a little entertainment for you. Actually we devised it within the last few hours. I am going to tell you a story called "Genesis—according to Melanie Klein, according to Donald Meltzer". Then Dr Negri is going to read her observations of a little boy's first day at nursery school. In his first day at school, we can trace remnants of his first day outside the womb. The story of Genesis-according-to-Melanie Klein finds its final form in her *Narrative of a Child Analysis*, the story of Richard, which was written a few years before her death. The story of the therapy and the notes that accompany it contain implicitly her theory of infantile development.

The story of that theory goes something like this: once upon a time there was a little creature who lived in a world of his own that was extremely comfortable, particularly because he had a very good friend there to whom he was very attached by his navel and who seemed to understand him perfectly, and whose name was Placenta. This little world of his own had qualities which suited him in every respect: there was enough room to move around him, there were no sharp or dangerous objects, there was a very pleasant dim light and muffled sounds, a slight taste to the medium and gentle stimulation to the skin. The world was so pleasant that he would never have wanted to leave it, were it not that as time went on it became smaller and smaller, more and more constricting of his movements. And, as it became smaller, he became more and more restless, and felt that he had to somehow stretch or enlarge it by exerting the full force of his musculature.

Then something terrible happened: the whole thing began to explode in some way. He found himself hurled or dragged or somehow propelled out of this pleasant environment into a most unpleasant one, containing all the qualities that his original home had not had. It was full of sharp sounds, sharp light, sharp objects impinging on his skin; it was cold, and worst of all, his friend Placenta seemed to have been left behind. Naturally he screamed for his friend; and to his amazement, his friend *immediately* arrived—not by his navel, but somehow came into his mouth and filled up his chest, and he felt much better, for a moment. For a moment he thought he had recovered his first home, and was able to fall happily asleep, but he kept waking up and discovering that it was not so; in fact, each time he woke up he felt more and more miserable. It was true that his friend seemed to have gone somehow *inside* him; and together they seemed to be able to get back inside their original home. But now, there were other, constant discomforts. At last, to his great relief, his friend came and attached himself to his mouth. He had never really seen his friend clearly before, and was astonished by his beauty—by the whiteness, and the succulent, delicious dark place in the middle of his friend.

But he couldn't really understand why his friend didn't just stay in his mouth, the way he used to stay attached to his tummy. And it soon became clear to him that this very succulent dark area that brought the friend to him, could change its aspect and become rather nasty-looking, and then take his friend away from him. Furthermore, he noticed that when this friend was attached to his mouth, another aspect of the friend appeared before his eyes that seemed to consist of two dark places, which were very fascinating, but could also become very frightening at times. He further noticed that by this action of sucking on his friend while he was in his mouth, that brought him great pleasure and relief, the friend also reappeared inside him again, as had happened the first time he had screamed. But it wasn't only the good friend, with the succulent dark place; it was also sometimes the friend with the very frightening dark place; just as the eyes could change too, from being pleasant to being unpleasant. So he found he really had *two* friends inside, with rather different qualities.

Things were becoming very complicated. Outside there were good friends and bad friends; inside, too, there were good and bad ones. He felt very confused and insecure, until he decided that really it would be better to try to keep only the *good* friends inside, and to keep the bad friends outside—which he could do by expelling the bad ones, for example by belching or urinating or defecating.

This very clever device, which at first seemed very successful, had rather complicated consequences. When he had the bad friend inside him, it might cause him pain and distress, but at least he knew where it was. But as soon as he pushed it out of his mouth or bottom, it seemed to be everywhere—in every shadow; particularly when the lights went out, it seemed to be all around him. From this dilemma there seemed to be only two avenues of relief: one being that he could get *inside* this internal good friend and go to sleep, and that was just like being back in the original place; or, when his good friend outside was attached to his mouth, he could feel very safe and very content. Yet these, too, seemed to have their complications. When he went to sleep inside this internal friend, he sometimes had dreams about that terrible event that expelled him; so either he felt imprisoned there, or in danger of being thrown out again, and it could become a nightmare. Also, the friend outside who attached himself to his mouth kept going away, leaving him full of distrust and suspicion. He began to reach the conclusion that this was no longer his friend exclusively, but that it had other friends in the world.

Most of all, he noticed that it had a particular friend who in some way bore a distinct resemblance to this dark place in the middle, that looked so succulent when it came, and so threatening and dangerous when it took the breast away. He concluded that his original friend was no longer his possession or part of himself, and that he was alone in the world. But then he discovered a new friend—in fact, a better friend, one who shared the same body with him, and who shared his feelings of resentment and distrust: someone lot cleverer than himself, who seemed to know the *explanation* for all these changes. This friend, in fact, seemed very independent of mind, and kept telling him that he really didn't *need* that original friend—who was unfaithful and had attached himself to this other creature. Really he was better off without it. The new friend taught him how to put things in his mouth that were just as good as that succulent thing; he helped him to discover other parts of his body that by touching could give him tremendous pleasure. He really seemed to be a marvellous friend. Moreover, he had great power in the world: he knew how to scream and make people obey him. Following this friend really seemed the best solution: to let him scream and discipline that former friend, making him come and feed him whenever he wanted, and be his slave.

But somehow this was not satisfactory. He began to notice that being fed by a slave was not the same as being fed by a friend; and that being in a position of great power was not the same as being in the company of *good* friends. Although he felt very secure, he felt very unhappy. So he decided to sever his connection with this new all-powerful friend, and to discover yet another friend, very much like the first friend—white, smooth, warm, pleasant—with whom he could have a relationship very much like the one his first friend has with the thing constantly referred to as "daddy". When left alone together, they could cuddle one another in the same way that he imagined this mummy-creature friend and this daddy-creature did when they went away at night. He thought he had indeed found the secret of eternal happiness.

But then he began to notice that this also had complications. When he had a lovely time in bed with his new friend, his dreams were not very nice. They were not the nightmares he used to have when he got inside his inside-friend, but they were unpleasant dreams, in which this mummy-friend and daddy-friend seemed unfriendly to him, or damaged in some way, evoking in him new and terrible feelings. He didn't feel as frightened of them as he used to when they were slaves, but—well, really, it made him cry. It made him want to apologize, and promise never to do it again, and other strange feelings. When he was in this weepy state of feeling ashamed, his other know-it-all friend would reappear and tell him that he shouldn't feel that way—they were his enemies and he should hate them, and use every device and trick possible to evade their influence and control. He was very influenced by this clever friend, realizing that he couldn't think as clearly as he did about things, except at one time—and that was when this breast-friend was in his mouth. Then he seemed able to think very clearly, and to realize that here was his true friend, who was doing something for him that was quite different from the pleasure he had with his other little white friend.

In this way he began to realize something he had never understood before: that this friend, that came with his mouth, like the first friend attached to his tummy, *made him grow*. It wasn't that this mummy-friend was getting smaller and smaller, as he had originally thought was happening with his first home, but it was *he* who was growing. He realized that if this process went on, he would some day—perhaps quite soon—be just as big as his mummy-friend and be able to marry her instead of his little friend-wife, and live happily ever after.

Of course, it would be necessary for him to get rid of that daddy-person, but he was sure that his know-it-all friend would be able to do that. And then, of course, there was the problem of his little wife-friend, but she could be left to the know-it-all as a reward for getting rid of the daddy. And just as he felt he had it all figured out, so he could live happily ever after, a terrible thing began to happen. This mummy-friend started to visit his mouth less frequently. Instead of putting herself in his mouth, she kept shoving other things in there, which were in some ways quite interesting, but certainly not the same. A terrible realization broke in upon him that *it was happening again*—just as it had happened with his first home. Now, his first outside friend was going to disintegrate or go away or something bad, and he would live *unhappily* ever after. He searches in his mind for possible explanations for the incipient defection of this mummy-friend; and he realizes that this is what it is going to be like for the rest of his life. Whenever you had a friend who helped you to grow, you grew in a way that made it impossible for that friend to stay with you. And just now, things were growing in his mouth that were so sharp and so dangerous that his friend didn't dare stay with him any longer.

Even so, while he still has his mummy-friend in his mouth, making everything clear to him, it dawns on him that everything is going to be all right after all: he was going to discover new forms of happiness, not just suffer the loss of the old forms of happiness. But when he is alone, this know-it-all friend comes and tells him a different story: it was all a plot, a trick; they were keeping all the good things for themselves, and giving him all the bad stuff. Then, just as he had expected, it began to happen: his mummy-friend did not come into his mouth any more at all. He joined up with know-it-all and screamed and yelled and tried to force her back into slavery. But she refused; and he was in despair.

Yet when he was with her, and her two eye-nipples were smiling at him, while she was putting this other stuff in his mouth, it seemed all right again. In fact, that other stuff was very nice, and these sharp things in his mouth were very useful. He could see that it was true about the new kind of happiness opening up to him. Yes, it seemed all right. She was quite devoted to him and knew what she was doing, and this daddy-person seemed also to be quite friendly and to take good care of her. Perhaps he could go on like that until he was big enough to keep her in bed with him every night, and live happily ever after. As his trust in her begins to be restored, he finds that even when he is without her, there is another one of her inside him who can be with him and comfort him, and he can get rid of his know-it-all friend who told him they were all his enemies. He seems to be settling down.

But then another worrying thing begins to happen. He notices that something is happening to his mummy: her tummy is getting bigger and bigger. It suddenly occurs to him—that must have been his first home! And if so, it must now be somebody else's first home—and that is really the ultimate betrayal. Clearly the only thing to do was to find how to get in there and do away with this rival. He remembered that he had found ways of getting inside his internal mummy; so there must be ways of getting inside the external one also, if he could only find the secret, the key to entry inside mummy's tummy. And his know-it all friend turns up and tells him that he has the key—it is right there between his legs and he need only learn how to insinuate it, to get inside that place and eliminate his rival.

This was a terrible shock. He felt as if the goodness and innocence of himself and the whole world had suddenly been shattered. It was not a Garden of Eden where the only trouble was when this know-it-all friend kept turning up. There were bad things *everywhere*. One had to be constantly on the alert for bad things in oneself and in other people; and life was never going to be blissful.

Of course, this is a highly simplified story; but it contains within it the essential elements of the way the early narcissistic union with the mother gives way to differentiation, as Mrs Klein envisaged it, and there comes about a splitting between good and bad in the self and objects. Then the realization of bisexuality evolves; and finally, the depressive position arises and puts an end to any dream of living happily ever after.

So this story is a model or ideal version of the pattern of development in the first year and a half of life. The implication is that these primordial conflicts and primary movements to resolve them are repeated at every developmental stage in life—every time there is what Bion would call a "catastrophic change", imposed by either developmental processes or environmental changes. This cycle of conflict, from birth to the birth of the next baby, has to be run through each time, in order to regain a depressive orientation to one's objects and a picture of the world as a place where one may live happily, if not blissfully.

Now, for the next phase in our entertainment, Dr Negri is going to read us her observation of little Simone, aged two years and ten months, at nursery school. It is his second day there—so, two days after birth. Then Mrs Harris is going to go through it with you to see if we can cull from it traces of this primordial pattern of the period from birth to the birth of the next baby.

The second day at nursery school[5]

Twenty-sixth observation of Simone, age two years, ten and a half months

RN (*reads*): It is Simone's second full day at nursery school. I have notified staff through the child's parents that I would go and observe Simone at 10.30 a.m. I enter through the school's gate and I see that the (many) children are playing in the garden that is in front of me. The school is on my right; a lady comes out from a door and tells me that Monica (who I later learn is Simone's teacher) is coming out in a moment with her group of children, including Simone; so I wait outside. Meanwhile, two children come running out from their classroom. One falls down and begins to cry. Soon afterwards, two older children come out holding Simone by the hand; they go to help the child who has fallen down. Simone has not noticed me. The cook—whom I had spoken to earlier—came out too. The little group go back inside.

Some children go towards the cook, who is just outside the kitchen door, and ask her about lunch; she replies there is no lunch today so they will go home to eat. Then Simone comes out running with an older boy to whom he calls, "Let's go!" Simone stays on the grass together with three other children; they form a circle. They look at their clothes for a while and then run towards the bottom of the garden. Simone is the last to get there and his three companions start playing with a big ball. The child stops, looks about him quite seriously, then goes towards an older boy (whose name, I shortly learn, is Alexander, and who is five years old). Simone obviously knows him quite well, as he is the son of a chemist who is his father's colleague. Simone and Alexander go over to a small swing with two seats that are already occupied by two other children. He stops to watch; he is very serious, looks around him, then thanks to the staff member who is watching to ensure children take turns on the swing, he gains a seat on the swing with his friend. They sit facing one another. Simone smiles and speaks in a loud voice, saying "uh" and looking at the other children who are jumping around the large garden. One has the impression this is quite a traditional nursery school; the children, teachers, and cook are all dressed in white; and the relationship between staff and children is necessarily limited by the fact that each teacher is in charge of more than thirty children.

Simone has not yet noticed me, even though he is looking towards me. Now he is watching his teacher on one side, who calls out, "Change over!" He gets down from the swing, holding on to his friend. He stops near a very big tree and watches the children on the big swing, then— still holding his friend's hand—he goes towards a roundabout consisting of several small seats, and finds a seat for himself and his friend. Meanwhile, four big children form a circle around me and ask me what I am doing; they follow me when I move towards the roundabout. Simone talks with the other children on the roundabout. He looks serious, worried. At one point, when going round, it seems to me that he notices me; then he looks several times in my direction. "*Ciao*", I greet him, but he does not respond.

Some girls come by dragging a cart, and when they pass near me they ask me what I am doing. Simone now has a smiling expression, but it seems to me that he is also worried, and tells his companions, "Let's slow down!" He looks towards the centre of the wheel and calls out laughingly, but also very fearfully, "Stop!" and he slides down before the roundabout has altogether stopped. He falls down; the teacher goes to the rescue and calls "Stop!" Simone picks himself up, touching his bottom with one hand and his head with the other, wincing meanwhile. Then he joins his friend, takes hold of his hand, and speaks to him, while keeping his other hand on his bottom. I am sitting on the grass and I swivel round to watch him; he seems annoyed. He goes with his friend towards the big swing. He holds one hand on his head, and begins to rub his eyes. He cries for quite a long time and seems rather cross. The teacher sitting nearby tries to console him, saying he is "spoiling his beautiful eyes". "I want to go home to mummy, I don't want to stay here for lunch", he retorts.

Meanwhile, another child near us who has been watching the scene bursts out crying desperately. Her teacher says to her: "Rossana, why are you crying? Your beautiful eyes!" But she is not consoled at all. Simone takes his friend by the hand and begins to speak to him; I hear him saying in a serious tone, his cheeks wet with tears, "I won't come back—when mummy and daddy come, I won't come back!" He keeps in close physical contact with his friend and never looks at me; it is as if I am not there. They go off arm in arm. The teacher explains that Simone's upset started when he did not want Alex to leave him alone while he went on the swing for bigger children, and Simone was afraid to go on it with him. She also explains that Simone can also relate to other children, when in a small group; but when he finds himself in bigger surroundings, like the garden, he insists on staying with Alessandro, and also that Alessandro must stay only with him.

Now Simone is sitting down on the grass with Alex who is playing with a green plastic accordion. I approach them, and Simone glances quickly at Alex and clings to him, stroking his neck. "I'm going now", says Alex. "What about me, where are you taking me?", asks Simone; he hardly looks at me and talks all the time to Alex. When two big children come along and start talking to me, Simone also turns towards me, and I hear him say, "I'm going home, you know", while he holds on to his friend by the back of his head. The girls do some acrobatics to show off. One asks in a loud voice, "Who is that child who is on his knees?" "Simone Paolo", Alessandro replies. Simone says, "This is my friend . . . this is my friend and you mustn't touch him because he is naughty."

Simone is still kneeling, and as he continues to stroke his friend's hair, he watches the girls, who are close by me, playing with conkers. One of them goes up to Simone and offers him a shoelace but he does not want it. He comes nearer and seems to be interested in the conkers. Then, still holding his friend's hand, he goes towards a group of older children playing with a big cart that can be dragged or pushed along while three children ride on it. A girl near me calls out "Simone", but he shows no sign of interest in her. All this time, Rossana has been a constant, silent figure at my side. She, too, had been feeling homesick, at more or less the same time as Simone, saying she wanted her mummy and wanted to go home. After her crying subsided, she remained near me throughout the rest of the observation, without saying a word.

Simone is still physically inseparable from his friend, who appears to be talking rather angrily to him. Simone is really worried; his mouth trembles on the verge of crying. Alex wants to go on the cart, but Simone does not want him to, so Alex says, "Come on, you have to learn!" He goes up and sits on the cart while Simone stays at the back of it, holding on and pushing it. A big blond boy takes the horse's place and plays his part quite well to begin with. Then instead of remaining a horse, he seems to turn into more of a tiger, turning towards the children on the card and raising his arms and shouting to frighten them. Simone seems to like this game, because he laughs and shouts along with the other children, "Come on, horse, gee-up!" When the "horse" turns towards his companions to repeat his aggressive gesture, Simone is quite amused: "Aha!", he laughs. One of the children on the cart grumbles at "Furia the horse". Then "Furia" asks Alessandro to come down and take his place. Simone tries to defend his friend, and calls "Go away, you ugly beast!" and, fortunately, "Furia" just smiles at this insult. Another child, sitting next to Alex, imitates Simone and calls out, "You ugly beast of flesh and bones . . . Mr Horse President!" Simone is delighted by this. The "horse" says in a menacing tone, "I am a big fierce beast!"

Simone climbs up on the cart and sits next to Alessandro. Rossana, who is still at my side, smiles while she watches the children playing the horse game, and also quite often looks and smiles at me. She stands up, holding a large conker and a small book. At the signal given by the "horse", a child cries, "Off you go, you ugly dinosaur!" Simone pretends to whip him, saying, "Gee up!" The "horse" moves out from the shaft, pulls up some grass, and throws it at the three children sitting on the cart. Simone shouts, repeating what he has just heard, "Off you go, you ugly dinosaur!" He brushes the grass off his friend and repeats words he has just said, "Get in the cart, gee up!" He watches the "horse" and laughs at his antics. The "horse" says, "Grass, the horse's favourite sweet!" as he throws more grass over his friends. Simone laughs happily while he picks the grass off Alessandro. Alex gets down from the cart and runs off.

Simone says to me, "I'm going off with the big cart now." It seems that he has just noticed Rossana, and invites her to go on the cart with him, then he shouts, "Gee up, off you go!" From the cart he watches Alessandro, who is playing near the big concrete tunnels. He orders Rossana to climb down, and shouts at the boy in the shaft of the cart, "Come on, dinosaur . . . gee up horse, turn that way!" Simone looks at me, lets a big boy climb on the cart, then comes down, saying, "I've got to tell the horse something." Indicating a child on the cart, he exclaims, "Come on horse, eat him up, come down." He takes the cart's shaft and shouts, "Go away, you pirate!"

After that he leaves the cart almost immediately and begins to run towards the tunnels. He falls down, picks himself up, and starts running again. (I realize he is looking for Alessandro.) He goes into a tunnel where he sees a child sitting; it is not Alex so he comes out again. Then he sees Alex playing out in the garden. He leans over another tunnel and remains there for some time with his hands outstretched, clinging on to it; he seems embarrassed. He finds the green plastic accordion on the grass, picks it up and then throws it down again, shouting out, "Look, what a beautiful thing!"

My hour's observation is over and I go to thank Simone's teacher. Rossana follows me and when she realizes that I am saying goodbye, she bursts into tears. "Your mummy is coming", I tell her (the children are going home at noon today because it is a local holiday), but she is not consoled. As I leave I notice Alessandro fighting with the big blond boy who had been "Furia the horse". Simone runs towards them, and though the two older children have already detached themselves, Simone advances towards the blond boy with a menacing expression and fist clenched. The boy takes no notice of him, avoids him, and goes away.

MH: I think it is important to say that Simone knows Dr Negri very well; she has been observing him weekly from the time of his birth, in the context—of course—of his home. This is the first time she has seen him at school, and it is his second day there. That suggests that his not seeing her, or seeming not to see her, for quite a long time during the observation means he is trying to cut off his feelings of home and of being a child at home. He seems to have attached himself to this older boy whom he already knows, Alessandro, in the way of the "friend" that Dr Meltzer was talking about—an ever-present companion who makes him feel he does not need his

mummy or his home. He attaches himself in a somewhat tyrannical way to this friend, who is meant to accompany him everywhere
and is not allowed to go off and play with the bigger boys. It is a
way of defending himself against the anxiety of being with all these
other children—there are about thirty in the class. He doesn't seem
able to use the teacher as a mummy-person, because she has *so
many* children to look after. She says that Simone is all right with a
small group of children, but finds it difficult out in the playground
with so many children.

> The good mummy is unavailable

It is notable that he seems to get worried on this roundabout, going
round fast with the other children, almost as if he were reaching
above himself and things were getting out of hand, so that when he
eventually falls and hurts himself one has the impression that he is
not so much hurt physically as toppled from his position of being
omnipotently invulnerable together with his friends. He feels
humiliated, reduced to being a little helpless boy who needs his
mummy. Then when *he* begins to cry, this little girl Rossana also
breaks down and cries for her mummy. It is noticeable how later on
she becomes closer to Dr Negri and can use her as a mummy-
substitute, whereas Simone is not able to do so, even though he
knows her very well, because he is hooked on this friendship with
Alessandro, the older boy. This relates, one would think, to his
anger at mummy for sending him to nursery school; Dr Negri
becomes his bad mummy, while his good mummy is somehow
unavailable.

But towards the end of this observation, when the children are
playing with the cart and this tiger-horse, Furia, it seems that
Simone manages to express—or have expressed for him in a
contained form—his own *real fury* at being deserted by his mummy
and sent to nursery school. He does manage to work out some of
his anxieties and fears through the game.

DM: I think it is very noticeable how the relationship between
Simone and Alessandro changes during the course of this observation. At the beginning, he is *attached* to him, as an object of security,
holding his hand; he is also very tender with him, stroking his hair
and so on. It is in relation to this attachment—to a previous friend

from his home environment, who has come with him into the school—that after losing touch with him he then goes and looks for him *inside this concrete pipe*. It is also interesting to see how this little girl Rossana attaches herself to Dr Negri, partly because she is interested in her as a mummy-person, but also partly because she is interested in Simone, and would like him to be interested in her; and the two of them function together here *vis-à-vis* Dr Negri as the *bisexuality* of the personality, as it were—its little-boy and little-girl parts.

Narcissistic attachment to a big brother

When Simone loses his *infantile* anxiety and becomes involved in the play, Alessandro changes meaning for him and becomes an admired older boy who knows his way around; he becomes to some degree interchangeable with the boy who plays the horse. His change in attitude to Alessandro seems to be brought about in part by his accident on the roundabout: as if he had attempted to attach himself to this breast-object and once again had the experience of being thrown off and getting hurt. Then, turning against the mother, he attached himself in a narcissistic way to this big brother figure. Of course, he gets very caught up in this marvellous game with the cart, which seems to be a perfect representation of the ambiguity of the daddy or tiger-horse's relationship to the mummy-cart full of babies. There is a good daddy drawing the cart at one moment, and a bad daddy the next, turning into a tiger and attacking the babies. It is pretty clear that it is the tiger-daddy that is admired, and turns into a dinosaur-daddy. Simone then gets quite carried away, becoming one of the boys, one of the gang, fighting and so on. From the beginning of the observation when he is this lost baby, to the end of the observation when he is one of the gang, is quite a sweeping metamorphosis.

MH: I think it is significant that Simone has only recently had a baby sister at home. Now he is plunged into nursery school with so many other children, when he has not yet quite adjusted to his home where he is no longer the only child. Also he has not yet forgiven Dr Negri for observing his sister at home, on several occasions, as we have seen in other observations. I therefore feel that the moment he turns to Alessandro as an elder brother can also be seen as turning to the figure of his father and against his mother who has betrayed him.

DM: From the viewpoint of the story I have told you, the essential difference between the boy and the girl is really only to be found—as you have recognized—at the moment of having to cope with the birth of the next child. Up to that point, the development of the boy and the girl is very similar. You can see it in this situation in the difference between Simone and Rossana: Rossana is walking around playing with her chestnuts, then with the book in her hand; later she adds the plastic accordion, and then attaches herself to Dr Negri.

Problems of boys and girls

According to this story, the little girl lives in hope and the little boy lives in despair. That is, a lot of his masculinity is built on the attempt to overcome his despair at not being the only baby, while he is unable to compensate himself by imagining that he will become the mummy and have a baby some day. He thus has a much more difficult task of identification. He has to work out an identification with a good daddy to whom he has been highly ambivalent since the very earliest days of his relationship to the nipple—which is succulent one minute, and the next minute takes away the breast. His masculinity tends to get stuck just where you find Simone, who is not even three years old. It is what Freud called "phallic masculinity", or, in the Kleinian story, being "one of the boys", a member of the gang, who show off to one another by demonstrating their muscular, phallic capabilities, using the girls as trophies and a playing-field for their exhibitions. The overcoming of that phallic gang-type masculinity is a very difficult task for men. From this point of view, in relation to problems of love and separation, the boy has a difficult problem in terms of developing his masculinity in response to this terrible experience of the next baby—which is even more dreadful if the baby doesn't come, because something must have happened to it.

The little girl, however, on the birth of the next sibling, encounters a dreadful problem in relation to her envy of the mother. If her love and admiration for the mother has been seriously interfered with by envy of the mother before this next baby comes, then its arrival quite knocks her over. The envious relationship to the mother can become an absolute impediment to her ability to wait in hope, in identification with her.

In summary, the little boy's main problem is jealousy and the identification with an ambiguous figure—the father, whereas the little girl's main problem is envy, struggling with her ambivalence towards a good figure—the mother.

Q: [about castration anxiety and the Freudian model]

DM: Now of course the problem of castration anxiety is simply the problem that arises as the successor to the earlier anxieties about loss of the womb, loss of the breast and so on, and is the form that separation and loss anxiety takes in the boy in his genital–oedipal complex and is not a very complicated problem in itself if the previous pregenital problems have been reasonably resolved.

The problem of penis envy turns out to have really two different aspects to it. The first is a problem that comes from a woman's masculinity, and the yearning for a masculine relationship with the mother. That isn't really penis envy—that's just her masculinity manifesting itself. Where "penis envy" really *is envy* is where the hostility and envy toward the mother takes the form of the wish to have male attributes in order to tyrannize and brutalize the mother; that is the *real* penis envy, and is very malignant really.

> Masculine and feminine parts of the personality

As far as the bisexuality is concerned, this model envisages a splitting of the bisexuality, and the projective identification of the contra-sexual part with siblings, with the parent of the opposite sex, and eventually with the lover, spouse, and so on. The place that it finds in life directly, as far as sexuality is concerned, is through the capacity to empathize and identify with the partner. But, on the other hand, of course the little girl, or woman, has plenty of opportunity to exercise in the world aspects of her personality that have, for her, the meaning of masculine. They may not mean the same for somebody else; but for her, they are part of the masculine side of her personality, and she has ample opportunity to exercise them and enjoy their functions.

A difficulty arises when one starts to talk about men and women instead of the masculine and feminine parts of the personality. The problem of envy toward the mother is a problem of the feminine part of the personality. The problem of envy of the father is a problem of the masculine part of the personality. In so far as these two problems compare with one another, the problem of envy of the father is a far less difficult problem for the boy or the masculine part of the personality than the problem of envy of the mother is for the feminine part of the personality, partly because *the father is a far more ambiguous figure.*

Melanie Klein and the model of healthy development

Q: [about the model of development in the story]

DM: This model of development is based on the assumption that we are dealing with perfectly adequate parents, and, of course, is subject to infinite variation according to the actual personalities of parents and the eruption of traumatic events, and so on. It assumes that the mother does not need to be satisfied by the child: that she is not a problem to the child because of being depressed or unhappy. It is an ideal model, on the basis of which variations, based on understanding of parental psychopathology or immaturity can be comprehended; but it is an ideal model, like the stories of the fall and the expulsion from paradise. It is highly simplified: it is an ideal model, and all the complications that you envisage can be construed in the light of modifications of this model.

Therefore, it is a model for thinking about phenomena; but it is not a model for construing psychopathology. The model for construing psychopathology is a very different kind of model. The one we have worked out (which will be published in Italian next year) is called "A Model of the Child-in-the-Family-in-the-Community". This is a model that attempts to give one a basis for construing the interrelation of the psychopathology of the child in relation to that of the family structure, and the parents as individuals in relation to the psychopathology of the community and social relations. It is a very different kind of model.

Models are not intended to convince; they are meant to be used, and a model has to be taken and used so one can see if it is, in fact, useful. There is no possibility of anything being convincing about a model. A model is not a theory; it is a way of thinking about phenomena.

The purpose of the entertainment today was to tell you a "Biblical" story according to Melanie Klein, and to demonstrate to you how much of its fundamental elements can be discerned by careful observation of normal children in their everyday environment. So it is really a story about *normal development*, and an encouragement to you to keep your eyes and ears open, because, if you watch children and pay attention to them in everyday life, you will see all of this story revealed before your very eyes. It was not the intention to give you a theory from which psychopathology could be construed, but to give you a model of healthy development to help you to recognize the significance of the play and behaviour of children as it goes on in everyday life.

The reason for doing this is because between Freud and Melanie Klein there is this very great methodological gap that is very important to understand. Freud attempted to understand by reconstruction the normal development of children by studying the psychopathology of adult patients. Mrs Klein attempted to understand the meaning of psychopathology by building up a model of normal development. It seems to me that the first method leads to rather grotesque results and comes to a rather dead end fairly quickly in the study of psychopathology, whereas the method of studying normal development and its variations as a basis for studying psychopathology seems to be proving endlessly fruitful. This is the reason that, for instance at the Tavistock, the training of child psychotherapists begins with the observation of mother and baby, with the aim of building up a concept of normal development as a foundation for the later attempt to understand psychopathology.

The other reason for presenting this entertainment is to demonstrate to you that in order to gain access to children's phantasy life, which is the matrix in which their development take place, one does not have to establish any kind of laboratory situation—as, for example, that of psychoanalysis. This information is available to everyone in their everyday life, if they have some model in their mind that enables them first of all to notice, and second, to think about the behaviour. Once you are able to do this, you see it all around you. One of the troubles is that we tend not to notice things unless they are psychopathological. We don't notice them because we have *no way of thinking about them*; we just take them for granted. We have presented this model in terms of a story because, in contrast to theoretical formulations, a story can simply stay in your mind, and just *be there* as a basis for noticing and thinking about the children that you encounter in your everyday life.

So, in this model, there is no problem about the child satisfying its parents. The only thing the child needs to do is to accept and make use of the parents' services and the ambience that the parents provide in order to grow and develop. And *that* satisfies the parents.

Thinking about emotions

I want to add a very brief addendum as to how one would fit Bion's theory of thinking into the story of Mrs Klein's model of normal development. The fundamental addition is Bion's emphasis on the examination of the individual emotional experience, and how it is dealt with in the mind in a way that contributes to development. In the story I have told you, the baby still *in utero* has no need to think about anything: the experiences he is having are generally so pleasant that he is not obliged by conflict and anxiety to apply any process that could be called thinking about them. But these experiences may become important in retrospect, later, when he has need to think about his relationship to his environment. Not only has the baby *in utero* no need to think, but he also does not have the essential equipment for thinking, because his friend that is there—the placenta—is not a thinking object; it is a servicing object. But once he is born and encounters this breast-friend, and the arms that hold him and the eyes that watch him, he is encountering a thinking object that makes it possible for him to think about his experiences and to fill them with meaning. Bion envisages this process of thinking as commencing with the infant using this object initially as a container for the expulsion of his confusion and anxiety. Through its behaviour it is able to expel into the mother its state of mental agitation and confusion, and the mother is able through her reverie to think about it and to return it to the baby in a form that enables him to think about it, namely in the form of a dream. And by a process of introjection the baby internalizes this thinking breast-mummy and becomes gradually able to think for himself. In other words, the capacity to think for oneself is an internal object relationship: a relationship with an object that knows how to think, and that can help and teach you how to think.

> The thinking sequence

This thinking process that is done for the baby or person by the internal breast-mother, involves a sequence of events, the first of which is the creation of symbolic representations of the emotional experience that can be used for making dreams. From these dreams it is possible to reconstruct what Money-Kyrle calls "a picture of his world" and a hierarchy of concepts for construing the world which he has defined as man's "cognitive development". From this dream picture and the dream concept the child can gradually step towards a passive or verbal transformation of these dreams into a language that facilitates communication and learning by communication, that is, by verbal and other means; and provides the primitive mechanism of thinking by communication through projective identification. Furthermore, the picture of the world that he needs to build up is a complicated one because it involves more than one world. An internal world has to be built as a basis for comprehending the meaning of the external world. This has to be differentiated from certain phantasies of the world existing inside objects (external and internal). So it is a complicated picture consisting of four types of world.

So, the fundamental addendum to the Kleinian model made by Bion is that the mother is not just a servicing object but a thinking object, and the communication between infant and mother proceeds by this primitive mechanism of projective identification, and is only much later replaced by verbal means of communication.

Bion has given an entirely new significance to dreams, and really has defined the area of "dream life".

This area corresponds in many ways to Mrs Klein's concept of unconscious phantasy (including dreams) as the foundation of mental life. But it is different to the extent that it emphasizes the primary place of dreams in the *creation of meaning*. Dream life is the fountainhead for the creation of meaning. Mrs Klein took meaning for granted, really. But Bion recognized that people have difficulty suffusing their emotional experience with meaning—they have what he called "thought disorders". He saw that people can live part of their lives outside the realm of symbolic functioning. It is the same problem we discovered in our work with autistic children—they live outside the realm of symbolic function, or in a two-dimensional world that has form but no meaning. They live in a world of signs, but not of symbols.

The third birthday

Twenty-seventh observation of Simone, three years old today

RN (*reads*): I see Simone after a fortnight's gap because I had been at a congress the week before. The door is open, so I go in without ringing the bell. I find Simone's mother in the kitchen, feeding Francesca. The aunt and Diego's father are also there. I go to hang my coat up in the hall, and notice through the open door that Simone is sitting on the sofa in the sitting room watching television all by himself. While I hang up my coat, the aunt enters the sitting room and I find her asking Simone whether Pufi's programme has finished and she can now switch off the television (advertisements are now showing on the screen). Simone seems to notice me at this point; he turns towards me and asks, "Are you staying for lunch, Romana?" I say I am sorry but I cannot, that day. He gets up and tells me that Giancarlo has come to see him and has brought him some things.

Simone leads me into the hall and points out a cardboard box covered with a towel. He lifts the box and shows me its contents: boxes of biscuits and other things from the supermarket. He covers the box again and goes back into the sitting room. Meanwhile aunty explains to me that their cousin Carla, together with Giancarlo, her fiancé, has come from the Marche to see them. Simone seems rather excited now, and throws himself on the sofa several times. While he is on the sofa a friend of the family, Alfredo, comes in and sits near him. I say that very soon it is somebody's birthday, and Alfredo asks whose it is; Simone smiles quite happily and holds up three fingers, to show us that he will soon be three years old. Aunty Augusta explains that there will be a party at the nursery school on Tuesday.

At that point, cousin Carla and Giancarlo come in. Carla is holding a parcel and she gives it to Simone, while Giancarlo goes out to meet the father in his pharmacy. Simone opens the parcel and gets very excited; it is a real camera. He holds it up while Carla puts the various parts together; meanwhile everyone tries to give him some advice. Simone goes to show the camera to his mother, who is seated near me holding Francesca. "You must handle it carefully", she admonishes him. Aunt

Augusta comes in holding Simone's toy camera, and compares it with the new real one. The toy camera is then given to Francesca, because Simone does not show any interest in that one any longer.

Simone says that as soon as Kelly comes, he will take her photo (Kelly is the five-year-old daughter of his teacher, and also attends the nursery school). He seems slightly annoyed by all the advice that Alfredo is still giving him about the camera. Cousin Carla wants to teach him how to look through the viewfinder, saying, "I'll show you the little eye (the viewfinder)". The child then goes to his mother and asks her, "Smile for me", and takes her photo. He is happy, but irritated by everyone's instructions. He presses the flash button from the bottom upwards so it flashes directly in my eye. Aunt Augusta wants to teach him how to use the new camera correctly so she gets him to play with the toy one, but he becomes impatient. The flash bulb has burnt and Simone now plays with Carla. She tries to teach him to take photos. "You need to be able to see aunty inside here—you couldn't see her, could you?", she says. Then he appears more willing to listen to Alfredo. He says to his mother, "Mummy, turn round because I'm going to take your photo", and he takes it with his finger over the lens.

He goes to his aunt and asks, "You do it for me", referring to the camera. "*Please*", emphasizes the aunt; then she adds, "If I don't you will break it in a minute." She explains about the necessity for the word "please", and Simone repeats the request more gently as she had asked. Then he lies on the sofa and begins to sing "Happy birthday to you"; his aunt remarks that he is thinking about the party he will be having at the nursery school. She also says that when he gets angry at home he threatens his parents, saying, "I shall stay there all the time!" Francesca, now on her aunt's lap, plays with the toy camera. Simone, still on the sofa, calls out "smile" to Alfredo and takes his photo. "What shall we do when the film is finished?", asks the aunt. "We'll go to the photographer's", replies Alfredo. "Have you taken one of Romana?", he adds. "Yes, earlier on", I assure him.

After that, Simone goes to his bedroom; I find him on the bed. "A bigger one would have been better", he tells his mother. "You must take care of it—it's like daddy's", she answers. "There are no more photos; it doesn't click any more", he says. He listens carefully to what his mother is teaching him. "You must turn it all round . . ." "All of it?", he responds. She says, "You can take this off-pull", and Simone asks, "Shall I take it off?" (referring to the burnt flash bulb), and smiles happily. Then, pointing to the new camera, he says to me: "It's mine and I won't give it to Francesca", and he puts it on the shelf near the television. "It's made of iron," he says, "and when Daddy comes I'll show it to him and take his photo."

Then he asks his mother, "Will you do me a camera?" (asking her to draw him a camera on the little blackboard lying on the carpet). She asks in return, "Do you want me to draw it for you?", and showing her a small piece of chalk, he asks again, "With this?" Mother asks, "Would you like to draw it yourself?", and takes a duster to wipe the board clean (it has some white dots on it). "Are you cleaning the rain?", asks the child. "Who drew it?", asks the mother. "I did", Simone replies. The blackboard is on the floor in front of the window, and it is in fact raining heavily outside. The mother seems to suddenly become aware of this fact and to be impressed by the child's intuition. She draws a camera and says, "Here is the little eye," pointing to the viewfinder; "do you want the flash, too?" "Now, will you do me a tank?", asks Simone. Mother says she will draw a tractor as she does not know how to draw a tank. "I don't like it, I want a tank, a tank with a cannon!", he cries.

The aunt comes in carrying Francesca, who has a dummy in her mouth and kicks her legs. At this point Simone asks his mother, "Draw me a hen, but with its legs!" She explains to me that yesterday, while she was drawing uncle John's tractor, she couldn't find room for the hen's legs. Francesca, in her aunt's arms, gazes at me, while the mother asks Simone, "How many little legs?" Cousin Carla comes in and the mother tells her she is doing a picture of a hen and Simone is commenting on the drawing. Francesca is now handed over to Carla. Meanwhile the mother says that "the hen is ugly, but it has got legs". She finds some nuts on the floor amongst Simone's toys (pieces of chalk, wax crayons, pencils and "the little tail"—a small piece of a real fox-brush from mother's fur coat). Simone had taken the nuts from Aunty Nana's.

Francesca starts whimpering, and the aunt says she is a terrible baby; she takes her from Carla and goes towards Simone, asking, "Is there room for Francesca?" He immediately replies, "no". He does some drawings on the blackboard and Carla asks, "What are you drawing?" "The cannon", he replies. Father comes in from work, and Simone greets him saying, "*Ciao* Mister" (in English). Francesca starts whimpering again until her father picks her up. He leaves the room soon afterwards, carrying the baby.

Simone jokes with his aunt, who is still in the room with me. She is drawing a tank for him: it is "more beautiful" than that drawn by his mother; "it has strong chains". Mother comes in and wants to see the drawing. Now Simone begins to draw on his aunt's shoes, and she says he is naughty. Cousin Carla enters and takes Simone's drawing from a shelf. She goes to the window to see it properly, and asks her little cousin to describe it. Then Simone tries to draw on his aunt's tights, but she does not let him, so he draws on her shoes. She suggests that he clean them up but he does not want to, and she sighs, "Now I can't go out", to which he replies, "So you have to stay here." She talks about borrowing his mother's shoes, and tells me that Simone has taken her big shoes/boots. She asks him what he has done with them. "In the land of the sharks", Simone replies. He gets excited and begins to jump about in the room. Aunt asks him how old he will be on his next birthday, and he replies by showing three fingers. She explains to him how to use the pencil without dropping it so as not to break the point. Simone doesn't want to do what aunt suggests. Augusta asks him if she can clean the blackboard, but he replies "no". "What do you want me to draw?", aunt asks; but Simone doesn't want the garden that she offers; he doesn't want anything at all. At this point aunt Augusta tells him to tidy the crayons, but he throws them over her. He says, "I'll grab your neck in a minute!" She tells him the circus will be here in town today, and she would like to take him to see the show. He says, "I'll make you walk with the tigers and then . . . there's the lion that hides itself inside a bush."

> ## Confronting his limitations

MH: The emphasis seems to be on his wanting something *strong*. And on his resentment about being in any way treated as a child. With the camera, he says to his mummy, "a bigger one would have been better". Is it he who says "you must take care of it, it's like daddy's"? ("No, the mother.") So she intuitively realizes that he would want a bigger one just like daddy's. Later he says, "It's made of iron; when Daddy comes I'll show it to him", as if the camera has the meaning of the penis, and he wanted to have as big and strong a one as daddy. Then when he asks his mother to make him a camera . . . it is as if he wants to continue to seize his mother's attention in relation to this camera, and to teach him how to draw one.

There is a feeling that the camera he has been given isn't *quite* the one he wants. What he wants really is to have this daddy-camera that would make him the most important person in the world for mummy. You can see his recurrent annoyance when people keep telling him how it works and how to take care of it—he doesn't take instruction very well.

You can also see how this is bound up with the thrill of being three years old; he is very proud of this when he holds up his three fingers. But there is also disappointment—that this doesn't mean he is quite grown up. Just as children so often look forward to birthday parties, yet they are accompanied by this terrific disappointment, and tears ensue. In his very first greeting to Romana—"Are you staying here for lunch"—he is behaving as if he were the host in the family; and after that he shows the box with all the things that have been brought.

Now when aunty Augusta brings . . . who was it who actually gave Simone the camera?

RN: Carla. The toy one had been given by aunt Augusta.

MH: Because it is mainly his aunt who starts to instruct him on how to look after the real one, there is a certain irritability in his reception of this present—as if he vaguely feels that he has been given something that he *doesn't* really know how to use. Rather than allowing him to pretend that he can work it—pretend to be like daddy—this really brings him up against his limitations. This is one of the problems in giving presents to children; if you give them something that is more complicated than they can understand and operate, it can become a liability. He is also going to have to wait a long time before the photographs are developed. I suppose the question is, whether he is old enough, realistically, to have the patience to learn how to take the photograph in the right way, and wait till it is developed—rather than *pretending* to take photographs. That may be why he wants his mother to *draw* a camera for him afterwards. I don't know what your feeling about it is, Romana?

| Mother helps him overcome his frustration |

RN: He did seem a bit clumsy with it. Sometimes he had his fingers in front of the lens. He understood very well he had difficulty with it . . . though at the beginning he wasn't interested in having advice, in the end he asked his mother, as though he really wanted to learn from her. There were two moments, one with his aunt and one with his mother, when it seemed he really did want to learn.

MH: One can imagine it would be difficult for him, a three year old. . . . He does seem to feel that the gift of the camera is something that *exposes* his childishness. When he asks the mother to draw him one, he seems just a little disappointed that she began by cleaning off his drawing of the rain. But she seems sensitive to this, and asks him who did it, giving him the chance to say, "I drew that"—so that it is noticed before it is cleaned away.

Now, after the camera he wants a tank; he doesn't want a tractor, he wants a tank because of the cannon, as if that would register something really *explosive* that he is feeling. Also this time, she should draw the hen, but *with its legs*—because its legs weren't drawn last time. I would think the cannon and the legs represent different aspects of his penis that he would like to have recognized, and not to be made to feel impotent because he can't work this camera properly.

Later he feels annoyed that his old camera has been given to Francesca—he doesn't seem to protest, doesn't seem to notice; but I think he does seem annoyed. There is this irritability afterwards, particularly with the aunt. This is the aunt with whom he has usually been great friends, and who also in a way seems a bit annoyed that he has been given a better camera than the one she gave him. She keeps on telling him how to work this new one, and to be careful with it.

Afterwards it is really *brought home* to him that you have to *learn* to use this more complicated thing: that being grown up brings more responsibilities. It means putting aside former, more childish things. He realizes that he is not really as big as he thought he was; but it is not so easy to just go back to being the baby again. I think this is what forms the basis of his irritability here. The aunt does rub it in: she instructs him in how to use the pencil without dropping it and breaking the point. As if to say, "Now you're a big boy, you must use it properly and not break it." When she tells him to put the crayons in order, he throws them over her.

Becoming three years old is not all fun and games.

RN: There was a cake for Simone but he didn't want it, and didn't enjoy his birthday at all.

An intrusive adult

Twenty-eighth observation of Simone, age three years and one day

RN (*reads*): When I enter the house I find Simone seated at table in the kitchen; mother is standing up and Aunty Augusta is also standing, with Francesca in her arms. Almost immediately Simone says to me, "I'm eating, and here I've got the stories of Pinocchio and Gattinger superstar." I have brought a present for his birthday; it is a memory game, and as I hand it to his mother I remark that it says on the box it can be played by anyone from five to ninety-nine years old. Simone stretches his hand and displays three fingers wide open. Then he asks quickly, "How do you play it, Mummy?" Francesca is watching me from her aunt's arms. Simone's mother reads out the instructions. "Shall we play it afterwards?", Aunty asks her nephew. "Now!", the boy replies. "What are we going to do?", says the aunt, "This little one keeps throwing her dummies about."

Simone is now standing on his chair looking at the cards of the new game. Aunt Augusta goes round the room carrying Francesca, who continues to watch me. "Little scamp!", aunt exclaims. "Isn't it time for you to go to sleep?" Simone runs outside, gets on his tricycle, and meets his father in the hall. "Arturo," says his father, "give me a kiss!", and the child runs back into the room, yells, and clings to his aunt. Simone runs off again to his father, who promises to tell him a story— "How about Ciccio the donkey?" Simone hurts himself and goes to his mother to be comforted. Father calls out, "How about this story about the hen, or the musicians of Bremen?" They both sit down at the table; father is on Simone's right hand. The child seems happy and eats his dinner. The story is about Pippo, Mickey Mouse, and Donald Duck. "Do you want some potatoes, Simone?", asks mother. He shakes his head while he continues to watch the book that father is reading. Augusta is in the bedroom, singing softly while she rocks Francesca— "a terrible baby"—to sleep. Simone raises his head from the book and laughs, looks at me, and eats his potatoes.

Aunty comes in again with Francesca in her arms. "I'm afraid you'll have to put her to sleep", she tells her sister-in-law. Mrs P is cooking, but she consents and takes Francesca. Meanwhile, father is telling the story of the Little Red Hen. Simone's mouth is full, but he stops chewing and leans forward to hear better, then resumes eating with a fork. "Here are the lazy creatures", exclaims father, as he shows the picture to Simone. "They refuse to do the sowing, the reaping, or the grinding." The child continues to eat. Now and then he lifts his head to look at me, then goes on eating greedily. Mother is still looking after the cooking while holding the baby. Alfredo, a friend of the family, comes in (he is the father of Diego and Flavia, a baby now five months old); he announces that he would like to eat, too. Simone tells his aunty he doesn't want to eat any more, but she tries hard to distract him from the book and get him to eat his apple. Father tells him to finish and he eats pieces of apple while looking at the book or out of the window, or at his father or sister. Alfredo asks him for a piece of apple, emphasizing "only a small piece". Simone gives him a piece that has already been chewed. Alfredo does not want it and Simone seems unwilling to give him another; finally they agree, and Alfredo gets a whole slice. "Is it sweet or sour?", he asks, and Simone answers that it is nice. "Why don't you eat it with the peel on?", asks Alfredo. Mother replies that they are given it peeled at the nursery school.

Then the father takes the baby and Simone asks him to "read the story"; then he asks his aunt. Alfedo offers, and prepares to read it, but aunt Augusta interrupts and tells him Simone is very fussy—he wants to see all the pictures in the book. Meanwhile, the adults have a discussion about how the stories should be told. I learn that when Simone had listened to some stories on tape, he had been frightened on hearing the voice of the ogre.

Simone stands up and asks his aunt for a drink. "Let's go to Brema", Alfredo suggests. "To Crema", Simone quickly corrects him. Augusta tells Alfredo that Simone is "terrible", and the child points to his mother. "I'd like to spank him", Alfredo exclaims, and again Simone points to his mother. I ask Simone, "Who is cleverer, Alfredo or your daddy?" "Daddy", he replies. Then he goes to fetch one of his small cars to give to Diego. Aunty tells me that the other day he gave one of Francesca's toys to Flavia. Simone wants to give a car to Diego because Diego does not have any, and he counts the cars on his fingers—ten in all. "You're rich", says Alfredo. "Do they run on petrol or on diesel?" "No," says the child, "they go on wheels."

Mr P wants his dinner, and asks who has dropped the potatoes on the floor. "I've eaten my apple, you know", says Simone to me. Then he goes into the sitting room with his mother and starts complaining because there are no cartoons on television. "We need something to read." Alfredo asks why Simone had his meal so early; mother says it was because he usually eats at 11.30 at the nursery school.

| The child's struggle to maintain his integrity |

MH: This again sounds a somewhat dissatisfying and frustrating session for Simone. Simone himself is a bit irritable and dissatisfied. Alfredo somewhat usurps the conversation, does he? He does then say to his aunty that he doesn't want to eat any more.

RN: He ate well, sitting beside his father, until the friend came, and asked for a piece of apple; after that he didn't want to eat any more.

MH: Not only does he ask for a piece of the apple, he asks whether it is sweet or sour; he seems to be talking to Simone in the way that grown-ups sometimes do, interrupting his relationship with his daddy. Simone then asks the aunt to go on with the story, but again Alfredo puts himself forward and says "*I'll* read it to you!" Then we have this discussion among the grown-ups as to how the story should be read—and the story gets lost. But we hear that when Simone listens to a story on tape, he is frightened of the voices. Then he gets difficult and Alfredo offers to spank him. Alfredo does seem to be a thoroughly disruptive influence—he wants Simone to pay attention to him, and when he doesn't respond he gets cross with him; then Simone becomes difficult.

To go back to the beginning . . . I was wondering about the present that you gave him, which he asks his mummy to show him how to play. Then his father comes in and starts joking with him, and he seems quite pleased to become involved with his father and not to have to learn how to play this new game at that moment. His father coming in, and talking to him in a natural way as his son, relieves him of the necessity to become a "big boy" and play games like daddy. Then he eats his meal harmoniously while his father talks to him, until Alfredo comes in with his intrusive comments.

RN: That was why I asked the question who is better—Alfredo or Daddy.

MH: Yes, your feeling was that Alfredo had come in and pushed Daddy out.

Comment: He gives the little car to Alfredo's son Diego, almost as if to say—"Take it and go!"

MH: It is almost as if he were saying, "I've got plenty of cars; I can give one to your little boy—I don't need you." I would think in this observation, Alfredo becomes the central problem, by *talking to Simone like a grown-up thinks little boys need to be talked to.* Simone reacts to this, when he gives the car, as if to say "Your little boy needs attention more than I do; *I've got ten cars*—I've got all these people here to pay attention to me, and I don't need you." Alfredo is behaving a bit like a school inspector, asking why he is having his dinner early, rather than with the rest of them.

RN: He is a school inspector!

MH: In real life as well! But Simone does put him in his place; when Alfredo asks if his cars run on petrol or diesel, he says "No—wheels!" I suppose that also explains how the grown-ups get into this discussion about how you ought to tell a story—Alfredo no doubt has ideas about how you ought to tell stories to children. Maybe Romana can tell us whether there is a general problem of Simone being a child who is surrounded by so many adults that he suffers from having *too many instructions* as to how he should grow up. His mother doesn't instruct him, nor does his father much; but the aunty seems to, now. It seems to me that when he was a baby, she petted him; but now she is carrying Francesca around—she seems to be her pet now, and Simone is the recipient of instructions on how to do things properly.

Good children eat their food—he says, "You know I've eaten my apple". Had Simone dropped the potatoes or not? ("Yes.") He had, but he'd eaten his apple.

Notes

1. Bergamasque dialect: "oh dear . . . this one".
2. Used to make a loud noise at carnival time in Italy
3. In Italian also, *lonza* is technical, not childish, vocabulary.
4. *Hamlet*, I, v: 196.
5. In Italy children start school at six years, so the nursery school will have children up to five years old.

CHAPTER FOUR

A three-year-old uses the gang as container[1]

T his case is of particular interest since it provides an opportunity to observe the containing function of the gang in a
child as young as three years of age. It demonstrates the
difference between the defensive qualities of the gang as "second
skin" and somatic symptoms. In the fourth session, the parents'
unfulfilled childhood becomes apparent.

Introduction and summary of first two observations[2]

When talking to Mrs Harris about young-child observation, I
explained the difficulties that arose as a result of my work not giving
me the opportunity to often visit nursery schools. Then it occurred
to me that I might be able to observe a young child who was recov-
ering from a physical illness in the paediatric department of the
hospital where I worked as a consultant, and where parents are
allowed to stay with their children. Mrs Harris said this was a good
idea, and I then made inquiries about the 2–3 year old children who
were in hospital. I excluded one who was in the isolation ward with
an infectious illness because I wished to make the first observation

in a room with other children present; and I chose Angelo D because his home was near the hospital. As I walked with my colleague down the corridor towards the day-room to find his mother, my colleague called to her and she came out. She was young, pretty, and sensitive in expression. While I was explaining what I wished to do, a small child emerged from the day-room and came up to her; I realized this was Angelo, a well-coordinated, generally fine-featured child, though with a slightly broadened mouth and nose. His olive complexion and light chestnut silky hair enhance his deep dark eyes. He was three years and two months old.

Later (on my first visit to their house) his mother told me that Angelo had not been a planned baby; his parents decided to marry after the mother found herself pregnant. She assured me she had never considered abortion and had subsequently welcomed the pregnancy. He had been born at term and happily breastfed until five months, and was a "very good" baby until eight months old. She had been helped in looking after the baby by her sister-in-law, who was very much older than her husband, and played the part of a mother towards both of them. The real mother-in-law also lives on the ground floor of the same farmhouse. I also met Angelo's father on that visit. He was a pleasant young man, but seemed rather less intelligent and sensitive than his wife. He butted into the conversation freely and told me the history of his family, who were farmers; he is proud of still living on the farm where he was born, and where his grandparents used to live. He brought his wedding photograph album to show me some members of his family, in particular the two foster brothers his mother had breastfed. The mother then showed me Angelo's photo album. At age eight months, she said, when cutting his first tooth, he had started to become disturbed and to demand more attention from his mother. She said many times that she couldn't cuddle her child enough because she had a lot of knitting to do. There were no signs of sleep or feeding problems, but from the age of one year he started to have frequent colds. From age two he always had a runny nose. Nothing stopped it, not even a series of thermal inhalations that were recommended by a doctor and tried in the summer, so they were advised to admit the child to hospital. He stayed for five days at first, then returned home, but had to be readmitted for a further five days owing to a febrile convulsion.

The mother said Angelo had recovered from his bronchitis, but there were problems about returning to nursery school. On the morning of the second day back she had had to tell a pack of lies to convince him to go, and once there, she hid and ran away, whereas before she had said goodbye to him openly. The child had numerous episodes of diarrhoea, so after a day or two the nursery teachers advised that he should stay at home. Now he said he did not wish to go back to nursery, and yesterday told his grandmother he would never go back. (Later I learned that Angelo never called his mother when he needed to do a pooh.)

Angelo had been staying the night at his aunt's as his parents had been out to dinner. I went with them to collect him, and when his mother asked, the aunt said that Angelo had done poohs twice, and they were of normal consistency. While she was talking to me about these sphincter problems the mother added that Angelo's genitals seemed rather large for his age. She seemed happy enough about that, but meanwhile both she and her husband were worried because they had noted he had some erections. The mother said Angelo seemed spoilt as a result of her being with him day and night in the hospital—the first chance he had had to enjoy such a continuous intimate relationship with her. Now he did not wish to be left with his grandmother even for ten minutes, though she is only on the floor beneath; while before his illness he had stayed much longer than that "very willingly". Soon after coming out of hospital, he had started calling his mother bad names like "stupid" and "idiot", and she seemed very hurt by this and did not understand why he was doing it. In response she often threatened to send him back to hospital, but he did not react and seemed unmoved.

The *first observation session* with Angi (as the boy came to be called) took place in hospital when his date of discharge was already fixed.

Angi is sitting on a bookshelf next to the television being fed by a woman whom I did not know, but who introduces herself as Angi's aunt. The child is watching television with close attention, appears not to see me, and taps his hand on the glass of the television. The other children are sitting at little tables with their mothers, placed in a long line in the room, and I note the empty place that Angi is not occupying. The aunt seems a little nervous about my being there and asks me the reason for the observation, murmuring, "He's fine, he's just very lively." Angi is glued to the television, watching the Pink Panther. The aunt goes to his little table to cut his meat and invites him to come over; instead he leans against the television set, swinging his legs, and opens the panel covering the television controls. He says, "Change the channel", and starts to do so, but the aunt says, "Wait."

I have the feeling the aunt regards the observation as a type of medical check. (Beta Copley has underlined how this kind of apprehension can influence one's observation. On the other hand, she says there is no difference between observing the child in a hospital and in an everyday life situation.) The aunt knows the baby is to be discharged, but clearly does not understand the point of the observation and whether it is related to the discharge. She seems angry with me, supposing that I am an obstacle to the discharge, and inviting me to take a look at the child so that then they will let him leave. Angi concentrates on his own activities, defending himself against the confusing messages that he senses in the situation. Mother is not there; he wants to go home. So he keeps changing the television channels, since that is a situation he can control. However, the aunt insists he must eat, and puts food in his mouth. The aunt says (referring to me), "She will tell you off if you don't eat!" But he remains glued to the television.

He seems to want to know about the world, but not about his present situation, which makes him feel uneasy.

Angi gets a book down from the shelf, an encyclopaedia that he also knows from home, takes it to the table and turns the pages. He has lost interest in the television. "Look at the soldiers!" While turning the pages he points out to his aunt a surgeon in an operating theatre: "There are no children to operate on." Perhaps he is worried about where the children might be—by the fact that he cannot see other children who were with him in the hospital ward. He lingers over a picture of a bull with a lance in its back and says, "What's going on here?", touching the lance with his finger. The aunt, rather embarrassed, says, "Yes, the bullfighters do that so they can win the cup." He looks at more pictures—a dentist at work, then a picture of a child using a torch in the dark, searching for something. The aunt invites him to comment and he says, "It's dark." He is concentrating and alert. There is a vague sense of anxiety; he seems troubled by these three things—the aunt not wishing to explain what happens to the bull, the thing that enters his mouth, and the observer who arouses a feeling of persecution. What is the relation between the teeth, the bullfighter's lance, his mouth, which has been investigated in hospital? He asks, "Are my teeth like swords?", as if asking, what do they want from me? These are diffuse paranoid anxieties compatible with his situation in hospital. The torch in hand is related to the mouth examination he has had—the light and eyes looking into him.

Then a doctor comes in to say Angi can go home now. The aunt telephones Angi's home but no one answers, so she asks Angi which uncle they should phone to tell the news. He says promptly "Uncle Agostino." The ward sister asks loudly from her telephone at the end of the corridor, "D . . . who is D?", and he runs quickly towards her, saying "Mummy, Aunty, who is it?" It is his mother on the phone and he seizes the phone before his aunt and speaks: "Do you know I'm coming home?" Both Angi and his aunt are in the corridor now, and a nurse accidentally knocks him to the ground with the food-trolley. He seems to have banged his head rather badly. The nurse is very sorry; he gets up again, and does not cry or complain.

In the *second observation*, which took place a week later, at home, Angi was sitting with an middle-aged man called Sapelli, a great friend of his whom he likes a lot. He showed him a book from the same encyclopaedia series that was in the hospital day-room, and insisted on it being read to him at the same time as eagerly eating the meatballs his mother had prepared for him. It was evident that this time he wanted Sapelli to tell the story, and did not wish to recount his own version as he had done in hospital, when he related it to his own experience.

The gang and circularity of time

Third observation of Angi, age three years, two and a half months

RN (*reads*): My appointment was for ten, but I arrived at a quarter past and saw Angi's mother outside in the road, apparently waiting for me. She greets me warmly and we go into the farmhouse's courtyard. She says she must go to collect the child from her sister-in-law's as he is playing with his cousins. I say she may leave Angi there and ask if it would be possible to me to go and observe him at his cousins'. She accepts my suggestion immediately. On the way she tells me that Angi has been unwell again, and had a lot of diarrhoea during the past week. At nursery school they advised keeping him at home. Mrs D had her son's faeces analysed because she feared he might have contracted salmonella while in hospital from the child in the bed next to his. (I had the impression they thought I would know all about all the patients.) She also hold me that Angi recognizes me now. She described me to him as "a friend who comes for my work" and he replied, "A friend of yours, yes, but not one who comes for your work." She said, "You see, he obviously knows the ladies who come here for my knitting."

We go into the in-laws' kitchen, which is on the ground floor, opening into the courtyard. Angi, together with his two cousins aged five and eleven, is sitting by the large television, which is on. The five-year-old has the same name, Angelo, so they are known as "little Angelo" and "big Angelo". Mrs D tells me that the two Angelos quarrel incessantly, but her son is always with his cousins none the less. Big Angelo is saying, "You mustn't look!" and Angi replies, "You mustn't put out your tongue. Do you see? Move over!" On the television screen there are aeroplanes flying and Angi exclaims, "It's a monster with a beak, it's a space ship!" "Shut up!" retorts big Angelo. The two little children are sitting side by side half a metre from the television, and Franco, the eleven-year-old, is sitting next to them, modelling a small candle in plasticine. A robot monster appears on the television and big Angelo wants to change the channel, but Angi says, "No, I want it."

I am sitting at the kitchen table with Angi's mother, and her sister-in-law is standing up, busy with the cooking. Mrs D talks to me about her son's stay in hospital. Meanwhile, big Angelo picks up a box and Angi says, "That's the doctor's!", then, leaving the television, he follows his cousin towards the sofa at the other side of the room. Mrs D tells me the children like to play doctors; yesterday they played at operating on a small doll. Big Angelo wants his cousin to wear the oxygen mask and Angi goes along with this to a degree. "I am going to give you an injection", Angelo tells his cousin, and the latter repeats his words, saying that he will give *him* an injection, then turns and points to the television which is behind them. Franco goes up to the two younger children and hands a wire to his cousin, who is standing by the wall; Angi is holding a toy electrocardiograph. Franco is cross because Angi should have placed the wire under his clothes but he does not want to do so. At the same time Angi turns to his mother and says ,"Don't look." Mother tells me he has been behaving in this peremptory way lately: yesterday at the dinner table she was discussing something with her husband and Angi interrupted, saying, "Mummy, daddy, eat, and don't argue!" She says he has been having problems urinating; he has not been passing enough wee. The aunt says that in winter one drinks less in any case.

The three children go out into the courtyard and run around. They are called back but take no notice. I go out and see them sitting at a table in the yard. The two younger children observe Franco with admiration as he focuses the sun's rays through a lens on to a piece of toilet tissue. Then Angi follows big Angelo into a storeroom facing the house, where the toys are kept. Big Angelo hits some big cardboard boxes on a shelf with a stick. They all come out again and Franco puts his finger under the lens to test the sun's heat, then removes it sharply, saying he is burnt. Franco goes back into the storeroom and writes "Death to the little one" on a big box. He says to his cousin, "You must die", and that they will take him out and burn him up with the sun. Meanwhile, Mrs D asks Angi if he wants to do a wee, and her sister-in-law remarks that she is "getting obsessed with the wee-wee business". However, Mrs D tells me that yesterday the child called her when he wanted to do it. Franco is still focusing the sun's rays on to his finger and on to the piece of toilet paper, which, however, does not catch fire.

Angi's aunt calls us into the kitchen saying that coffee is ready. While we are having coffee, she talks to me about Franco and how he loves gadgets (like the lens) but hates school; this morning as a punishment his father did not take him fishing. Now the children, still in the yard, are playing with a tortoise. Angi's mother tells me he is afraid of it— he is even afraid of flies. Then, since the kitchen door is open, I can see that Angi is holding his younger cousin's hand and they go into the storeroom. Soon afterwards the two of them come into the kitchen and ask for some crayons. Mrs D gives them a pencil case and they go back to the storeroom with it, where Franco fixes a coloured pencil on to a stick and uses it to draw on some cardboard boxes, commenting on his designs as he does so. Angi seems fascinated by his younger cousin when he takes hold of the stick and writes on the boxes. Then he takes the stick himself and tries to write, saying, "This is a . . ." Big Angelo cries, "Leave it alone!" Franco draws on the boxes saying, "This is the sun with all its rays, here is the little planet, we go in the space ship . . ." The two little cousins observe Franco with wonder, and he continues, "We shall put the moon here and the games here." Then he says he has finished, and pokes the crayon into the box. "Look Angelo, that's good, it's stuck! Now we can kill our enemy or shut his mouth." He turns towards his cousin and covers his mouth with a piece of ribbon, which he ties at the back of his head. Angi objects, saying, "No, you idiot!", and Franco retorts, "You're the idiot!"

Out in the courtyard again, Franco tries to frighten his cousin with the tortoise. Angi's aunt comes to the rescue and encourages him to touch its shell, saying, "You see, it's like the lady's shoe", and she points to my foot. Mrs D explains that her son is afraid of the cat, too. Meanwhile, she has noticed a bee flying between his legs and she says he will also be afraid of the bee. As soon as Angi sees it, he covers his ears with both hands and runs towards his cousins, a few yards away, and cries, "There's a bee!" Then big Angelo goes into the kitchen, having quarrelled with his brother. Franco is showing Angi the lens. "You shit!", Angelo calls out from the kitchen. "Screecher!" (*pigoloide*) retorts Franco. Mrs D says, ironically, "That's right, teach him some new things—some nasty words like *stronzo pigo*—he only knows a few so far!" Franco asks his cousin, "Do you want to go for a ride on the mountain-bike?"

We are still standing in the yard and Mrs D recounts to me how her son was very healthy until he was nine months old; he used to eat and sleep. When she returned from hospital a few days after his birth, he had four feeds daily, and was breastfed until five months old and after that used to have a homemade soup (yes): "He never had any processed foods." Now I can see Franco riding on his cross-bike round the courtyard, followed by his younger brother on his bike; Angi goes after them on foot. Hastily, Mrs D goes into the garage and brings out her son's little bike; now all three children are riding their respective cycles. Franco collides with his little cousin who, however, does not cry or fall down; he cycles fast on his bike with its stabilizers. Then his foot gets entangled in the chain; he seems to have twisted his foot badly, but his mother sets him free. Franco stops and says, "Come, Eagle Number 2, let's wait for Little Eagle!" Angi calls out, "Wait for me, I'm coming too!" and resumes riding very fast. I ask Mrs D if he knows how to use the brake and she replies that he does not and is very reckless, but he is good at using his toes to stop (and a little later I see this in action).

While Angi is going round on his bike, his mother explains that he can also use his fists; in fact he can defend himself pretty well against the attacks of his cousins. I ask her if there are other children living round the courtyard, and she points out a flat in the middle of the first storey where there is a two-and-a-half-year-old girl whose mother always keeps her indoors, never letting her go out to play with other children. Mrs D says this woman suffers from psychological problems and used to beat her baby until she was a year old, then, fortunately, she stopped. She had tried for six years to have a child, but when eventually her child was born she became very aggressive towards her.

We find the three children with their bicycles in the garage that belongs to Franco's father. Franco pretends to be the garage attendant and checks the petrol and tyres of the three vehicles. They are standing in line: Franco's bike first, then Angelo holding his bike, then Angi at the rear. Mrs D laughs to see that her son has taken his place in the queue.

Big Angelo wants to start off but his brother exclaims, "You can't—I have to check everything", and adds that he will give the signal when all is ready. Then he calls, "Off for big Angelo, off for little Angelo—oh no, off for Eagle Number 2, off for Little Eagle, turn on the engines . . ." While Franco is getting on to his bike the chain slips down and he is obliged to turn the bike over in order to fit the chain back in place. Angi's mother remarks that now Franco is bound to get his hands dirty. Straight away the two Angelos cluster round Franco to watch the procedure. I go to say goodbye to the three children and Angi gives me an interested, almost cordial response.

Supervision with Martha Harris and Donald Meltzer

MH: [asks why and when Angelo had been in hospital and is told there were two periods, each of five days, the second owing to a febrile convulsion].

DM: Has he ever been toilet trained, or has he always soiled himself?

RN: I don't know, I did not ask; but I think so.

MH: Maybe we should have the observation, then we can put it together.

> Contamination anxieties

DM: It sounds as if he discovered how he could stay away from school by dirtying his pants; all you have to do is to get ill then you can stay in hospital with your mother. How that makes his mother a "stupid idiot" I'm not sure, but I suspect it has something to do with feeling he is cleverer than she is. His toughness and assertiveness comes from a culture where you gain control of your mother and then treat her like dirt. But it seems to include his father as well.

MH: Yes, you have to be in with the big boys. The little eagle is just dying to become Big Eagle.

Comment: It is interesting to see how when the bees fly between Angi's legs he covers his ears.

DM: Then his name-calling—*aquilino* and *api*—it is as if the bees and the pieces of faeces were all things that go into your ears. The bees have something to do with these powerful dirty words. Like this beautiful thing that can pierce the box and kill the enemy.

MH: Then, when he gets very anxious, he becomes incontinent, as if he can't hold himself together and his faeces pour out; and he partly deals with his anxiety by projecting himself on to or linking up with these big boys, and doing as they do.

DM: Yes, in the gang all fear goes away; they become dangerous and everybody is frightened of *them*.

MH: As if his little bicycle is the precursor to one of those great "vroom vroom vroom" *motorinos* that the adolescents have.

DM: So when he gets his foot caught in the chain it doesn't hurt! It doesn't hurt because he is not frightened—if he were frightened, it would hurt. It shows you how the gang is counterphobic.

Comment: If these things come from the gang it is all right, but flies and bees terrify him.

DM: And he is very proud of his membership of the gang. What a competent little mechanic he is!

RN: It's Franco—the mechanic.

DM: Oh, that was Franco!

MH: They are all watching Franco, all learning from him.

RN: There is an aspect of his illness that struck me—he was diagnosed with asthmatic bronchitis. It is true that his nose was always running—perhaps this was the same problem as his faecal incontinence. However, at nursery school his illness changed into asthmatic bronchitis.

DM: Let us tell you about this one-year-old child we were hearing about in Bologna—a one-year-old going to nursery school. When his mother brought him to school he cried and clung to her, but when his father brought him he ran around with the other children, ordering them about, pulling their hair, and so on. So this split between the baby and the little phallic boy can start very early, particularly if it is reinforced by the father on the one hand, by the mother's admiration for these phallic qualities, by big brothers or cousins around. You see this split in the way Angelo clings to his mother, and treats her with contempt.

MH: And this is a beautiful child, his mother's joy, and he has both her and her sister-in-law in attendance on him.

RN: However, I've noticed it is strange how the mother is distant from the child; she is brusque with him and does not have an emotional, tender contact with him.

DM: There is probably the same split in *her*, between her relationship to him as a baby, and her relationship to him as this tough guy.

RN: She told me she wasn't able to cuddle him much because she was so busy with her work, and besides he had been so good until he was eight months old.

DM: Too good.

MH: It does look as if he may have had the sister-in-law also to perform services for him—picking up something when he dropped it.

RN: All the same, the mother was interested in him, and concerned about him; she did not have much affectionate contact, but she was interested—that's my impression.

MH: She observes things about him that are rather important: when he was one year old he got his first tooth and then became very nervous. The tooth cutting through was experienced by him as something really persecuting. Then he had frequent colds. She seems to feel rather badly about being so preoccupied with her knitting that she didn't cuddle him. It looks as if the diarrhoea, the bronchitis, together with his fears—because he is a cowardly little boy, by the sound of things—are all linked with his difficulty in holding his emotions and expressing them in some more individual way, as if the mother herself had never been very close to him emotionally.

> The difference between phobias and paranoid anxieties

DM: I wouldn't say "cowardly" is right, in the sense that this isn't a child who is easily intimidated and likely to knuckle under to bullying, but rather that his infantile anxieties have just been split, and split off pretty early—which is why they manifest themselves in psychosomatic things rather than in well-structured phobias. His fear of flies is not so likely to be a phobia, in the sense of having a symbolic basis, as it is to be a paranoid anxiety related to primitive fears of contamination and penetration—as in his ears. They may be loosely called phobias, but they don't really have that symbolic structure.

MH: The mother was overjoyed to have him, apparently, and breastfed him for five months. I am wondering whether he was weaned in just a week, as some paediatricians recommend, and whether the breast was his main physical contact with his mother, in which case it would be pretty traumatic. Weaning isn't usually so traumatic when there are other close ways of relating to a mother, who holds and talks to the baby. She was preoccupied with her knitting, and she herself may have felt cut off from him in some important respect.

RN: But I think that the mother, working at home, was not obliged to be far from the child.

DM: On the other hand, she is not an unobservant woman. But she probably has no way of thinking about it—she admires it, or it frightens or worries her, but she has no framework for thinking about it. One doesn't imagine her breastfeeding him while watching television; she seems to have enjoyed it; but probably she just fed him, they both enjoyed it, and that was that. It was probably quite a strong erotic love affair that just came to an end.

RN: His attitude to his mother is rather deprecating—she is just a woman.

MH: We haven't seen the parents together, but the father doesn't look as though he obviously bosses his wife around.

DM: He is less sensitive than the mother.

RN: The mother is more intelligent, more sensitive; and the child resembles her in physiognomy.

DM: But he sounds a gentle fellow. It doesn't sound as if the boy is modelled on his father. There is something very shrewd, observant, in him. And he is no slave to the gang—he lets them play their games with him up to a point, and then he says no. Even Franco quite respects him.

MH: I take that. He is not really cowardly at all. I was feeling prejudiced because he called his mother stupid!

DM: Little boys are like that. I know all about them!

RN: One day at nursery he left his towel at home, but he refused to dry his hands with his friend's towel.

DM: That is the contamination anxiety.

RN: And then he has this continuous motor activity. When he sits at table, he is always moving his body and legs. Not only during the first observation in hospital, but also at home.

DM: Shadow boxing, karate . . .

Constant movement, second skin, and circularity of time

MH: It looks as if his constant movement on the bike has some-thing of the second skin phenomenon described by Mrs Bick. He has to be always on the go to keep himself together. If he kept still he could be invaded by these unmanageable anxieties.

DM: It is the kind of restlessness that, if he is alone, he has to *pretend* to be with the gang. Because the moment he is really alone, then he will be invaded by these anxieties, this loneliness.

MH: The gang, I was just thinking, is a rather primitive gang, a kind of gipsy gang—always keep on the move so your enemies don't get you.

DM: It is very important to have a vehicle—preferably a noisy and smelly one.

MH: He finds it difficult to really attend to any one thing—only with television does he seem to get a bit absorbed. He has to split his attention all the time.

DM: Because of this *perpetua mobile*. Children in therapy play the most endless, endless games: football, cowboys and Indians . . . that have no beginning and no end but just go round and round in circles. Time is absolutely circular.

RN: Is this form of containment and circularity of time connected with the "second skin"?

DM: I think the circular time has more to do with going in and out of projective identification. I think the second skin is a more meaningless relationship to the world. These games, if you watch them carefully, are all about going into the cave and out of the cave, into the house and out of the house, into jail and out of jail. This in-and-out is projective identification. In two-dimensionality time really hardly exists; it just isn't a dimension. Things are much more superficial and meaningless. There is hardly any story at all—it is just imitation of surface conformity. The second-skin muscularity is in people who do weight-lifting, body-building, things of that sort. Their muscle-tone makes them feel held.

RN: And in this child?

DM: He is intelligent, shrewd, and with the potential to take an interest in something and be pulled out of the gang by his intelli-gence and capabilities.

RN: So how would you interpret his muscular activity?

DM: It is part of the continual phantasy of being *in the* gang and not isolated, by himself. It is to do with the narcissistic organization of the gang and its endless activity of killing and escaping its enemies.

MH: I was just wondering about the diarrhoea, suggesting some kind of collapse of internal holding-together.

DM: I would have thought his diarrhoea was much more a psychosomatic expression of his anxieties about contamination, being penetrated by bad stuff.

The parents' unfulfilled childhood

Fourth observation of Angi, age three years, five months

RN (*reads*): I go to Angi's house on Christmas Eve at about 11.15 in the morning. I ring the bell at the little gate down below, then go up to the flat. His mother is in the hall, and she says, "He's hiding, he's hiding." I go into the sitting-room and there the boy's grandmother tells me the same thing; she goes into the hall saying, "Angi's not here any more, what shall I do?", and a moment later he comes in, with a runny nose, looking very smart in long trousers held by braces over a woollen shirt. He has a pair of gym shoes on his feet. I give him my present: a car transporter with a movable tailgate that can be lowered, and a red snowplough that can go up on the vehicle. Angi opens the parcel and seems very happy. "It's a lorry and a digger", he tells his mother, and she offers to help him with it. Angi, kneeling on the carpet, exclaims, "It comes off, too; this one goes up . . ." and he makes the snowplough ride up on the truck, then makes this run across the floor. Mrs D confides to me that, unfortunately, Angi is again not feeling very well and has had a fluey cold for the past two days. Angi is stretched out on the floor, resting on his side and playing with the truck, saying, "Brr . . . brr . . . grr . . . grr." The mother asks him, "Show your pictures to Romana", and the child brings me a drawing and points out the Christmas tree, the Madonna, the sun, and baby Jesus; "And here," he continues, "it says Angelo D." Then he resumes playing with the truck and says, "It goes along the road like this . . . then the digger goes up", and he makes the snowplough go up on the truck and closes it inside with the tailgate, saying, "Meh . . . meh . . . neh." He had previously taken the little bucket off the back end of the snowplough and left it on the sofa.

Mrs D takes me to see the paper construction her son had made with other children (yes) at nursery school, and Angelo points to the bottom of it and says, "I've drawn on here." Then he turns towards the box that contained the transporter and says to his mother, "Next time she comes she'll buy me lots of lorries—look how many there are", and he shows her the picture on the box of many motor cars and a child playing with them. He puts the truck near the sofa, then on the small table, then on the floor. "It goes up here", he says. "What goes up?", the mother asks. "The sand", he replies, and makes the snowplough go up and down the truck. Then he raises and lowers the tailgate. "I want *mem*", he says to her, then goes to the sofa and says, "You can call it water" (yes, he calls water *"mem"*). "And you call it water", his mother exclaims. He looks at the box that contained the toy and says it is violet. "Well done", says his mother. "Here it says Angelo", continues the child. "Who told Romana about it?", mother asks. "Giuseppe", he replies, and then "Daddy." "You fibber," she says, "who gave it to you?" "Daddy gave it to me for a present", the boy answers. Mrs D corrects him, saying, "My friend gave it." Angi, kneeling, looks up at his mother and comments on the colours. "What's this?", asks mother; *"Ro-sa* (pink)", he replies. "You fibber—come on, you know it quite well, what is it?"

Somebody knocks at the door, and mother and child both run to see who it is. Father comes in carrying a plastic bag and immediately asks his son if he has a temperature. He sees the new toys and asks his son who gave them to him. "Romana", the child answers, and jumps about. Angi sticks close to his father and seems totally absorbed by him. Then, looking at the truck, Angi tells his father, "The sand is going up; I pick it up and put it on the truck . . . I put all the plasticine on it, close it and then it goes." (Probably he is referring to the holes in the car ramp.) Mr D sits down on the sofa and asks if the digger is going up. Angi shows him the vehicle and puts it on his father's knees. "You try", he asks. Daddy remarks that it is quite heavy and that it is not a digger but a snowplough. Angi puts the vehicle on the sofa and goes into his father's arms. Mother comes in from the kitchen and says, "Show him the car-track—what a lot of toys there are!" Angi stoops down under the sofa where his father is sitting and with some trouble pulls out a track of the sort that will support two electrically-operated cars. Some pieces of the track come off and mother says, "It's fallen to bits." She says that the musical instruments have arrived, too, "and heaven knows what will happen when he starts playing those". "I'm strong," Angi asserts, "and then you get frightened." Then father starts to put the track together again. The child says it won't "go in"; mother reassures him that it will, and the child points to the places where it fits together saying, "here" and "here". When it is done, father says, "I'm going to get the long lead", and Angi asks, "What?", and puts the two cars on the track. When his father returns he asks Angi three times if he has been a good boy at Granny's. "Yes", the child finally answers after the third time, then after a pause he adds, "I've been naughty too." Then Angi takes the finishing post for the track and asks, "How do you fix it?" "Hey, move a bit", he tells his father as he puts the cars on the track again. "You play too, daddy—I'm the blue one." He tries to start the car by pressing the button, but it does not work. Mother intervenes saying it should be going in the other direction, and the child changes it, but the cars do not run at all. Mr D explains it does not work because the track is on the carpet. So the track is placed on the floor, mother dusts the cars, and they start to move. "Angi's is going fast—come on, press!", calls mother. The boy complains his car is not working and the two cars collide. "Accident!", cries mother. The child repeats the word, and puts the car on the track again. However, he puts it facing the wrong way so his mother puts it back properly. "Come on daddy", she urges, and then, "Come on, Angi." The child watches the game very carefully, with his tongue between his lips. "Mine is going", he says, but then it collides with his father's. Mother keeps up a commentary on the game; now Angi's car is going too fast and gets stuck at the bend; he puts it back in place and it restarts. Now the blue car blocks father's car and the latter pushes the former off the track; the child gets angry with his father, and mother says he always wants to win when he plays with his cousins. Angi's car comes off the track again and he folds his arms crossly and starts moaning at his father. "Mine has come off too", his father points out. Then the child's car goes on the wrong side and blocks the track for father's car; he laughs, but little by little father's car pushes his one off the track and so he gets angry again, saying, "Oh! (*uffa*)—mine's coming off!" When the child's car is completely off the track he cries, "I don't want to play any more— I'm tired." Lying on the floor, he smiles and then coughs, then calls again, "Oh, look here", and takes hold of the box containing the electric lead. Mother scolds him, saying, "Don't—it's still connected."

Angi then asks his father to go and get him his helicopter, saying, "I can't get it." Mrs D urges her son to fetch it himself, but he replies that daddy told him not to (which was not true—meanwhile, his father had gone out). Mother says, "You go", and they all go out of the room. I hear mother saying that Big Jim is in the car. As they walk back towards the sitting room I hear Mrs D talking to her husband about Angi's cold, or flu. She turns to me and says that it is a great pity, since he has just got over his asthma. Mr D carries in a very large helicopter, and his wife suggests he goes and fetches Big Jim. She tells me Angi always wants to take his best toys to nursery school, but when he is in the car he thinks it over and decides to leave them, "in case the other children break them". "He is quite happy to go to nursery school again now", says mother. Father is back; he winds up a big train and lets it run over the floor, emitting whistles and flashing coloured lights. It is heading towards Angi, who is standing on the carpet. It seems to me that he moves away, quite suddenly, a little frightened, as if he had just seen a snake. He stands with his hands in his pockets, watching his father, who is getting Big Jim ready to put in the helicopter, raising the front window and placing the large toy inside.

Mother comes in carrying Big Jim's motorbike and a large toy tank. She encourages her son to "shoot" with the tank. He gives a few shots but leaves it almost immediately and begins to play with the motorbike. "This is the motorbike", he says. Then Mrs D asks her husband to "go and fetch the boot". (Big Jim had indeed only one boot on.) "Where are you going, daddy?", asks Angi. "To get his other shoe", replies his father. Meanwhile, mother makes the tank start moving on its own, and Angi, who is kneeling down, says it "won't go any further". Mr D comes in and says he cannot find the boot. "He dropped it on the way", mother remarks. Mr D sits down on the sofa and tries to make the tank move. Angi puts Big Jim on his motorbike and, moving the tank away, puts the bike next to the helicopter. He takes a gun in one hand and aims it at Big Jim, who he is holding in the other hand. Then he puts the gun down by the bike and helicopter. He puts Big Jim on the tank and then near the other toys, and puts the train with them also. He starts the train and places Big Jim astride the top of it. Mother laughs and so does her son, as he watches the train carrying the Superman around. Angi overtakes the train, removes Big Jim, switches off the train, and places it alongside the other toys. He is standing up holding Big Jim, then he puts the doll on the tank while his father picks up the snowplough and puts it on the sofa. "Let's find the digger", says Angi, putting Big Jim on the tank. He also puts the car transporter with the line of toys, holding the snowplough in one hand. The child stays near his father, who comments on the fact that Big Jim's calves are turned round the wrong way, and he also wonders what happened to the other boot. "It must be lost", says Angi; then, referring to Big Jim's legs, explains to his mother that "I did it". "What did you do?", she asks. She goes back into the kitchen, and father and son discuss the lost boot.

Father suggests they dress Big Jim in his trousers, "otherwise you can see his pants"; but Angi wants to undress Big Jim completely. "You'll break him", says his father, meanwhile touching Angi's forehead to see if he is hot. Mrs D intervenes, saying, "That's not how you undress him—lift the clothes and then pull", and she undresses the doll speedily while her husband and son look on. "All bare", says Angi. "It's cold now", says mother. "It's just like they show it on TV", exclaims the child, making the doll hop, then make swimming movements; then he says, "Now you can change it and get it dressed." "There you are", he says, giving it to his father, who tries to dress it. "Come on", calls Angi. His mother, sitting next to her husband, resolves the problem and says "Do you know, daddy, that Big Jim can use his hands?" "Yes, he does;" says Angi, "he's made them work himself!" Then he talks about the missing shoe and mother says, "It's not a shoe, it's a slipper." "No," retorts the child, "it's a boot." Then Angi gets angry with his mother because she wants to dress Jim beginning with his shirt, while he wants to put on the waistcoat first. "It's true, daddy", says Mrs D to her husband. "Look at daddy", she says to her son. "He's got his shirt underneath—he knows . . . how stubborn you are, can't you see?" Father suggests that perhaps Angi has got it wrong because he is "looking at the colours". "I will put this on him", says the child, putting the shirt on Big Jim: "I can do it". "See, he does understand", says mother, putting on the waistcoat. "Oh dear, the buttons!", Angi calls out. "Look, there aren't any", his mother replies. The child is kneeling near his mother, watching. She carries on dressing the toy, puts on its jacket and asks, "Where is his overcoat?" "No, his jumper", says Angi. But she insists and tries to explain to him: "Look, see how long it is—the shirt comes up to here, the waistcoat up to here, and this is the jacket." But he does not give in. "No," he insists, "it is a jumper." Mother says Big Jim has still not got his boot, and Angi replies quite calmly, "I have lost it."

DM: They play quite nicely really. Was all this for your benefit—a demonstration to you?

RN: On the part of the mother, yes, but not the child.

DM: And I suppose these are quite expensive toys.

RN: Yes, he had them from his entire family—aunts, grandparents; he is much loved, this child, not only by his parents.

> A family phantasy about the male genital

MH: Near the end there, when the father says "you'll break it", and then touches Angelo's forehead to see if he is hot . . . I wonder whether at that moment the father has some excessive concern about whether the whole atmosphere was getting too feverish for the boy. That seemed to follow on the undressing of Big Jim and the talking about the lost boot. It seems very important to all of them that Big Jim lost his boot—his penis—and seems connected with some sort of competitive masturbation feeling. Big Jim's calves can be turned around . . . is this a toy you can put together?

RN: No, the joints can just be turned round, in different positions.

DM: There is a general feeling of maintaining a very excited atmosphere, while at the same time worrying that it will burn out the little boy's circuit. There is a very mechanical concept behind it.

MH: There is very little that's really *maternal* about the mother in this game—the way she joins in. She plays as if she is one of the boys.

RN: Yes, she gives the impression that she is a little intimidated by Angi and his way of behaving. He has a clear predilection for male figures—his uncle Gianni, his father. One time I came in just after his mother had given him a light smack. He was furious and said, "When papa comes you'll see what will happen, I will tell papa!" Then he said to me and his mother, "Go into the kitchen, both of you." Then he changed his mind and told only his mother to go.

MH: He puts his name on the toy that you gave him; then he says it's Giuseppe, and then that Daddy gave it, not you. It is a way of dismissing both you and the mother.

RN: He likes to play jokes on his mother; he often hides himself.

DM: It is part of his concept of masculinity—when women don't behave, you send them to the kitchen. There is certainly an impression that his parents experience this little boy as a really super electronic toy. But there is a danger when his penis lights up that the system is overheating. There is a very strong emphasis on *performance*: on getting this little boy to perform just like a grown-up daddy, but not his penis—that has to wait.

MH: With the toy, he does seem immediately to be preoccupied with how it works, how the back lets down . . . the workings of the toy, like the workings of his bottom and genitals, are really preoccupying him. Big Jim seems to become a focus for the concern of all three with the performance of the genital. I wasn't quite clear who said, first of all, "Big Jim can use his hands—"

RN: The mother said it to the father—

DM: Could you explain a little how the calves of Big Jim's legs can be turned around—does it mean turn around top to bottom, or turn around right to left?

RN: They rotate, but they can bend, too.

DM: There is a certain feeling that when the child gets tired, he is not allowed to stop playing. The toys require to be played with because they cost so much, as it were—that seems to be part of the economic structure of the situation.

MH: They do seem to be invested by both parents with a terrific importance. I was thinking of the little argument at the end about whether it is a shoe, or a slipper, or a boot that Big Jim has lost. Mother says it's a slipper and Angelo says no it's a boot, as if emphasizing the masculinity, as if she were demeaning his genital. Then he gets angry when she begins to dress Big Jim, as if *he* were the one being treated as a little child, being emasculated by these feminine things. He insists that she follow his dictates about the order of getting dressed—what you start with and so on. Then again she has to address him saying, "this is just like daddy", as if to say she is not trying to make him a little girl, she is trying to help him be just like daddy—almost placating him.

> The impact of the culture

DM: I was thinking about the impact of mass media and mass purchasing on family life. Certainly in the United States the way in which the mass media hold up and image the idea of family life and the way in which this is slavishly imitated in terms of the kind of entertainment, the holidays, the toys, the relationships . . . One gets the impression that the economic system that depends so much upon people spending—wasting—their money, so that the money passes around—has a tremendous impact on family life. In the past, of course, family life has been just as enslaved to the culture. But the techniques for achieving cultural accommodation in children were primarily the techniques of discipline—of exacting obedience. These of today are quite different. They are techniques of excitation and stimulation. It seems to me that the techniques of discipline— which were in a certain sense tyrannical—attempted to draw children into projective identification, so that they set up tyrannical systems of their own, controlling the younger children and so on; whereas the methods of today seem to depend much more on the *parents'* projective identification with the children—projecting child parts of themselves into the child and controlling the child from within. In that sense it has much more resemblance to what one is accustomed to see in immigrant families, where the parents remain relatively unassimilated in the culture but project into the children their ambitions regarding education, language, and so on.

RN: I think this could well be a feature of this family. Originally they were a farming family and relatively poor. They live in the old farmhouse belonging to the father, now totally renovated, and their style of living has changed enormously.

DM: What does the father do?

RN: The father is an artisan; the mother works with her knitting.

DM: The general trend is that the immigrant families that push their children on through education tend to produce pseudo-maturity and obsessionality in the children. The kind of thing we are seeing here will produce perpetual adolescence.

> They are all children

MH: It could be that when the parents feel all the attention, all the toys the child is going to have—all the things they didn't have as children—they project their own unfulfilled childhood or adolescence into the child and indulge it through the child. There isn't a parent there.

DM: The idea in the 1960s, particularly in the United States, was that mother and daughter were like sisters, and father and son were *pals*. The ideal was a two-children family—so you had to get the sexes right, otherwise you were in danger of producing two little homosexuals!

> The risk of drug addiction

Q: I was wondering how this connects with the problem of drug-addiction?

MH: I would think it certainly does. It would go with the tendency to try to meet the child's needs before they even have time to feel frustrated—to encourage some quick or easy solution to any kind of problem, boredom, or unhappiness. But I wouldn't be inclined to imagine or prognosticate drug addiction for little Angi; I think he would be more likely to manipulate people through his intelligence and charm—get lots of girls perhaps.

DM: Yes, thinking in terms of culture and its impact on patterns of family life and general impact on character development, you can see that the emphasis here (and it's not even very covert) is on sexual potency—and it's conceived in very mechanical terms. While in a certain sense 007 was an anti-hero, a send-up of the western hero, he was also a new kind of hero in the sense of being somebody who didn't really take anything seriously. It made a joke of it—there was never any real anxiety or real danger. Things just exploded all around him.

Comment: Nursery teachers always complain of the children's incapacity to really pay attention to what is offered.

DM: I think what I'm saying is—given that nobody knows how to rear children—the cultural pattern of bad rearing changes.

MH: That's putting it a bit brutally!

What is a good upbringing?

DM: People who have been well brought up don't know how to do it, but none the less they do it relatively well. It's all based on unconscious identification. What we seem to come up with is the impression that the main factor in good upbringing is interest in the children. That is different from what we thought twenty years ago in psychoanalytic circles, and that was different from what was thought forty years ago.

Learning from the child

MH: I would think that that is, in fact, what does break the mould of identification with not-very-good parents sometimes. The mould can be broken. A mother or parents can look at their child, get interested in their child and *also learn from the child*. They learn what the child is like, think about it, and so have their *own* experience. It does seem to me, in this observation, that both the parents are more interested in the toys and their working, and in getting the child to be happy with them, than they are in what the *meaning* might be of what the child is doing with the toy. They are both so involved, projecting themselves into the game, that they are not able to stand at a little distance in reverie, thinking about how the child is playing.

RN: That is true, and reminds me of what the mother and father told me about their own experience and their own history. But this happened only once, because it was a special occasion at Christmas; they do not usually play like this.

DM: They've been bombarded by merchandise and yielded to it, so they've got to get their money's worth. That's why people go on holiday and have to use the facilities they've paid for. It is also true that this family would seem at this point to represent well the modern ethic of *mastery of the machine*. You master this machine culture by first of all getting enough money to buy the machine, then you learn how to read the instructions so you can operate it properly, and you learn when to trade it in before it breaks down. There is tremendous pressure on the educational system outside the family also—to follow the course of producing children who will be technicians and who will know how to operate this machine culture. We see it in Great Britain at present with the cutting of funds for the humanities and the tremendous encouragement of computer studies, for example. People get a degree in English literature in order to become an accountant.

MH: Well, it's better to get the degree in English literature first rather than not at all.

DM: Every family is caught up in needing to prepare the children to survive in the culture. They can't escape that. So there is tremendous pressure to interest the children in playing with machines. You can see with this little child in this observation his *fatigue*—the feeling of being driven, and not allowed to stop playing. He can't stop playing because these toys are expensive.

> The child's primitive anxieties about the penis

MH: I was wondering about that moment when considerable anxiety comes through—when he moves away suddenly as if he had just seen a snake. It seems to come after the mother has been saying how happy Angelo is to go back to nursery school; he takes his best toys, but then decides not to because the other children will break them. He doesn't appear to notice what his mother is saying, but undoubtedly he is hearing it all. It also follows the moment when the father with the locomotive in his hand goes towards Angelo. I don't know whether the anxiety is to do with daddy with his locomotive-penis going to run him down, or with mother talking about the nursery school and the idea of the other children breaking his toys.

DM: It would seem to me not quite correct to say "as if he had seen a snake". With Angelo, it would be more correct to say "as if he had seen a locomotive out of control"! His dreams are more likely to be with machines out of control than with snakes. He reacts like children who are frightened of dogs because they see them as uncontrolled little machines. A patient of mine found himself suddenly terribly distressed and weeping, during the Christmas holiday—he had a dream that I was sitting in a jump-jet and was about to catapult him into space. There was a book called *The Jet-propelled Couch*! So the form of anxiety changes. But, of course, you are quite right in thinking that it has something to do with his father's penis, fundamentally. It is the symbolism that changes. The alternative culture—the adolescents who want to grow vegetables free from chemicals on their own plot of land—is a rebellion against being controlled internally and is a real hatred of this machine culture.

MH: I'm not sure that I agree with you about this. I think that, basically, to everybody, it may be more frightening to see something that moves and has got life. I think it is to do with the most primitive anxieties that are there already in the mother's womb. Something that actually has a life of its own is potentially more frightening than a machine that can be operated.

DM: I agree about that. But that's at the non-symbolic level. I was talking about the symbolized interpersonal anxieties and how the form of the symbolism changes.

MH: I would think that this little boy has a great deal of anxiety about his penis and about losing it, as when he says it won't go down and fit into the toy cupboard. He may even himself have some anxiety about enlarged genitals and so on.

DM: But where a boy thirty years ago might have gone in for body-building and getting big muscles, he will go in for motorbikes.

Tyranny and collusion

Comment: [on the connection between Angi wearing nappies at night, the bees, and the incontinence]

MH: One would think that this child has got some kind of fear about his basic instinctual impulses, which could be heightened by the sort of flirtation that he gets from his father—like another big boy. There is almost a collusion between him and his father to put mother into a secondary position, and the mother herself even goes along with this. They don't look as if they ever had a real *fight* with one another, in a more open way; Angi has his ways of contemptuously bypassing mother and turning to father, in this boys-together collusion. . . . Because of this collusion between him and his father, it seems that something very tyrannical in this child has never been met head-on and stopped. Any chance of a fight is always diverted; and if a child doesn't come up against something that is *not afraid* of his omnipotence and tyranny, he continues to be a bit frightened of it himself.

This is one of the great problems that everybody has in bringing up children. You don't want to say no to children, to stop their initiative any more than is necessary—you don't want to crush them. On the other hand, you have to sort out when it is not initiative but tyranny, and they need to learn when to stop imposing upon other people. No doubt Angi gets that at the nursery school— you can't have twenty or thirty little tyrants in a class.

DM: I was thinking also that where the child's formation is being directed primarily by stimulating his interest, and where the interests are of *this sort*—playing with mechanical toys—the dependence upon keeping the child in a state of excitation must interfere with the development of control. There are children whose incontinence is of the sort that they are *so busy playing* that before they know it they have soiled themselves.

RN: Last time you spoke about this circular time, where the child is constantly engaged in some activity.

MH: Another problem is that when a child is being constantly entertained in order to keep him in a good mood, he never learns how to cope with being in a *bad mood*. Therefore he has to keep active in order to fend off the depression and anxiety that he does not have a chance of feeling.

RN: [on the mother's difficulty holding and cuddling the child]

DM: We don't know why the incontinence stopped—it stopped about fifteen days ago? ("Yes.") I wouldn't have thought it has much meaning, really. I wouldn't have thought it to be a neurotic symptom. I think it is more likely that it has not achieved any *importance* for him—he is so busy with other things.

MH: I'm not too sure . . . it seems to me that he is a bit preoccupied with it, not just with his penis but with his defecation and what comes out of his bottom—with the sand, and the truck. I was actually wondering whether this playing, with your watching him and paying attention, may have helped him to unconsciously feel that he was working something out in his play about the way that his own bottom and body works, and his fear of losing bits of himself—being incontinent.

DM: I would think that once this child has *noticed* this was a problem, he would set about mastering it, and would do it. What he does seem to be in conflict about is this question of his penis becoming erect, because it does not seem to have been greeted with great delight, although the size of his genitals is pleasing to them. The fact that he came back with an erection and couldn't get it down seems to have aroused a paradoxical reaction in his parents. You might expect him to approach it as a problem of how to control his penis becoming erect, and to discover the techniques of erotic fantasy for making it become erect, and of punitive fantasy for bringing it down—to *find the switch*. These are some of the techniques of sex therapy for men with impotence—with pornographic pictures and so on they are taught how to concentrate their minds so they can simulate potency; and it is quite in keeping with this mechanical age—how to operate your body as a machine. Just like going to the optician—they put one glass in, then another glass in, until you see it clearly. In these therapies they show you one picture after another until they get the one that does it—that's what *turns you on*. It could be a picture of a concentration camp with one of those bulldozers pushing the bodies into a pit—and that would be all right if it was the one that worked. Making the best of small means.

MH (*to chairperson*): You'd better keep us in order—remind us when it's time to switch to the next one!

Notes

1. The following observations were presented during the 1982 programme on "Young Child Observation" on the Tavistock-modelled Psychotherapy Course organized by Professor Lina Generali Clements at the Department of Infant Neuropsychiatry of the University of Milan.

2. The first two sessions on Angelo were supervised by Beta Copley, and subsequent ones by Martha Harris and Donald Meltzer.

CHAPTER FIVE

Play observation in a hospital setting: some diagnostic implications

The work recorded in this chapter was carried out by Martha Harris with doctors from the Institute of Infant Neuropsychiatry at the University of Milan between 1970 and 1973.[1] There are three cases of play observation which were conducted in the hospital by Romana Negri and (in one case) by Laura Musetti; followed by two infant observations which were presented for supervision in the context of the same clinical group. Each of the children in play observation had posed particular problems in terms of diagnostic evaluation.

In psychiatric practice, above all in infant neuropsychiatry, it is quite frequent to encounter symptoms which do not conform unequivocally to any single diagnostic picture but which may belong to quite different and distinct clinical situations. In considering a child's inhibitions, for example, we need to judge whether psychotic or neurotic elements are dominant. The various psychical tests and instrumental examinations used in the traditional clinical approach do not always permit this type of differentiation, so it often happens that the neuropsychiatrist is drawn into abstract theorization, without necessarily realizing it, and so loses sight of the concrete elements that define the meaning of that particular case.

At the Institute it was recognized, therefore, that there was a need to develop observational tools that were more adequate to getting a picture of the child's mental life at a deeper level. This need became more acute the more serious the illness or disability, and the younger the child (therefore less able to communicate). It was for this reason that Mrs Harris was invited to conduct some clinical seminars, as a way of demonstrating how to understand a child's unconscious phantasies, following the methods developed by Esther Bick on the basis of the psychoanalytic practice of Melanie Klein.

Only seven or eight doctors took part in the seminars and each of them reported a case from time to time. We realized that only those directly involved in this type of work were interested in a way that could contribute to the discussion and derive practical benefit from the session. Ultimately, however, the principle of play observation became a recognized part of the overall assessment of a child admitted to the Institute.[2] It was taken into account together with the history, psychical examination, and complete test evaluation—intelligence quotient, projective tests, neurological evaluation, and instrumental examinations such as the EEG (electroencephalogram). The play observation method turned out to be a precious instrument for arriving at a correct clinical diagnosis.

The play observation sessions that follow here concern three girls aged nine, ten, and twelve, respectively. They were in hospital at the Institute owing to significant symptoms. Mrs Harris's supervisions here are of particular interest, since they allowed the psychiatric diagnosis to be modified, in the first two cases, and to be defined more clearly in the third case.

Following these are two infant observation cases, which were supervised in the hospital group and which shed light on the early introjection of the object, the origins of speech, the significance of the baby's hand movements, and of the mother's look.

Play observation—Eleonora: redefining a diagnosis of child psychosis as neurotic anxiety[3]

Eleonora was in hospital at our clinic with a diagnosis of severe mental illness (*psicosi infantile*). Her symptoms are frequent fits of crying, refusing school, refusal to go out alone since "some bad men had hurt her", sleep disorders, gestural repetition of a compulsive character, perception of inner voices heard as "voices inside you, the same as when you think". As a result of the little girl's behaviour during the interview and the observation session following, it was possible to modify the clinical diagnosis as neurotic anxiety (*nevrosi d'ansia*); and the validity of the diagnosis was confirmed by the subsequent course of the disturbance.

Observation of Eleonora, age nine years

> **RN** (*reads*): The little girl accepts the sessions willingly and seriously. She looks worried because she wants to create a good impression and she starts drawing (Figure 1). During the session she does the three drawings here reproduced. At this point I want to underline their different characteristics: with the first one, a fine typical drawing according to predefined school models, Eleonora seems to offer the best image of herself; in the second one, with less accurate and precise strokes, she expresses her worries and troubles more explicitly, and in the last one she reveals her real inner situation.

Figure 1.

She draws with great care and silence on the first sheet. Then she takes the second sheet (Figure 2) and she draws a skyline, mountains, clouds, rain, a small lake. She says she will not draw a little house because it is raining. She will draw two little houses instead.

MH: It is interesting to note that she does not want to draw a house, saying it is raining; while children usually like to draw a house so that when it rains, it is possible to find shelter. The house usually represents the mother who contains. Eleonora, instead, does not seem to consider her mother as a containing figure; if it rains, the mother does not seem able to protect her, to help her with her depression. This situation finds some correspondence in her external situation: when her elder brothers argue furiously, "when the weather is bad at home", she is terrified, and her mother is not able to defend her, she does not offer an adequate shelter.

RN (*continues reading*): At this point the girl says she does not like the mountains, because where she went last year there were a lot of meadows and horses. The horse seems to represent something frightening,

Figure 2.

which makes her anxious. Then she adds, "Now I'll draw a horse, but I am not so good at this, I can't do it", and while saying this she seems to show her difficulty through expressing her worry. Then she draws two human figures: a woman who goes and asks for some salt, because the shops are closed, and a little girl who is going to pick up the washing.

MH: The fact that it is the girl who picks up the washing and the woman who goes and borrows some salt is quite strange because, usually, it is just the opposite. From the case history and from the interview it appears that the little girl hears voices telling her that the mother is not her real mother. Children like playing pretending to be the mother, but here the fancy seems to be lived in a particularly intensive way. She lives being her real mother; while her mother is a woman who is lacking something, who must go and ask for some salt.

RN (*continues reading*): While finishing this drawing, Eleonora tells me that once, in front of her house, a car ran over a woman; nobody helped her except her mother who went out and aided the victim. I realize that it is really Eleonora's mother who is the victim of the "road accident"— the aggressiveness of her father, who struck his wife in Eleonora's presence. The mother, who helps the woman run over by the car, is Eleonora herself, lived here as the helper of the mother run over by the father. So, in this fantasy, Eleonora is no longer the mother of herself but she is the mother of her own mother.

It is interesting to notice that only now, after talking about the accident, does Eleonora pay attention to the doll provided for her, which is on the windowsill of the room. She takes it in her arms and asks me if it moves, as if the doll were alive and could move and she even says that the doll needs a toy—thus projecting the infant part of herself on to the doll. She then selects a toy car.

MH: It is strange that she chooses such a dangerous toy, since it was a car that ran over her mother. Her own aggressive part seems projected into the toy car; her hostility to her mother is projected into her father and experienced as something dangerous (first the horse, then the car), enabling her, through a destructive fancy, to take her place and to become the mother herself.

RN (*continues reading*): At this point, running the car and a small plastic truck on the table, she makes them crash into each other and the damaged car is then towed away by the truck. In the meantime she says that the child is hurt and must be taken to hospital.

MH: Once her aggressive part has crashed into the mother, Eleonora feels ill: she needs to be taken to hospital, and the doll represents the part of herself which is not well—the poor little girl, the victim who must be helped and protected.

> **RN** (*continues reading*): Now Eleonora puts a soft rabbit into the doll's arms, it represents something soft and comfortable, and so she expresses her need of attention, of affection, of the reassuring care of her mother for this little girl who needs help. (When she feels hurt, ill, small, she can give herself a consoling mother.) Then Eleonora, pretending to be a nurse, gives the restored child back to her mother. When the mother expresses worry that the child seems small, the nurse answers, "Don't worry, madam, when it is grown-up it will be bigger than you" (so revealing once more the ambition she has already expressed through the story of the woman asking for salt, to be considered older and more grown-up than her own mother). Then the little girl mimics the siren of an ambulance, and another hurt child arrives, suggesting again the theme of suffering a wound in the infant part of herself. She dandles her doll and says, "Here, darling, now sleep", and she rocks it to sleep. Then she takes a sheet of paper and says she wants to do another drawing (Figure 3). She explains to me that she is a mother in her nightdress with her hair messed up, picking up her child who has awoken her.

MH: This drawing seems to refer to her sleep disorders: the little girl sleeps badly, she suffers from nocturnal agitation and needs to be comforted and reassured by her mother, who must leave the door between her room and Eleonora's open.

What is she afraid of during the night? Why must she be helped by her mother? What troubles her? It may be necessary to go back to the episode of the horse and the car that ran her mother over. The little girl has shown for some months a compulsive repetitition in the form of dusting the chairs, her own shoes, and her mother's bed continually. These actions seem to express a mechanism of denial, of repression of her anxiety about her mother's sexual intercourse, something dirty having to do with her mother in bed. Cleaning the chairs and shoes reveals worry about her faecal attacks on her parents' relationship. She can express it only by enacting something

Figure 3.

that she can't communicate directly. Her wish to clean all the dirt—
her faeces—can be connected to the brown animal she experienced
as dangerous and which must be fenced in.

What seems to be very important is that lamp lit over the child.
She is terrified of finding herself alone in the night, in the dark, with
all her fears. Light is very important for her: it represents the wish
to have light inside herself, but it also takes on a persecutory meaning, because she is afraid of the possibility of throwing light upon
all that frightens and terrifies her.

Eleonora is pathologically depressed because she is frightened,
terrorized by her own bad, faecal, aggressive part, which, projected
outside her, is experienced as terribly persecutory. She cannot go
out into the street because "some bad men want to harm her"; and,
in reality, the father does hit the mother. The "bad men", that represent her faecal, bad part, split and projected out of herself, chase her
to hurt her; she feels pursued by her aggressive, hostile part, and
her anxiety to run away from it is then expressed here in the
session.

The little girl knows that she cannot take out her aggressiveness
on her mother, owing to her fragility and the aggressiveness of her

brothers; so she prefers to live in a fantasy world. Her complete immersion in fantasy expresses her difficulty in communicating with her mother. Eleonora is so frightened by her brothers' quarrels that she believes her own aggressive feelings must be something absolutely dreadful, uncontrollable. Because of this, it seems really useful for the little girl to be able to express her aggression during the psychotherapy sessions and to have some experience of a figure outside herself who is able to contain her attacks, taking her projections without being too damaged by them—instead, interpreting them and helping the child understand the damage caused to her internal objects. Now Eleonora can introject the figure of the therapist and so begin to work through her depressive anxiety.

Play observation—Daniela: redefining a diagnosis of epilepsy as psychosomatic illness

Daniela is a ten-year-old girl, sent to our Institute for having frequent and serious fits that started when she was eight years old. The EEG shows alterations in the central–parietal–temporal regions on the right, with typical epileptic features at the start of the trace. Mrs Harris's supervision of this observation session enabled us to exclude a diagnosis of epilepsy and to move towards one of psychosomatic illness.

History

The little girl's parents are working people: the father is a bricklayer, the mother a housewife. Daniela is the second of three daughters and they live in a farmstead. They seem both fond of her and interested in her problems. It is important to note that all three girls present with the same clinical symptoms as Daniela and are treated with anti-epileptic drugs without any result, the EEGs remaining abnormal. Daniela's mother, while explaining this, says that she should have taken all three daughters to hospital but that she has chose Daniela "because she is the only one who would tolerate being separated from the family". The girl's history also shows the persistence of bedwetting beyond seven years of age, and an episode of extreme drowsiness (semi-consciousness) lasting for many hours that occurred when Daniela was nine years old. On that occasion the little girl, who was at school, started to behave strangely, to answer the teacher's requests at a tangent and to confabulate. After some hours she fell deeply asleep and the next morning, on awakening, complained of headache and could not remember anything that had happened.

The child is very intelligent and there has never been a problem with her school results. The first six or seven days after entering hospital, Daniela kept up a quite authoritarian stance; she tended to be the boss among the others on the ward and to keep them in strict order. Her desire to seek out grown-up attention and to do well became evident. She liked showing she was "grown-up", and was very happy when praised for the "maturity" of her behaviour. The fits persisted, however, with daily episodes, and were not relieved by drugs.

After a week in hospital Daniela started to behave in a disorderly and confused way, wanting to sleep during the day, and remaining awake at night, demanding the doctor on duty; she refused the nurses' requests, lashing out at them, crying, then flopping on the floor. She became particularly touchy and aggressive with the other children and, in some circumstances, she seemed to have hallucinations. Her behaviour was strictly analogous to that of a fourteen-year-old on the ward who was suffering from a serious form of hysterical neurosis and with whom the ward staff were heavily preoccupied. Daniela had established a close but emotionally ambivalent relationship with this girl. The beginning of these serious behavioural problems coincided with the complete cessation of the fits. Still, despite the anti-epileptic drugs, the EEG continued to be abnormal and was no different from that on being admitted to hospital. At this point I came to conduct the observation session.

Observation of Daniela, age ten years

> RN (*reads*): I come to collect Daniela from the day-room. She does not appear to see me and hurries towards the door. I invite her to come with me but she replies that she cannot because the teacher has taken away her belt. Meanwhile, the teacher comes up, followed by another girl who tries to hit Daniela. After asking whether she would be going

with me, the teacher gives back the belt that Daniela had been using to hit other children. Daniela goes with me into the corridor and says in a pained tone that she cannot breathe: "make me breathe", and veers into the ward sister's office, embracing her and saying, "I want to stay with you." The ward sister tries to persuade her to go with me, but Daniela clings to her ever more strongly and begs her to put on her belt. Daniela opens the exercise book on the desk that contains the drawings she had made during the clinical evaluation, and comments, "What lovely drawings." While the nurse threads the belt round her trousers, the girl says she is thirsty and wants some tea. The nurse says she will have some after she has been down to play with me. Daniela takes off her belt because she "can't sleep" and goes towards the kitchen, ignoring me, waiting for the nurse. The kitchen is closed and there is no one in. I catch up with her and say that by behaving like that she wants to show that she is afraid of coming with me. She leaves the kitchen and follows me to the lift.

On the ground floor, before entering the room, she meets a nurse and calls to her, "Old witch, old witch!", then she enters the room reluctantly. As soon as she is in, she is attracted by a doll; she picks it up and says, "What a nice little doll, I want it!" She looks at the sheets of paper on the table and says, "I don't want to draw." I say she can do what she wants—she can talk, play, and so on. Immediately she says she wants to sleep. She takes the doll, hugs it, and curls up on the sofa with it. She asks me if I will let her keep the doll but I explain that it is for all the children who want to play with it. She insists, then says she is thirsty, very thirsty, and complains that I didn't let her drink her tea when she was upstairs. I tell her that she can drink if she feels like it. She goes to the sink, holding the doll away from it, saying she doesn't want it to get wet because "it is beautiful", then she drinks a sip of water. She curls up again on the sofa and, looking at me, says, "I've got tummy-ache"; then she adds, "Why don't you take me to my bedroom? I'm so sleepy, why do you make me come down here? . . . I want Corbetta (the ward sister)". I tell her that she wants to make me realize I am useless at my work, I can't do anything for her. She rises a little from the sofa, looks at the doll's dress and says it is nice, lifts it a little and adds, "It's got knickers on too'. She covers the doll, hugs it and says she wants to sleep. She closes her eyes but she can't sleep; after a little she says: "I want to go home, when will you let me go home?" I answer that she will be allowed to go home when she is better. After a while, still with her eyes shut, she says to me, "I can feel butterflies flying round my head, take these butterflies away, doctor, take them away!" I answer that I understand perfectly how bad she feels.

After some minutes in silence, still with eyes shut, she asks, "Who are you?", and then, looking at me, "Look, look, my little lamb is coming, bring me my lamb, doctor!" Looking at the doll, she asks. "What's its name?" I answer, "What do you think her name is?" She immediately says, "Monica." She gets up from the sofa and says she wants her mother and that the light in the room is bothering her. She lies down again, saying her arm is still aching, and that Nicola (the teacher) has hurt her arm. "I don't want to stay with Nicola . . . here everybody hates me." With her eyes shut, she asks me if she can sleep. I repeat she can do what she wants. She raises herself a little from the sofa and asks, "Can I even mess up the room?" I confirm she can do what she wants provided she doesn't damage the objects in the room. She says again that the light is bothering her and orders, "Switch off the light!" I say that if she wants, she can switch it off. She asks me where the switch is; I answer that she can easily find it, if she looks around. She gets up and switches off the light. She lies on the sofa hugging the doll and repeating, "This doll is really beautiful!" Then she says, "I'm cold", keeping her eyes shut and pointing at the floor, saying insistently and a little dreamily: "There's the sea, look . . . the sea. I am in hospital, I don't want to stay in hospital . . ." We can hear a piano playing in the ward and she says, "Who's playing—Nicola? She does plays well!" And, still with her eyes shut, "A ship is coming, miss . . . a wave is coming . . . there, I want the doll, I want to sleep." Looking at my stockings she says, "Give me your stockings, miss, I'm cold, my arm aches, here is the sea, it is coming, the waves, look at the waves . . . you see?" She rises from the sofa and kicks out violently against the wall: "I want to go home!" She goes up to the desk where I am sitting and says, "I want to draw, miss." I tell her she may do so, then she says, "I want to go away", and leaves the room.

After a few moments I go out to invite her back in. I find her in the "quiet area" where she is fiddling with neurophysiologic instrumentation; she says she wants Corbetta (the ward sister) and then that she wants to stay there. Then, after urging her to come back into the room with me, I ask a nurse to take her back to the ward. She refuses, calling her an old witch and saying she wants to go back to the room with me. I ask an attendant to take her upstairs and then I leave.

Summary of supervision[4]

From a first look at this material, the difficulty of working out the nature of Daniela's disturbance is evident. Here is a little girl who, from the history and from her behaviour in the ward, shows that she has to control all situations. We can ask ourselves to what extent she realizes this need and, then, what kind of fantasies she has to control things inside herself. In this way, we can understand the little girl's fear and terror when she knows she has to come into the observation room with me. She is so frightened that she can't breathe: "Let me breathe!" The idea of coming with me corresponds, for Daniela, to entering an extremely hostile place. Because of this, the girl keeps asking about her belt; wearing it may give Daniela the physical impression of having something around her body, "a skin" that she can control and that can protect her. Despite her efforts to pull a protective "skin" around herself, she seems extremely worried she might lose control of the situation completely. Looking at her own drawings, she says, "How nice they are!", as if, by clinging to something good of hers, she is making a further, desperate attempt to re-establish certain control over what is happening to her.

For Daniela, entering the room seems to mean entering me, and this is experienced as bad, as dangerous, as a breast that oppresses, crushes. The child clearly expresses this worry when she projects this situation, which is extremely persecutory for her (me, the room), into the nurse we meet in the corridor and whom she perceives as an "old witch". After entering the room, Daniela is so attracted by the doll that she completely blocks out the possibility of using any of the other play material; through the doll she can express her infant part, the part of herself that is "so thirsty", that needs to be fed, to drink. Not only this: when she hugs the toy so tightly she shows how, at that moment, the doll is for her the breast she would like to stick to. And when she wants to sleep it is as if she is expressing her wish to split off everything that prevents her from entering the breast and becoming one with it. This regressive fantasy allows the little girl to possess her mother completely; Daniela seems at this moment to be dominated by the omnipotent fantasy of being herself the breast that is feeding her.

Daniela has been in hospital for a fortnight and it seems that she wants to express the very intense jealousy she feels for the other children, showing her extreme need to possess her mother and get inside her, to control her from the inside and thereby shut out any other potential experience. When she said her own drawings were nice, she wanted to demonstrate her wish to make nice things; in fact she knows she dirties, she wets—she had bedwetting problems until she was more than seven years old. Hence the need to reassure herself about what she does—beautiful things, her drawings. The doll, which she does not want to get wet because "it is beautiful", represents the idealized part of herself. But Daniela, when she wets, seems to be particularly worried about not being able to do good things; her extreme fear of urinating can be connected to her way of taking, of possessing, which is so intensely greedy that what is seized cannot be digested, elaborated and assimilated, and is instead immediately eliminated as urine. The little girl shows that she has to control this fantasy through the doll when, later on, she wants to reassure herself that "everything is all right", that the doll has knickers on and is dry.

At this point Daniela tells me that she feels "the butterflies flying around her head". The butterflies can be connected to the "headache", to the fits that she suffers. They are the persecutory fantasies she tries to put away; when these are projected outside, they are the hospital staff by whom she feels persecuted ("everybody hates me"). Out of this comes up once again the wish to "go home"—to get inside a mother who loves her, feeds her, takes care of her. This seems to be a dominating idea for Daniela; but it is a fantasy that cannot be realized, and for her, the idea of being separated is so intolerable and felt in such a persecutory way that it transforms into the "butterflies", the fits. She seems so little able to bear separation that she experiences herself as terribly bad. For this reason she warns me that she could destroy the room and she is so frightened that she wants to switch off the light: she cannot bear the persecutory feelings deriving from her aggressiveness and, only when the light is off, does the doll—herself inside the doll—become good. "The doll is so nice!" Daniela shows such fragility at the level of thinking, regarding her persecutory fantasies, that she must transform her anguish into physical illness through somatizing processes. Maybe it is not accidental that Daniela's sisters have the same problem: somatization frequently requires a particular type of organic receptivity. This intolerance in the face of frustration and persecutory feelings is frequently found in very small children suffering from psychosomatic troubles.

Then Daniela tells me that she is cold, that she's got a pain in her arm, that she wants my "stockings": in this way she expresses her wish to get inside my "skin". Wanting to be inside mother, to feel completely protected, seems to be for her—as well as a defence against needing a mother—also a way of protecting herself from the danger of being submerged by her fantasies, which are like "the sea, the waves" advancing onward to submerge her completely in coldness, in death. But her wanting to stay inside is so intensely greedy that it provokes damage to her internal objects. Daniela seems to deal with this part of herself—which is under the sway of persecutory fantasies so strong as to make her feel a poor helpless little girl—by behaving like a big, grown-up girl, who can do fine drawings, who can produce good things. In this way she manages to hold herself together, self-controlling, keeping the infant part of herself split off.

A hospital environment facilitates the externalization of a child's psychical illness. It does not require either any scholastic performance or particular behavioural patterns; here a child finds many more people to take care of him by comparison with a family environment, and he finds himself in a situation where he can express his own inner situation more freely. So Daniela has been able to slow down her control mechanisms and so to reveal, for the first time and quite clearly, her jealousy problems with her sisters as well. It seems very important for this girl to express her own feelings, even if only through play sessions like this, and to find outside herself a "mother" who can listen to her and understand her, but who at the same time does not allow her to take everything for herself or to "mess everything up". Daniela has the opportunity to express and externalize her greed, but in such a way that the object is not totally controlled by it.

Play observation—Vittoria: redefining a diagnosis of brain pathology in terms of mental insufficiency
Observer: Dr Laura Musetti

The following observation material also demonstrates the diagnostic usefulness of the play observation method.

History

Vittoria is twelve years of age. Her fifty-year-old father works abroad, far from home, and he goes back home only once a year. The forty-seven-year-old mother is impoverished both intellectually and emotionally, and cannot give very much to her children. Vittoria is the seventh of ten children and she did not have any pathological symptoms at birth. Her psychomotor development is described as normal; she was breastfed for the first six months; a slight delay in controlling sphincter and bladder and some difficulties in feeding were noticed. When she was three years old she was sent to a nursery school, where she seemed to feel at ease. At age six she started to attend primary school but she seemed to take little interest in what she was doing and so her results were poor. At seven she had a very violent nightmare; she woke suddenly in the night and said she saw some dark-haired figures threatening her, whom on subsequent days she kept identifying with her mother. From then on she could not fall asleep alone but only with another person present, and she started being afraid of the dark, of moving around where there was no light, etc.

From seven to eleven years of age she attended a boarding school far from home, because her mother could not keep her, or at least this is the reason given by the mother, and until the age of eleven she remained there almost all the year round. She went home for a few days once a year. We know little of this period; it seems that she had occasional moments of intolerance, excitability, or aggressiveness towards the other children. She failed her academic tests many times at school. Now she attends the third year of a normal primary school (in class with eight-year-olds), without being able to learn much. During the past few months she has had some episodes of excitability and panic, calling for help. She said that all this made her want to give up and so she refused to eat. These crises have occurred more than once and that is why she was admitted to hospital—first at Parma (where they happened several times) and then at our clinic. Altogether she had about ten of these panicky crises, but only once with us, when the anti-depressive treatment was suspended. For us, Vittoria presented another diagnostic problem. In an attempt to throw light on her condition, therefore, Dr Musetti conducted the following play observation with a view to discussing it with Mrs Harris.

Observation of Vittoria, age twelve years

LM (*reads*): When I go to the ward to fetch Vittoria for the observation session, she runs towards me smiling and says, "Let's go!", but once in the lift she throws her head back and looks back, clenching her arms as if she were frightened, flattening against the walls of the lift. We go out and along the corridor. Vittoria enters the observation room with me: she is immediately interested in the family of dolls, saying, "Aren't they lovely"; she picks up the mother and the father and holds them in one hand while with the other she points at the other members of the family and says, "This one is a man, and this one is a man too, isn't it?" (pointing at the grandfather and at the elder child—the younger child is further away and she doesn't see it). Then she looks at the two characters she is holding in her hand and (referring to the man) says, "This is a dancer!", and tries to make it walk and to undress it. Then (referring to the woman) she says, "This is a dancer, it's a woman, isn't it?" Then she looks at the grandfather, picks it up, and says, "He's bald, why is he bald? Why has he scribbled on his head?" Then, after keeping silent for a while, she says, "Why has he got lice? I don't know!" Then she immediately adds, "I've been ill today." She looks at me and sits down: "My lungs hurt from running and I don't have any breath and I must go—oh, oh" (she takes two deep breaths); then she gulps more than once and says, "I have to go like this"; then she half-closes her eyes and bends her head right back. Then, raising her head a little, she says, "I've sat down and got my breath back."

She stands up and goes towards a box of dolls on top of a cupboard. She looks at them and says in a frightened way, "No, not the devil—all men—I'm afraid!" She makes a gesture of pushing the box away from her, and turns herself round, then, however, looks at the box again and says once more, "No, no, the devil makes you afraid", and makes a movement as if to throw away from her a dark-skinned doll (but she does not actually throw it): "They're men, I'm scared! They all scare me." And she turns her back so as not to see it. Then she looks again into the box and asks, "Where's the woman?" She can't see it and then she takes two other dolls, sits down again and says, "These two are nice, aren't they?" She tries to make them work and says, all the time in a monotonous voice, "Good morning, sir, are you well? Good morning!" Then she puts them down saying, "No, no!", placing them in the box, and starts again to search for something. She finds the woman and smiles. She takes it and says, "This is beautiful, it's a woman, isn't it? Who's this?" She makes it work and says again, "Good morning, madam, good morning."

Then she hears footsteps outside the door and starts as if frightened. She turns towards the door and says, "What is it?" Then she looks around, upwards, turns her head back and in all directions, keeping silent. She repeats, "What's this?" And after a moment: "This is a playhouse." And she laughs. Then she takes the yellow plasticine; she doesn't know how to use it, she touches it a little, she rubs it on a sheet of paper. She realizes it marks yellow and says again, "No, no, I'm afraid of yellow, I'll take the white one." She takes a piece of white plasticine and rubs it on a sheet of paper: "Why doesn't this one mark?" Then she suddenly picks up a pencil, handling it awkwardly, and says, "I'll draw you." She sits down and starts drawing. After drawing an eye she says, "No! I got wrong. This is the eye and this is the *pipilla*." I say, "*pupulla* (pupil)". She answers, "*Pipilla*, I can't say *pupulla*." And she spells just those two words. Then she starts drawing again and says, "I'll draw your face." She makes two holes in a piece of plasticine with a pencil, she turns it up and shows it to me: "This is you." Then she takes the red plasticine, breaks it into pieces and says, "I can't do anything with this—it's in pieces!", and goes on breaking it into smaller pieces. Then she takes a pastel from a box, first a white one that she puts away at once, then a red one. She passes it over the drawing and says, "I'm a messer and I like making mess." Then with a black pencil she writes my name under it, says "clearly", and then "don't throw it away, will you?"

Then she looks at the family characters again, notices the small child and says, "It's a family then!" And she looks at me, satisfied. She points at each of them in turn and says, "This is the father, this is the grandfather, the mother, the uncle, the child." And she tries deliberately to put the child into the mother's arms. First she makes it cling to the mother then she places it carefully in the mother's arms. Then she puts them down, stands up, and takes a big doll out of the box and says, "What's this?" She looks at it upside down and tries to make it sit and eventually succeeds, but she hits it and says, "Stupid! You know, I haven't got patience", and goes on hitting its head. Then she looks at the big doll's navel and asks, "What's this?", and points at it. "Have I got one too?" She touches her belly with a finger and after a moment she says, "No, I haven't", and then she goes on hitting the head of the doll. Then she hears a noise, jumps up, takes her head between her hands and presses as if to crush it and says, "It hurts." After a little silence she repeats, "It hurts, you know!" She closes her eyes and looks very tired.

The little girl's IQ (intelligence quotient) is 72.

MH: So Vittoria had failed to progress from one class to the next ... I am wondering what the immediate problem is—why she was referred to the hospital?

LM: She had symptoms of fear and agitation, calls for help accompanied by running round in circles continuously, and no one could stop her. These symptoms occurred in the last few months seven or eight times.

MH: Do I take it that she was living in an institution until she was eleven years old, and that since then she has come to live at home, and she goes to a school near her home?

LM: Other children from the family were also in the institution, mostly for economic reasons.

MH: So she was brought up in a state institution where the mother didn't have to pay, and that was from seven to eleven. She probably also thinks that her difficulties are due to leaving this institution and coming home, going to a day school, after suffering the separation from her home of those four years, while having very little in herself that can really help her to cope with this less protected situation.

LM: In the institution she did not have these crises, though there were moments of excitation when she would hit some other child, but nothing else.

Problems of distinguishing psychosis from mental deficiency

MH: She is probably of poor intelligence and slightly defective constitution too.

Q: Could these things be linked together?

MH: Yes, I would think they are linked together. There doesn't seem to be any history of her developing relatively well, and then some sort of regression afterwards. It looks more like a lack within herself than like things developing in the wrong way. She seems to be one of those children who—if they are going to function at all or even earn their living when they are grown up—do need to have a fairly continuous protective environment. It is sometimes very difficult to determine from the behaviour of children like this those who have a lack of ability—who are deficient mentally—and those who are actually psychotic. I can't pretend to talk about this with any authority. If one compares this child with the one in the previous session there were indications there of a rather better development before he regressed, when separated from the mother with the new baby. So there was something more promising to return to.

Shall we go through the observation and consider this child's words and actions? In the first paragraph—she runs to meet you smiling and says "let's go", then in the elevator she looks back and stretches her arms as if she were frightened, leaning against the sides of the elevator. I take it from this that she knows you already, when she runs to welcome you?

LM: Yes, for some days, and she got attached to me immediately.

MH: She feels uncontained, and leaning against the sides reassures her—which any child might do. In the room is the doll family, and she says how nice they are . . . the father, the mother . . . "this one is a man, this one is a man too isn't he . . . this one is a dancer—she is a woman isn't she?" Then to the grandfather: "he is bald—why is he bald? Because he has scribbled on his head". I am wondering, why do you think she said the man was a dancer, and why did she say the woman was a dancer?

LM: There seems to be no reason—they don't look like dancers.

> Lack of thought or phantasy

MH: There is something very *thoughtless* about her enumerating—a man, a man, a woman, a dancer . . . there is not much thought or fantasy in this. Then with the grandfather who's bald—is he bald because he's scribbled on his head?

LM: In fact he has white hair.

MH: There is no obvious connection there at all. You see, a remark like that could be an extremely *bizarre* connection. The movement of scribbling is a little bit like rubbing, or rubbing out, which could mean rubbing something away. But the fact that the grandfather isn't bald but has white hair—

LM: —not completely bald—

MH: I see, he is both bald and has some white hair. This might connect a bit with her feeling about her own head, when at the very end of the observation she hears the noise and presses her own head. She may see the grandfather as having rubbed off, scribbled away his head. I would think this may have something to do with feelings of erasure—trying to rub out things that hurt. Then she links it with lice. Probably she knows about lice—she may have had lice herself. In her mind, lice that make her head itchy, and sensations in her head that are troublesome or painful, probably get equated as things to be *rubbed out*. Because she then goes on to say "I've been ill today"—there seems some link between scribbling, lice that have to be rubbed out, and feeling ill or unwell in the head. Then from ill she immediately says "my lungs hurt from running and I don't have any breath and I must go—oh, oh". The lice in the head link with her breath being taken away. When she says "I have to do this" and she half-shuts her eyes and bows her head, looking overwhelmed, and says "then I sat down and my breath came back" . . . it does look to me as if she is doing a *running commentary* on sensations that she is feeling at that moment.

Undigested sensations

These sensations somehow pass through her and she puts them into words. I get the impression from this that very little actual thinking takes place. It is more that she has a sensation, and she verbalizes it. It comes in as a sensation, and it comes out expressed in words. There is very little digestion or organization. Again, when she sees the doll and is frightened by it, she says immediately "no, not the devil—all men—I'm afraid". The doll makes an impact on her and immediately her expression comes out.

So far she does give the impression of a child with a very poor capacity to hold and organize her experience in herself, and to make something of it. If one compares her with the little boy in the other session, who is traumatized by seeing the baby and locks his hands, there is some feeling of a *conflict* inside him. He does not simply have the sensation of seeing the baby and immediately it comes out again. There is an impact—something goes on inside him though he is not able to organize it well. Even if he can't think about it, the impact remains within his personality. With this child, it straightaway comes out again. In order to develop and progress, there would have to be a much greater capacity to hold and make something of her experience.

Next, when she says "no not the devil—all men", the devil becomes "all men" and she is frightened. She tries to push the box away, turns to the opposite side, then repeats to herself "no, the devil frightens" and she tries to toss it far away. Then "men, I'm afraid, they all frighten me". She tries to push away and escape from this experience of being frightened. She turns to the woman. It seems there that the woman might be connected with something better, a protector. But not finding this she takes two dolls at random and says "these are nice aren't they". She tries to make them work, saying "good day gentlemen, are you well, good day". It seems there as if, when she can't find the woman, she tries to control the dolls and make them do what she wants. Then when she finds the woman she says "she's a woman—she's beautiful isn't she". There again there is very little differentiation, very little fantasy connected with these objects. She repeats "good day gentlemen, good day". There is something very mechanical and impoverished in her characterization of these dolls.

Now here come the footsteps outside the door. She gets on to the chair; she turns to the door and says "what is it?" She looks upwards and throws her head silently backwards in all directions. That's the sort of movement she made in the lift, isn't it—throwing her head back?

LM: Stronger and more sudden than before.

MH: It seems again to be a movement of getting herself away from something frightening. Like that newborn baby observation today—the baby made that sort of movement, straining his head backwards. Shortly afterwards she says, "What's this? This is a playhouse". Did she mean by that, a place where you can play? She tries to comfort herself by repeating that this is a place where you can play—a place that is all right—to protect herself from her fear of the noise. Then, when she rubs the plasticine, she says "No no, I'm afraid of yellow, I'll take the white one", and says "why doesn't this one mark?" It doesn't seem to occur to her that the white doesn't mark because it is the same colour as the paper. It does look as if her capacity to make very obvious connections between things is very poor.

> Seeing herself as a mess

Then when she draws you she says "this is the *pipilla*, not the *pupulla*"—what would that be, a pun on *pipi*?

LM: I didn't have the impression she meant *pipi* and *poo-poo*.

MH: Not at all? . . . I am just looking at this face. I would think that she has very little idea about differentiating when she is doing something that is good, or when she is doing something that is actually *pipi*.

LM: Yes, I have noticed this confusion.

MH: I wonder too about the yellow plasticine—whether the yellow links with *pipi*. Then she's doing a face and says "I can't do anything with this, it is in pieces", and she continues making even smaller ones. She takes some pastels from the box—a white one, which she immediately puts away, then a red one. Going back over the drawing she says, "I am a messer and I like making a mess", which would confirm this feeling that whatever she does she is making a mess, and she doesn't have any real control over what comes out of her.

LM: She is always afraid of doing the wrong thing. She draws herself as a goose.

MH: Yes, there is something very pathetic about this. In all of this, she does give one the impression of being a *bewildered* child, who doesn't know what she is doing, and very easily feels persecuted and intruded upon, and can't contain those feelings. She is a child who is very much in need of protection, order, structure—of some kind of continuity or sameness in her life.

| The observer's role |

Then she takes the black pencil and writes your name, and says the word "clearly", and says "you will not throw it away, will you?" She remembers the family and sees the small child and says "well then, it is a family", then she looks at you and says, one by one, "this is the father, the grandfather, the mother, the uncle, *and the child*". She tries to place the child in the mother's arms. I am just wondering what the doctor actually said to her before this . . .

LM: I hadn't said anything to her.

MH: Because I had the impression that by this point in the session she is feeling a little bit safer, and she is able to put things together in a rather less enumerative way. The people are a bit more differentiated; they are a family; they have relationships with each other—they are not just "a man, a man, a woman". She does seem to be a bit more at home with you, a bit held and protected by your *interest* in her.

Now ... the child falls from its mother's arms; then she takes the doll, turns it and looks at its bottom. It looks as if the child falling from its mother's arms has the significance of something falling out of the bottom like faeces. She feels the doll must sit down, but it won't, so she hits it ... When she tries to make the doll sit, what happens—does it fall over, at first?

LM: Yes.

MH: I would think this has the significance for her of faeces, so she smacks the incontinent doll for falling over. Then she touches the doll's navel, says "Have I got one? No I haven't", then she hits the doll again on the head. I wonder if the navel is equated there with a kind of anus. There again the noise; she springs on the chair; she takes her head in her hands, trying to crush it, and says "it hurts". At that point the noise that she springs away from must feel like some echo or return of her own aggression, as a result of smacking the doll, so she gets up to get away from it. The noise—the thing that she fears—seems to be something that comes from below, because she gets up on the chair to get away from it. I have the impression that with this child, sensations pass right through her—they come in, and they go out down below. She has very little capacity to hold her own feelings of anger; they come out as urine, faeces, or actions where she hits out or runs away. She has very little tolerance of her own emotions or aggressiveness; they are passed out as soon as they have been evoked.

> Environmental needs

Looking back at the history ... when she gets excited she says she is frightened. She asks for help because she is afraid of dying, and she also refuses food. I would think her fear of dying is probably related to her difficulty in tolerating painful feelings—a feeling that she will disintegrate. When she experiences pain for whatever reason, and gets rid of those feelings in the form of urine or faeces, it could be a situation where the whole world is filled with faeces and then anything she eats becomes bad and persecutes her; she cannot take anything in. From what I can see this is a child who is fairly defective in her intelligence and capacity for holding and organizing her emotions. She does need above all a protective, constant and kindly environment. I take it that during this period of age seven to eleven there weren't so many difficulties—when she was in the protected environment of the institution?

LM: That is so.

MH: At the moment, I would think her problem is being not sufficiently protected.

LM: The father is away and comes back home only once a year.

MH: She looks the kind of child who is going to need a protected environment all her life. Comparing her with the last child, it would be worth trying some psychotherapy in that case, but in this case it would be a waste of time, because what she needs is more of a constant environment. I won't say that a child like this could not be helped a little by psychotherapy, but I don't think that is primarily what she needs.

Infant observation—Matteo: early internalization of the object

The first two sessions with Matteo are of particular interest in their clear evidence of early internalization of the object.

History

Matteo, aged thirty days, is the second-born after his sister Grazia, aged two and a half. The father, a biologist, suffers from serious neurotic problems: he is always unsatisfied, he frequently changes his place of work, and continuously requires his wife's protection. The mother, who is a vet, has had to go back to work a month after her child's birth since she is the main wage-earner. At the time of these observations she seemed worried and depressed. She has had two nannies for Matteo: for the first twenty days an older woman whom, according to his mother, "he liked very much"; now he is looked after by a young woman who is described as a little "distant" towards him. The mother is sympathetic and justifies her attitude by explaining that she has had to give up looking after her own child, few months old, in order to take care of Matteo.

First observation of Matteo, age thirty days

RN (*reads*): The child sleeps lying on his back, perfectly quiet, for a long time (about ten minutes); he is late for his feed but shows no sign of waking up; he doesn't seem to have a regular routine. The young woman who is helping to look after him picks him up and he opens his arms but does not cry. He is put down on the changing table and starts to cry. He opens his arms, bends and stretches his legs vigorously. The mother puts him on the scales, the child cries more intensely and wriggles around. The mother says that he cries even when he has his bath and he also complains when he is being dried. He does in fact look quite cross during the process of bathing and drying. Grazia comes in and shows us she is eating a slice of bread spread with Nutella. She looks around then runs away. She makes a lot of noise outside, though, while playing with her grandfather. Matteo is picked up by the nanny and breathes deeply. The mother remarks to me that he looks like a seal, then she adds, "He's such a darling, look, he's hungry." Matteo is placed on the changing table to be dressed and starts crying again, but stops when the nanny picks him up.

Grazia comes in, marches around the room eating her bread, then goes out. The mother tells me about the problem of the cot: she would like to move the little girl into another bed but she is afraid of distressing her; at this period the child keeps trying to get into her brother's cot and pram, wetting herself, and so on. The baby is sucking, keeping his fists closed in front of him, making a loud noise. The mother tells me that he is a very slow feeder and she thinks it is because the holes in the teat of the bottle are very small. The child sometimes looks towards the light and frowns. Mother says he likes looking at a light, and when he is turned away from it, he cries. Grazia comes in, rides her bicycle around the room, calls her mother, speaks a few words to her, then goes away. The child, while sucking, keeps his hands joined together under the bib. The nanny removes the bottle from his mouth. The child looks sideways, drowsily. He starts to suck again even more slowly, looking sleepily in front of him. He sucks noisily and burps. He continues to suck very slowly. The feeding bottle is removed. He starts to suck again, still slowly.

He sometimes opens his fists, gazing as in a trance. He stops sucking for a few moments and looks sideways. The nanny agitates the bottle a little in his mouth.

Grazia comes in holding a toy car, which she hands to me and then goes out. The mother asks the nanny whether Matteo slept that morning; it seems that he did sleep for a long time. The feeding bottle is taken out, then given back and he sucks a little, shaking his head, then he closes his eyes, burps and falls asleep, with his hands open. He bends his head, possets a little (milk), then he wakes up and looks around. The mother, meantime, told me that he always did that and then would start to feed again. Now Matteo sucks well, looking forwards. Then he looks drowsy again. He sucks with eyelids lowered, opens and closes his hand. The bottle is removed; his hands slip on to his tummy and he protrudes his tongue. At this point his mother picks him up. He looks around, reclines his head on his mother's face, and seems to caress his mother with his hands. He does not stop looking around.

Summary of comments by MH

> The mother's distance

It is striking how, during the observation session, the mother stays away from the baby. She picks him up and puts him on the scales; but only at the end of the session is she able to hold him in her arms. As the following observation sessions show, the mother understands Matteo's needs very well; she sees he is a "darling" and knows that he likes to be cuddled. We may ask ourselves whether she stays distant because, owing to her depressed state, she cannot feel the child's need to be contained; or because she is actually afraid of establishing too close a relationship with her son, in which case Matteo might become excessively dependent on her and so separation might be too painful for both of them.

During the first part of this session Matteo looks restless and even when he has his bath he does not seem to calm down. Most newborn babies, even if they appear restless and irritable, calm down when they are placed in touch with water. One has the impression that Matteo connects the bath sensation with the previous nanny he "liked" and who was with him for the first twenty days of his life, when he seemed to like having a bath. The little sister, meanwhile, makes a lot of noise, and does everything possible to attract attention to herself; she seems intensely jealous of both the attention given to her brother and of the relationship her mother has established with the observer. Matteo stops crying when he is picked up; but, if put on the changing table, he begins again; the impression is that he likes to be held close, protected, cuddled. The impression made by his sister is very different. She comes in, watches, goes out again, and does not seem to want to be cuddled or to stay close to her mother. Towards the end of the session, when Grazia comes into the room holding a toy car and hands it to the observer, she seems to try to overcome her jealousy by identifying herself with the mother or nurse who gives the bottle, so denying her own need and dependence. Her behaviour would confirm the mother's report that from the very beginning Grazia, as a baby, had seemed rather tetchy and irritable and always wanted to do everything by herself, whereas Matteo, though he appreciates being picked up and cuddled, seems able to overcome his anxieties about being contained. He sucks hard, keeping his fists closed, despite the rather small holes in the teat. It is interesting that the mother thinks it is a good idea to have small holes in the teat to encourage Matteo to work hard to suck and to grow. It seems to relate to her desire for the child to grow strong quickly and her worry about the time when she will have to leave him. Matteo is a child who expresses quite clearly his vitality: sucking hard, keeping his fists closed, staring at the light or at the familiar objects in the room; all this is a way to contain himself, to find the stimulus to get on.

> The baby's internalization of the object

When the teat is taken away from his mouth he looks "amazed" and tries to see where it has gone. He doesn't seem angry or persecuted because it has been taken away. In that situation other children would get very angry and would start crying desperately. The nipple-teat, when taken out, does not become something bad or persecutory for him, and when offered again, it is accepted very confidently. This suggests that the child has already been able to internalize a good object. His self seems to develop greatly around this good object, and the identification with the mother's good characteristics becomes for the child the basis for further growth-promoting identifications.

The different levels of internalization of such an object enable us to comprehend how those who watch carefully the behaviour of very young children can say that each child does indeed have his "own character" from the first days of life. Returning to Matteo, we note how he sucks with his eyelids down; he opens and closes his hand as if he wants to show that things go and come back, get lost and found again. The bottle is taken out, and Matteo sticks out his tongue more than once, again as if he wanted to preserve the memory of the bottle that has been taken away. It is extremely interesting to observe how internalization of the object is taking place little by little, even through physical sensation: the child seems to be trying to face up to the breast going away and coming back, by opening and closing his hands. The same happens through movements of the tongue. When, at the end of the session, Matteo is picked up by his mother, he does not look frustrated or angry because he has been separate from her; instead he snuggles towards her and evidently appreciates the experience of being held closely.

Second observation of Matteo, age two months and three days

In the drama going on between hand, light and face, the hand appears to reassure and to be a source of strength for the baby. It is also possible in this session to observe the origins of speech in the baby.

MH: Could you give us a little summary of what you have been noticing in the period between these two observations?

RN: The nanny has changed again. First there was an elderly woman whom the baby liked but she only stayed for three days; then another woman came but the mother did not like her, finding her rude, and rough with the baby. At the moment there is a young woman who appears so severe that the observer thought, at first, she had rung the wrong bell.

MH: I wonder what effect you felt this was having on the baby?

RN: Apparently all these changes had no significant effect on him; the child showed the same qualities that had been observed in the previous sessions.

MH: I am wondering how much time is the baby spending with the new people, and how much with his mother?

RN: I do not know, but I know that the mother is with the child four or five hours a day, and is always present at the observation sessions.

RN (*reads*): When I get there I find the mother together with the little girl, Grazia, who has just got up after her afternoon nap. Matteo is sleeping deeply; then all of a sudden he makes some sucking movements with his dummy in his mouth; the dummy comes out, then is sucked in again. The mother asks me to sit with her and Grazia in another room while she prepares the baby's meal. Grazia is very noisy; she puts Matteo's fluffy dog in a plastic bag and demands her mother take her out shopping. The mother replies resolutely that she will take her out after she has given Matteo his dinner, and she repeats this several times. We go into Matteo's room; he is sleeping quietly without his dummy, his face turned on his right side. The light is switched on and his covers drawn back. He grimaces then goes back to sleep. The mother says she wants to see if he has done a pooh. Grazia, who has problems controlling her own sphincters, is greatly interested in seeing what "that dirty Matteo" is doing. Matteo seems not to want to wake up, and puts a hand before his eyes. Grazia says, "Chicco, pooh poon." And then, "Chicco wants to sleep", then "Chicco, good boy", when she sees he has awoken.

The mother takes him out of the cot and holds him in her arms. He nestles down between her arm and shoulder and looks around. Grazia demands in a loud voice, almost shouting, that her mother come and play with her; but the mother puts the baby on the changing table and undresses him. Matteo has not done a pooh. Grazia, next to them, seems surprised. The baby breathes deeply, looks around, stretches his arms. He plays with his right hand, slowly bending his arms and looking at the hand. Grazia repeats, "Let's go shopping!" Matteo breathes deeply, moves his mouth, protrudes his tongue many times, and laughs happily. He goes "Eh, eh!", looks at me and smiles, then looks around and sighs. Grazia says, "Chicco, dinner time!", and he sticks out his tongue several times, opening his mouth; he says, "Oh, oh." The mother cleans the child's nose with a cotton bud; for a while he lets her do this without complaining. Grazia says, "Chicco's neck is hurting!", then "Stop it, Chicco!" He seems to be complaining about his nose and when his mother stops cleaning it he calms down. She picks him up and, as soon as he is in her arms, he looks around. The telephone rings and the maid calls the mother, who asks me to hold the child for a minute. In my arms he is restless; he opens his mouth more than once and grasps my sweater with his hand. Meanwhile the sister says, "Chicco, bye-byes."

The mother comes back and takes the baby. He puts his hand in his mouth, then she sits down with Matteo and gives him the bottle.

Matteo sucks greedily with his fists closed, staring at his mother's face; while feeding, he bends and stretches his toes. Grazia comes up close to him and kisses his head and talks loudly into his ears. The mother removes the bottle then puts it back in his mouth. Matteo goes on sucking, looking in front of him and moving his toes slowly; he opens his hand and plays with his smock. He stops sucking for while and looks at the light in front of him, motionless, then starts sucking again, pulling his mother's finger from the bottle. He turns his head, frowns, and sucks greedily. He puts his hand under his mother's armpit. Grazia goes out of the room, Matteo goes on sucking, making a noise and looking in front of him meanwhile. He makes little sounds, "Eh eh." He lets some milk dribble from his lips; he looks up and stares at his mother. She says, "He drinks it all, to the last drop." While she talks to me he gazes at her face. She tells me that he started to like his bath again a fortnight ago, as he did for the first ten days after birth. Now Matteo moves his hand out in front of himself; he closes and opens his eyes, remains still for a little, then starts again to suck greedily. Grazia comes in and says, "Cover, Chicco", and she tries to settle the blanket around her little brother's feet. In the meantime the baby finishes his milk and the bottle is removed from his mouth. He opens his lips a little, sticks out his tongue, opens his hand and plays with his blanket. The mother puts him into his cot and then gets ready to go out with Grazia. Matteo stares in front of him, grasps his smock, makes some little noises, looks around with his eyes wide open, then he burps. His sister comes up to him and caresses his head heavily, talking to him in a loud voice. He does not cry, but tries to push her away with his hand.

MH: In this observation he does seem to be developing very much in the way that he was a month ago. He does seem to be a peaceful, self-contained baby. In the same way Grazia comes up and intrudes as she was doing in that earlier observation, and very clearly shows her jealousy, but it seems to be reasonably contained and is not something that interferes with the baby and the mother.

RN: Grazia in the previous observation succeeded in grabbing her brother's bottle and thrusting the teat into his mouth. The little toy dog was a gift for Chicco (Matteo) at birth. Grazia has never taken any soft toys to bed with her, but when Chicco was born she started to take his toy dog with her. Going shopping, she wanted to carry in her own bag the empty bottles her mother was returning to the supermarket, but the mother would not let her. So Grazia took the little dog instead in her bag.

MH: What are these—milk bottles?

RN: No, probably water bottles.

MH: It does seem here that Grazia partly manages by having her own mother-bottle or mother-breast, as represented by the little dog. In the shape of the little dog she gets her own bottle-breast and can revert a little bit to babyhood, which seems to allow the baby to have the mother without her interfering too strongly. But it is interesting how at least twice she wants mother to go out shopping with her, just when the mother is about to pay attention to the baby.

RN: In this observation Grazia appears to be much more intrusive than in the previous one. She wants to be a big girl, carrying plates, washing glasses, and that kind of thing.

MH: It is interesting that she wants to be grown-up and wash all the glasses, when she has a lot of difficulty in controlling her sphincters and dirtying herself. It would also seem that she very much wants to split off this dirtying part of herself and project it into the baby who is the "piggy". She is very much trying to take the role of Chicco, the baby's mother, trying to interpret what the baby wants to do.

Then he wakes up slowly, mother takes him in her arms, and he looks around very intensely . . . You describe him here as if he nestles very closely to the mother and feels very safe with her.

RN: It is true; in the previous observation the mother only picks him up at the end.

MH: It would seem this is a baby with rather a good disposition. I remember in the first observation, although he was a bit restless when being fed, under his bib he put his hands together. He has a disposition to come close to the mother and feel at ease in himself. This time when the mother takes off his nappy and unswaddles him and he stretches his arms, he is much more at ease than in the first observation when he was crying and kicking when he was unwrapped.

RN: So the mother is also getting better; they seem to be going ahead together, and have overcome the problems caused by the constantly changing nannies.

MH: It may be that she has developed partially *because* of those bad other people rather than in spite of them. I wonder to what extent she may have managed to split off and get rid of some of her own uncertainties about being a bad mother into the nurses, who are sent away, so that she feels she is a good mother by contrast. I just wonder about the baby who now seems quite composed when he is unwrapped. At the end of the observation the mother says that for the past (is it fifteen?) days, he has enjoyed his bath, as he had at the very beginning.

RN: For the first twenty days after birth the baby used to love his bath, with the nurse he liked. Then there was a period when he didn't like it, but in the past ten days he has begun to like it again.

MH: He has somehow managed to work through some of the uncertainties about being handled by the different nurses. He began to be persecuted by his bath after the first nurse left, but now seems to have developed enough in other ways to be able to enjoy it again.

The beginnings of speech

One sees him noticing his surroundings and also noticing himself. He stretches his arms, then plays with his right hand, then moves his arms slowly, and then he looks at his hand. He is sufficiently at home with himself to be able to notice his surroundings and also to notice parts of himself—how they feel and what they look like. Then he moves his mouth, puts his tongue out more than once, laughs happily, and then he says "eh—eh". That would seem to be the beginning of a kind of talking that he is doing with his tongue. You described first of all "eh—eh", then later he puts out his tongue again and says "oh—oh"—two different sounds!

Now I wonder, when mother is cleaning his nose with the little stick, and Grazia says "Chicco" . . .

RN: The mother was wiping the baby's nose and Grazia said "Chicco bad neck", referring to the stiff neck he had had a few days before.

MH: Was Grazia talking to you, or just generally?

RN: Generally.

MH: In the observation she does seem to relate mainly to her mother—she notices that you are there, but without making direct contact.

RN: When I was holding the baby she turned to me and said "Chicco go to sleep".

MH: It would seem she has a very proprietary air towards the baby, as if she is his mummy and saying how he feels and what he must do.

Now—he looks around, is given to you, in your arms he is restless and grasps your pullover, and that is when Grazia says "Chicco go to sleep". I don't know if you felt that the baby noticed the difference when the mother handed him to you?

RN: Yes—the restlessness.

MH: It is interesting that he notices, and gets a bit restless, but he does tolerate it; he doesn't cry. Mother comes back and takes him, he puts his hand into his mouth, she gives him the bottle, he sucks strongly, keeping his fists clenched before him; he looks intensely at his mother's face, and moves his toes. Then Grazia kisses him and talks loudly into his ears—trying to drown some of her feelings about the mother and baby being close together.

RN: Grazia's shouting in a loud voice seemed particularly aggressive to me. The mother herself speaks in a low voice.

MH: Through her loudness she expresses some of her aggressiveness, but also her constant talking is a way of trying to get rid of or cover up what she feels about the baby. She is very *active* about it. Through her loudness, and kissing of the baby, she is trying to get rid of feelings that she is danger of being overwhelmed by.

Comment: Grazia's hyperactivity seems to be a way of not perceiving these feelings.

MH: Yes, I would agree.

> A good enough feeding situation

It is interesting about the baby and the bottle. In your description of the feeding here, he is very involved in thinking about it and also about his surroundings; he seems to be able to go on sucking while not concentrating solely on it. He opens his hand and plays with his clothes; he stops and looks at the light; then he comes to his mother's hand; he turns his head and frowns; then his hand goes under his mother's armpit. So he has enough security in this relationship to the bottle to be able to also take in other things and do other things. It does not seem to me that he is *distracted* by other things in a way that would detract from his feeding, as if the feeding were not a very good situation. He feels the feeding is a *good enough* situation for him to afford to take his time about it and to savour the things around him while he is doing it.

RN: Some days ago he had flu, but he didn't cry or whimper. His mother noticed he was ill because of his noisy breathing. Even when he was ill he was fairly calm.

MH: Yes, that's true. He does seem able to tolerate quite a bit of frustration; he has enough security within himself to do that. The mother says he is drinking everything, foam included. So it is not that he isn't having a wholehearted, thorough, taking-in experience from the bottle.

> The hand, the light, and the mother's face

I was wondering, too, about his looking at the light, and how in the first observation the mother said that he got upset if he couldn't see the light. This seems linked with looking at the mother's face. Towards the end when he says "eh-eh" he looks upwards, then he looks intently at the mother's face, and goes on looking. Later on when he puts his hand up, is he looking at his hand? ("I'm not sure.") Because earlier he was both feeling and looking at his hand, and in the first observation the hand had seemed to be rather important in the feeding, when he put his hands together under his bib, so I was wondering if there was coming to be some connection between the light, the mother's face, and the hand. And this time, before he had the bottle and the mother took him in her arms, he first put his hand in his mouth before taking the bottle, as if there were some connection between the hand and the feeding.

RN: I think that is true, because when I was holding him he was very restless, and before taking and feeding him the mother said, "you can see, he's hungry."

MH: He goes on sucking, then Grazia says "Chicco", then the mother takes the bottle out; he opens his mouth, puts out his tongue more than once, then he *opens his hand* and plays with the coverlet. So when the bottle has gone, he turns to his hand. Like when he grasped your pullover. Then in the cradle he grasps his clothes and looks on intently with eyes wide and says "eh-eh". Grazia comes and caresses him and he doesn't cry, but with his hand he pushes away her arm.

I don't know if it is the same hand each time, but it does seem he feels he has a certain strength or confidence in his hand: he comforts himself with it but can also use it in his defence, and can push Grazia away when she gets too near.

RN: Nevertheless, he seemed more restless in the cot than in his mother's arms.

MH: With the cot, it seems a bit like the restlessness when you are holding him—he notices the difference all right, but seems to feel capable of dealing with it, not being overwhelmed by it. It's very nice. Despite all those changes that you reported at the beginning, the baby does seem to be developing ways of coping with them.

RN: He is beautiful, and so is Grazia—both of them.

Supervision following the third observation session of Matteo

The third observation took place when Matteo was three months and twenty days old. The transcript of the observation has been lost; however its contents may be deduced from the supervision, which focuses on the obsessional behaviour of the elder sibling, Grazia, age two and three quarters.

> Obsessional behaviour in children—some general problems

MH: I was wondering if there was anything particular happening at that time, when Grazia was a year old? ("No.") So it would be difficult to say why this happened—generally speaking this obsessional trying to keep everything the same, keeping her clothes on, suggests that underneath there must be a terrific persecutory anxiety about things changing. If they are always kept the same, then she knows exactly what is there; and nothing new or strange or bad can intrude. This method of trying to control and keep out persecution means there must have been some increase of persecutory anxieties at that time, for whatever reason—I don't know why.

RN: According to the mother, one is dealing with a situation that appeared gradually, perhaps even before she was a year old. From early on she was very insistent about things being in the same place and always wanted to stay in one place and was very tied to her routine. Going out of the house they always had to take the same route and so on. Recently, these symptoms seemed much ameliorated.

MH: Was it in any way related to weaning?

RN: Yes. Both Matteo and Grazia started to be weaned very early. From two and a half months she had a bottle and also was offered a spoon, which she rejected violently. The girl found the process of weaning particularly difficult.

MH: So she was breastfed for three months? ("No.") So she was weaned from the bottle at three months? ("Yes.") I would think it is almost certainly related to some increase of anxiety about some loss in her relationship with the mother, probably to do with the parental, oedipal relationship at that time. Keeping things the same and knowing exactly where they are means that she knows where mummy and daddy are, and if she knows that, then they can't be doing things together and creating the possibility of other babies.

> A barrier against emotions

In the observations you've already presented you say Grazia is there a great deal and is always intruding in some slightly hidden way in what is happening with the baby. She is not so openly aggressive and angry; her feelings appear in a more hidden way. Not so much when the mother is there, but rather quietly, you said. I think this obsessional behaviour that you've described as setting in around a year old is a way of putting up barriers against experiencing feelings of jealousy and aggression, stopping them from coming out openly and struggling with her parents. She tries to hide her jealousy both from herself and from her parents, and this rigid controlling is a barrier against feeling these emotions, as well as of trying to control her objects in an omnipotent way.

How is she now—is she still so obsessional and controlling? ("No.") Defences of this kind can be very rigid, or they can be more fluid, and be mitigated by a better and more secure relationship growing up with the parents.

RN: This child has improved.

> Characteristic defences

MH: I think these defences are those that probably most children would have at some point in their development. It is the kind of defence that is very characteristic of children generally in the latency period, say age six to eleven. One has only to think of the kind of games children enjoy at that time, with rules that cut off anxieties about uncertainty. Also in adult life, each one of us has some kind of obsessional defence to keep things the same, to stop changes that could be felt as detrimental or hurtful. If you want to take it still further, in adult life—especially perhaps when settling into middle age—those obsessional defences may well take the form of not really liking to let in any new ideas! People become rigidified to keep out the pain of uncertainty—the threat of some-thing new that might change their whole organization and attitude to life.

The threat of the new idea

To somebody who is very settled in their ways, a new idea is the equivalent of a new baby to a young child, that will displace it from its position of being at the centre of its world.

Comment: There seem to be two different things here: the first linked to change in the mother, and the second to the new ideas like new babies and the hostility to the new baby and desire to control it.

MH: Yes, it is different, but that in a sense really means a change in the mother, which also means a threat to the child's knowledge of where she is with the mother—knowing that the mother is her possession. If the mother changes she becomes a different mother, no longer within the child's knowledge and control.

Comment: The person in question experiences new ideas as a change in their relation with their internal mother; they are familiar with the old relationship and they fear change.

MH: There is quite a bit about Grazia in the observation. Here she is dirtying things . . . The mother seems to feel that Chicco is much less demanding than Grazia, and that Grazia gets more of her attention than does the baby. Now, you describe Chicco as being rather nervous a lot of the time . . . has that become more noticeable since the mother has begun weaning him from the bottle?

RN: Yes. From the beginning he took milky food well but had difficulty accepting savoury food. He became particularly irritable after his meal, especially when left alone in the room with a dirty nappy. But even before, in his mother's arms, he seemed restless and tired.

Secret aggression

MH: Perhaps we could go through the observation again, look-ing at what happens with both the children. The mother has had flu. Grazia wakes up and speaks very loudly, calling her attention. She has dirtied her bed, which she only does when she is asleep. She wants to know whether Chicco has wet his bed. Then she says, "Lina stinks", and the mother laughs. So again, she is being *secretly* aggres-sive—the dirtying happens when she is asleep, therefore she is not responsible. It is Lina the nurse who stinks. The mummy is dirty, not me. The mother doesn't seem bothered about Grazia soiling herself.

RN: No, because she is clean during the day.

MH: I think she is splitting off responsibility for her own mess-ing and for the feelings that go with it. Lina represents the servant-mother who is just there to receive the dirty things, so she is the one who stinks. Her anger and aggression are split off, with the fact that she is a little girl and has to learn to control her sphincters. The dirtying and the wetting are waste products, not really wanted, and they represent the child's unwanted feelings that it would like to get rid of altogether.

RN: Grazia pointed out that Chicco was dirty.

MH: Yes. The nurse (representing the mummy) is the dirty one, and the baby is the one who does the dirtying. Somewhere there will be an idealization of her faeces, pretending that they are really babies, something good. Faeces can mean to the child both an ideal-ized production and, at the same time, something dirty to be got rid of. The child's phantasy when she wets the bed may be that she is secretly the mummy who is producing the babies, or, if it is the bad side of defecation, she would disown it and put it on to the baby or on to mummy as the dirty one.

Comment: It is a way of splitting off the responsibility, the guilty feelings.

Idealization of urine and faeces

MH: Yes, but it is also a way of idealizing the pretence that urine and faeces are milk or babies. You can see young children playing with sand, feeling as if they are making babies from their bodily products. Somewhere there is this absolute denial of reality. Long after there is a conscious knowledge that babies are not produced from the child's own bottom, they will hang on unconsciously to their insistence that they are. This is very much in competition with the daddy and mummy, whom the child consciously knows produce the babies when they come together. Grazia here is not at all upset that she has dirtied the bed, whereas many children of three would be upset. I suspect she has the secret phantasy that when she does this she is producing the babies, the good things, whereas the dirtying qualities of the faeces are split off on to mummy or the nurse or Chicco.

> ### Intruding on the adults

In the dining room, when you and the mother are having coffee, Grazia wants a cup of coffee as well. She is very noisy, and mother tells the maid to give her a cup with a drink, but she doesn't stay in the room. So it looks here as if it is not that she wants to be together with the grown-ups; it is more that she insists noisily on her own cup, in a way that is really *intruding* on what the grown-ups are having together. She does not want the company of the two grown-ups, but insists on her own rights, and on interrupting them.

She comes in afterwards with her toy dog, and again comes in wanting her mother to have a walk with her. She is behaving like a little-boy daddy who comes in with mother's little dog (representing the baby) and announces "mother, I want you to come with me". So she is behaving in a possessive way, coming between the mother and the observer, to take the mother away.

RN: Often Grazia wants the mother to put the baby's bib on herself.

MH: So that would again be as if she is making mother be *her* little baby and her possession.

Comment: But this behaviour is normal for this age.

MH: Well, I think that to some extent every child manifests something of this kind of behaviour. But, as children go, I would think that Grazia is pretty possessive and controlling. It shows in her attitude. It is not that she is terribly disruptive; she doesn't make such a nuisance of herself that the mother can't talk to the observer, or be with the little boy. But she is always intruding, and always trying to get something from the mother. I would think that deep inside herself she is not at all reconciled to separating at all from the mother or allowing her freedom to be with the baby or the father. She is always trying to control and take her away.

MH: To answer your question: I think this is a very usual way for a child of this kind to behave, but the question is to what extent, and how strong is her possessiveness? I think she is learning to be more social and civilized, and her relationship with her mother would appear to be a good one—her mother accepts her as she is. So she is not caught in any strong obsessional *symptoms*. But inwardly she is unable to allow the mother to be free; she is very controlling of her objects.

Comment: A mother who is always blaming the child is liable to induce obsessive symptoms, neurotic problems.

MH: Yes, probably; or on the other hand there could be a much stronger, more open clash between the mother and herself. This is the kind of little girl who, if she had a mother who insisted on her being clean and behaving herself, could feel very persecuted by her secret controlling of her.

Infant observation—Giuseppino: the relation of the child's way of looking to the mother's emotional condition

Giuseppino is the first-born of a young couple. The two observation sessions reported here come from very different moments in the child's family life. In the first session, when Giuseppino is forty days old, the mother is at home all day with the child and the family are all together. In the next session Giuseppino is five months old and his father is away from home on military service while his mother is often out because has she has resumed her work as an architect. The two sessions together enable Mrs Harris to make important comments on the direction in which the child moves his eyes and looks, and on how this relates to the mother's emotional condition. The precise communication between mother and child that is achieved by this means bears witness to the primal language of projection and introjection.

First observation of Giuseppino, age forty days

RN (*reads*): Giuseppino is sleeping in his cot on his left side; the dummy is in his mouth and he holds his fist in front of it. He stays like that for about five minutes, then gives a groan and opens his hand. I ask if the main light—which had been turned on for me—could be switched off; the room is indirectly lit. In a little while the baby opens his hand and closes it again, then he gives a sound and opens his hand again, touches the blanket and closes his hand. While sleeping he makes a sound as if he were sucking. After some moments he moans, moves his head, but doesn't wake up. He doesn't open his eyes, goes on sleeping with his fist clenched. I don't see any sucking movement. The face is motionless. Giuseppino then shakes his fist, opens his fingers and moves his fist in almost rotatory motion. I can hear regular short breathing. The fist movements continue slightly and softly. The baby lifts his eyelids and adjusts his position. Still sleeping, he stifles a grimace and moves his fist. He is motionless again, then starts moving his fist. He moans a little then shakes his head slightly.

The mother comes in with the feeding bottles and prepares his milk. While shaking the bottle she says to me, "He should be woken up a little earlier, poor child! He makes so many faces when he's sleeping." She adds that for the first time Giuseppino cried a lot during the afternoon; she carried him around in her arms, cuddling him. She said he was crying because of tummy ache. The baby shakes his fist a little, his face motionless. While preparing the bottle she talks to me about the paediatrician, then she goes to the baby and says, "My little pussy."

She draws down the blanket and the child remains with his right arm stretched and the left one curled up; he stretches both arms but does not open his eyes. The mother takes him out of the cot and puts him on the changing table. Giuseppino is still asleep. She takes off his nappy and says disappointedly, "No pooh!" She puts baby oil on his bottom and genitals, which are reddened, and shakes some talcum powder. Once he is ready, Giuseppino curls up his legs, hold his arms close to his body and then kicks his legs about and wakes up. He looks, smiling. His mother lifts him up and in her arms he first looks down then he lifts his lids slightly and looks around; he also sticks out his tongue a few times and makes some little noises. His mother reassures him, saying, "I'll give you your feed, chubby fellow, just a moment." I follow her to the bathroom where she is heating the bottle. The child, in his mother's arms, holds his head up quite well and continues to stick out his tongue.

The mother brings the baby back into the room and sits down on the last step of the spiral staircase. She tells me, "I feel comfortable here, I always sit here to feed him." She gives Giuseppino the bottle. He sucks, making a noise with his mouth and keeping his fists closed. After some moments the mother says, without looking bothered, "Ah, he's done a wee." She does not interrupt the feeding and adds, "I never interfere while he is feeding." Giuseppino makes a little noise while sucking, his eyelids down. The mother says, "My pussy, you're eating too fast." The father comes in and looks glad that his child is feeding so well; almost immediately he is called out of the room by a colleague. The mother tells me that Giuseppino has now started making "those lovely sounds" that he made when he was breastfed (she breastfed him for the first ten days but then had to stop owing to mastitis). During the first days of artificial feeding the baby was "angry, agitated"; only now has he started making "nice noises". The baby continues to suck, looking downwards; as he finishes his arms relax and he falls deeply asleep without making any noise, staying motionless and perfectly quiet.

Second observation of Giuseppino, age five months

RN (*reads*): I go into the room. Giuseppino in his cot is lying on his right side sucking his thumb. As soon as he realizes I am there, he takes out his thumb and follows me with his eyes. He turns his head to look at me as I walk around his cot to go and sit on a chair; he carries on looking at me. He holds his hands open over the blanket, he touches for a moment the rubber dog that is in his cot, then he lifts his bib with one hand and puts the other into his mouth, still looking at me. He takes his hand from his mouth and handles the bib, then he covers his face with it. From time to time he looks at me. He moans a little and cries briefly, then puts his thumb back in his mouth, looks at me, and starts moaning again, his thumb still in his mouth. He takes the thumb out, he puts it back again and lowers his eyes. He opens his eyes, presses his hands on the blanket and moans. He makes a sound, looks at me then stares in front of him, looking thoughtful. He moans and puts his thumb into his mouth, touches the bib, sighs, and cries as if making an appeal. Then he moans, looks at me and touches the rubber dog. He is silent for a little, then moans again, looking in front of him. He goes on looking at me and moaning. He puts his thumb into his mouth, looking at me and making a sucking noise; for some moments he doesn't moan, then he starts again. He looks at me again, puts his thumb into his mouth and lowers his eyes as if to sleep. But immediately he opens his eyes again, still looking at me. His thumb is still in his mouth and he moves it around, exploring the cavity of his mouth with his eyelids down. Then he opens them, looks in my direction but not at me, and holds his thumb still in his mouth.

The mother comes in and passes quickly into another room. Giuseppino looks away from me and looks at her immediately. She comes back, goes up to him and says, "Hallo, darling!" The child smiles at her intensely, more than once. The mother puts him on the changing table and undresses him; the child kicks about, smiles, and puts his thumb in his mouth. After some moments he starts moaning and puts his thumb in his mouth again. He looks around, at the window. The mother says, "Today I'll try mixing his solid food in the bottle. A few days ago he was very good and ate it with a spoon willingly, now he doesn't want it any more. I want to see if I can trick him." The baby carries on moaning. His mother gives him the bottle and Giuseppino looks quite satisfied while sucking. The mother says to him, "My dear, I've played a little trick with you!" But the feed is too thick; the child has difficulty getting it down and looks troubled and kicks around. While sucking he clicks his tongue. The mother says, "It's not going down very well—perhaps that wasn't such a good idea", and she removes the bottle from the child's mouth to allow him to swallow the food. Giuseppino is moaning. The mother gives him back the bottle and he starts sucking again. At this point the mother, with an amused air, tells me that Giuseppino is silly because he is sucking without eating anything and she adds, turning to the child, "Go on sucking!" He looks at her, then at the other objects in the room, then turns to stare at the window. The mother now says, "It's true, it's no good deceiving him, I know he prefers milk to solids." She takes the bottle from the child's mouth and adjusts the rubber teat. He makes no noise and follows the bottle in his mother's hands with his eyes.

The maternal grandmother comes in. She says that Giuseppino is "quite thin" compared with other children she knows of the same age. The mother agrees and changes the bottle for another full of milk. After a few moments he starts to moan again; he puts his thumb in his mouth, is silent for a short time then moans. The mother dandles him gently in her arms; meanwhile he sucks his thumb. Then he starts to drink the milk, looking pleased and making some little noises "eh . . . eh . . .". He looks at his mother more frequently and she says, "Of course you would rather have this!" Giuseppino goes on, making a noise while sucking. The mother lifts the bottle from the mouth of the baby, who keeps it open, going "oh . . . oh . . .". He starts to suck again quite greedily, keeping his hand on the bottle. When the milk is about to finish the mother removes it, the child opens his mouth wide and groans. The mother says, "Now the milk is really finished!" Giuseppino follows the bottle with his eyes, staying quiet and still. His hands are not really relaxed, his arms are bent. He puts his thumb in his mouth, going "eh. . . . eh", and sucks it, looking out of the window. Meanwhile the mother talks to me and at one point the child turns to look at me. He takes his thumb out of his mouth and lets his arms lie down by his sides, his hands completely relaxed.

Summary of comment by Martha Harris[5]

These two observations give me the opportunity to note some things about the child's mental development and the mother's emotional situation.

> Sleeping as protection

From the description of the first session we can see how Giuseppino uses his "being asleep", his passing from sleeping to waking up, as a protection from unpleasant experiences. Closing his eyelids, sucking his tongue, seeking refuge in sleep seem to mean "I don't want to be hungry, to feel angry about being hungry and dependent; I want to do everything by myself". But this omnipotent fantasy does not satisfy the child when the need is too great. While "sleeping", Giuseppino frequently keeps his fists closed; he waves his arms, expressing in this way his tension, his uneasiness, his pain. At the same time the good experience—the comfort coming from the relation with his mother—leaves him relaxed, his arms by his sides, his hands open.

> The mother and the stranger

In the second observation I want to examine the child's relation with a stranger. Watching Romana while walking around the room, making small sounds to elicit an answer, closing his eyes, opening them again, pulling the bib on to his face, clinging to his clothes and familiar objects, putting his thumb into his mouth—all express his attempt to understand and adjust to what is happening around him. This watching and not watching, this quick alternation of quiet moments with noisy ones seems to express a comparison between the internalized previous experiences and the present external reality.

This behaviour suggests further implications. It is a reality test that Giuseppino makes on the basis of his mother's image; so at the end of the session, after repeatedly looking for and finding the proof that his mother and this stranger do not contradict one another, he can look at Romana and receive, through this, a new experience.

The way he directs his look is very interesting: Looking at my face and looking above my head are the two poles of uncertainty between the elaboration of a new experience and external projection.

Uses of the eyes

Giuseppino can either absorb what is perceived by his eyes or he can use them to expel the experience. In the case of psychotic adults we may commonly observe, quite glaringly, this way of looking forwards, looking away, looking crosswise, through which a person or object is expelled or put away. Projecting, expelling, throwing out without any pause for thought, are characteristic of such patients. The sensation of void that we frequently find in them comes from this attack against elaborating and then thinking. Giuseppino had already used this type of behaviour in the previous session when, once awoken, he looked around from side to side as if he wanted to throw out the unpleasant experience of the afternoon. But during the second session he remained thoughtful; it is interesting to note how he wants to expel the unpleasant experience but at the same time he tries to elaborate it in some way.

Now I want to examine the mother's attitude in some detail. In the first observation we can see how the mother has looked out a small, intimate environment in which to protect and contain her child: she always feeds him sitting on the same step of a spiral staircase, in front of a large, bright window. It is interesting to see how often Giuseppino looks at this source of light, which is certainly for him something related to feeding; he often looks at her (the source of light) as if he wanted to put something bright and comfortable inside himself.

| The basis of primal relationships |

In the second session a lot of things in the child's family life have changed; the father is far away and the mother has gone back to her work as an architect. During this observation the mother not only knows she is "tricking", but Giuseppino understands he is being deceived and the mother indirectly catches his mood. It is interesting to see how at one point the mother, making fun of the child and denying his suffering, really denies her own loneliness by putting it inside her child. Giuseppino's answer is very clear and appropriate: he cannot tolerate being left alone with solid food; by looking at the window and at the other familiar objects he shows he is clinging to his mother as she was before, so rejecting the child-mother she had (for the moment) become. This precise communication is based on the exchange of feelings and parts of the self between mother and child. It testifies to the way that primal relationships subsist on a basis of normal projective identification mechanisms. Mother and child help reciprocally and each offers the other a means of progression. Giuseppino makes his mother understand he is not happy and she, for her part, realizes she has been expecting too much from him when the father is absent: she has become distant, the food is too solid. In coming to understand this the mother shows she is again in touch with the child. Her true perception of his needs is shown when, giving him the bottle full of milk, she says, "Of course you would rather have this!"

Notes

1. Play observation sessions, on the lines of those practised for many years at the Tavistock Clinic in London, had been introduced to the Institute in 1968 by Professor Lina Generali Clements, who suggested that Professor Adriana Guareschi Cazzullo (the director) invite Mrs Harris to hold a series of six-monthly supervising seminars at the Institute.
2. This remained the case until 1992.
3. This case was approved by Mrs Harris for presentation at the Fourth National Congress of Infant Neuropsychiatry at Genoa in May 1971.

The tape is lost and the following account is edited from that presentation.

4. The taped supervision is lost and this is translated from RN's notes.
5. The taped supervision is lost and this is translated from RN's notes.

INDEX